Georg Büchner

COMPLETE WORKS AND LETTERS

The German Library: Volume 28

Volkmar Sander, General Editor

Georg Büchner

COMPLETE WORKS AND LETTERS

Translated by Henry J. Schmidt

Edited by Walter Hinderer
and Henry J. Schmidt

CONTINUUM · NEW YORK

2003
The Continuum Publishing Company
370 Lexington Avenue, New York, NY 10017

The German Library
is published in cooperation with Deutsches Haus,
New York University.
This volume has been supported by a grant
from The Marie Baier Foundation, Inc.

Printed in the United States of America

Library of Congress Cataloging in Publication Data

Büchner, Georg, 1813–1837.
Complete works and letters.

(The German library ; v. 28)
Bibliography: p.
1. Büchner, Georg, 1813–1837—Translations,
English. I. Schmidt, Henry J. II. Hinderer, Walter,
1934– . III. Title. IV. Series.
PT1828.B6A28 1986 832′.7 85-25561
ISBN 0-8264-0300-X
ISBN 0-8264-0301-8 (pbk.)

Acknowledgments will be found on page 312,
which constitutes an extension of the copyright page.

Contents

Foreword

The complete work of Georg Büchner consists of only a few hundred pages written by a man who died in 1837 at the age of twenty-three, yet its influence on twentieth-century literature can hardly be exaggerated. Particularly his drama, a century before Bertolt Brecht, is considered an important precursor of the major trends in drama today. His plays are not only performed in Berlin, Hamburg, and Munich, but in Paris, London, Rome, and New York as well. His novella *Lenz* is generally held to be an early example of modern narrative technique. Consequently, Büchner's works are used in most Humanities Departments in this country, yet almost all translations are out of print, including Henry J. Schmidt's *Complete Collected Works* (the first complete English edition; New York: Avon Books, 1977). The present edition is largely based on Schmidt's translations, reworked and revised according to the latest research on Büchner. The recent editions of individual works by Thomas Michael Mayer (*Danton's Death*), Gerhard Schaub (*The Hessian Messenger*), Hubert Gersch (*Lenz*), and Gerhard Schmid and Henri Poschmann (*Woyzeck*) have disclosed major changes in textual form which were taken into consideration in this edition. Moreover, this edition includes all the surviving letters of Georg Büchner and presents for the first time in English his letters of August 20, 1832, and August 31, 1833, only recently discovered by Jan-Christoph Hauschild. The bibliography contains a comprehensive listing of works on Büchner in English.

Henry J. Schmidt is responsible for the translation of the works, the chronology, the glossary for *Danton's Death*, the reconstruction and synopsis of *Woyzeck*, the notes on *The Hessian Messenger*,

Woyzeck, and on the letters, as well as the bibliography. The introductory essay on Büchner's life and work and the notes on *Danton's Death*, *Lenz*, and *Leonce and Lena* were written by Walter Hinderer. The editors have attempted to present supplementary material on Büchner's works and letters in as concise a manner as possible. They hope that this edition will be of use in the classroom as well as in the theater.

The editors would like to thank Dr. Thomas Michael Mayer for his prompt and generous assistance, Ann Rider for her help in updating the bibliography, and Karen Loaiza and Robert Norton for their translation of the introduction and for preparing the final manuscript.

WALTER HINDERER
HENRY J. SCHMIDT

Introduction

The noted German literary critic Wilhelm Emrich once said that "Georg Büchner's writings already contain in condensed form all of the fundamental compositional elements of our century's modern literature." In fact, Büchner's *oeuvre* is modest, consisting as it does of three dramas (*Danton's Death, Leonce and Lena,* and *Woyzeck*), a prose fragment (*Lenz*), a few essays, and some letters. Since the late nineteenth century, however, the influence of Georg Büchner's work has grown out of all proportion to its size. In modern theater, for example, the plays of Gerhart Hauptmann, Frank Wedekind, Bertolt Brecht, Max Frisch, and Peter Weiss bear traces of his influence, as do the operas of Alban Berg (*Woyzeck*), Gottfried von Einem (*Danton's Death*), Kurt Schwaen (*Leonce and Lena*), and Wolfgang Rihm, and some of the prose works of Hauptmann (*Gatekeeper Thiel, Apostle*) and Peter Schneider (*Jakob Lenz*). Yet Georg Büchner was not only an unusual playwright and novelist whose work, by the time of his death at the age of twenty-three, overshadowed that of many of his contemporaries. He was an idealistic yet pragmatic revolutionary and politician, a progressive natural scientist and philosopher. In his first lecture, entitled *On Cranial Nerves,* the young teacher criticized the idealistic philosophy of his time: "Philosophy, *a priori,* exists in a dismal desert far removed from fresh, green life and the question is whether it will ever be able to shorten the distance." Büchner's own philosophy was based on a "law of being." He did not share the teleological belief that everything is determined by its purpose. For him, "the entire physical being of the individual is not exhausted in self-preservation." As a schoolboy he formulated the principle that "*Development* is the purpose of life, *life itself* is development, therefore life itself is *purpose*."

Georg Büchner's philosophy was largely determined by the influence of Fichte. Politically, he owed his position to Rousseau and the Jacobins, aesthetically to Storm and Stress, and his own ideological position anticipated in turn the work of Søren Kierkegaard, Karl Marx, and Friedrich Nietzsche. He traced man's alienation and reduction back to inhuman working conditions; he analyzed the paradoxes in mankind's existence and pointed out the psychological and social strategies behind bourgeois morality. His theory of nature was inspired by the elements; politically, he was on the side of the people; in literature, he was interested in the individual's position in history and society. Not sharing the idealistic belief in the autonomy of the moralistic individual, Büchner abolished the classical concept of man, the artificial ideal of a social class, by depicting the contradictions within reality. Büchner's stage is a paradigmatic, rather than a moral institution, in which the classical moral is replaced by questions. Thus, rather than employing a dramatic method which resolves contradictions in order to demonstrate a moral, Büchner chooses to elucidate the contradictions without providing a solution for them. Each of Büchner's heroes—Danton, Lenz, Leonce, and Woyzeck—loses his belief in his own superiority over the outside world and finds himself in conflict with the forces of his own nature, of history, and of society.

Büchner's Life

Georg Büchner was born in 1813 in the Hessian village of Goddelau. His father, formerly a military surgeon in a French regiment and a fervent admirer of Napoleon, must have been dismayed by the defeat of his hero near Leipzig in the year of his eldest son's birth, but Büchner's mother was filled with national pride and patriotism. The decisive battle near Leipzig forced the French Emperor to retreat beyond the Rhine. But the German patriots who had helped their princes and their allies to defeat the Emperor, yet who hoped for a continuation of the civil rights they had received under the Code Napoléon, instead found themselves not only stripped of those rights, but also without the slightest realistic hope for the attainment of their original goal, the proclamation of a constitution based on personal freedom and national unity.

The elder Büchner advanced from district physician in Goddelau to chief medical examiner in Darmstadt. His admiration for the French Emperor remained firm in spite of the defeat. He continued to read extensively on the French Revolution, although he firmly opposed any defiance of political authority in practice. Enlightened in religious matters, politically the elder Büchner was "not just loyal and conservative but downright reactionary, with a deep-seated distrust of liberal, let alone democratic, tendencies," according to Karl Emil Franzos, the editor of the first critical and complete collection of Büchner's works (1879).

Eugen Boeckel, a friend of Georg, described Büchner's mother, Caroline Büchner, as "one of the most pleasant and entertaining people" he had ever known. Indeed, she appears to have been very different from her husband. The father's family background was modest, hers genteel. He appears to have been stern, cool, and practical, while she was friendly, endearing, and interested in the arts. He was influenced by French culture, she by German. Georg's brother Wilhelm Büchner described how their father read aloud revolutionary history to his family from the magazine *Unsere Zeit* (*Our Times*), while the mother exposed her children to Schiller, Jean Paul, the Romantics, and folk songs. Büchner had lessons with her until, in 1822, he entered school in Darmstadt. Two letters written to Georg when he was living in Zurich serve to illustrate the differences in character of his parents. The father's tone is stiff, dogmatic, self-righteous, and petty: his attempt at reconciliation falls far short of the mark. The mother is straightforward and concerned, describes the latest familial occurrences and ends humorously: "I hope you can read my scrawl—I'm writing in the midst of such a tumult that I hardly know where my head is."

In his family circle, with brothers Wilhelm, Ludwig, and Alexander and sister Louise, Georg Büchner seems to have been quite contented, but in school he was mostly just bored. From 1825 to 1831 he attended the Ludwig-Georgs-Gymnasium where he mocked the "philological rabble" whom he held in rather low esteem ("scholarly dung-cacti"), and passed the time as frivolously as possible, writing parodies of lines from Schiller's *Fiesco* and from *Hamlet*. According to his friend Zimmermann, Büchner "preferred

Shakespeare, Homer, Goethe, all folk poetry . . . , Aeschylus and Sophocles," read "Jean Paul and the major Romantics," devoured Herder's collection of folk songs entitled *Voices of the People* and Brentano and Arnim's *The Youth's Magic Horn.* He was also fond of French literature. The poems Büchner composed for his parents at the time were mediocre, and it is the spontaneous fragments in his school notes which point to the talent which was yet to unfold. In these, one notes his ability to turn a phrase, his talent for caricature, his critical attitude towards tradition, and his play with quotations and with words. In spite of his dislike for school, Büchner appears to have done well academically. Carl Dilthey, a well-known school master in his day, graded Büchner's knowledge of Greek with "good" and praised his fluent Latin. According to Dilthey, Büchner's interest in German literature was "excellent." He proved himself capable of independent thought in religion class and possessed particular knowledge of history and art history. But in mathematics, Dilthey continues, "[he] was unable to keep pace with most of his schoolmates because of a poor grasp of the basics and shortsightedness."

Although his schoolmate Luck describes Büchner as a "quiet, thorough, reserved observer," rather than a political firebrand, Büchner was not incapable of enthusiasm in this area and it was during his school years that he developed his thoughts on politics and aesthetics. He and similarly minded friends condemned the contemporary political situation in Hesse and championed the cause of the common people who, to their way of thinking, were tools exploited in the hands of the ruling class.

Büchner left school during the "Age of Restoration" which followed the Karlsbad Resolutions of 1819 and the resulting persecution of opposition leaders. A contemporary remembered how, after a short period of enthusiastic national unity during the war of independence, Germany "swiftly [fell back] into its parochial routine." Opposition to repression was stirring, though. In Darmstadt, the young Büchner discussed "the political needs of the people" with his friends. Undoubtedly, he and his political soul mates, Karl Neuner and Karl Minnigerode, eagerly followed news of the 1830 July Revolution in France: "toward the end of their high school years [Büchner and Minnigerode habitually greeted one another] with the words: *Bon jour, citoyen.*"

In the spring of 1831 Büchner took his leave of the Darmstadt Gymnasium with a talk in Latin on Menenius Agrippa (since lost), and, on November 8 of that year, began his university career in Strassburg, where relatives of his mother lived. The importance of Büchner's years in Strassburg can hardly be exaggerated. He studied medicine, became engaged to Wilhelmine (Minna) Jaeglé, and formed friendships with German and French revolutionaries. In Strassburg, where once Herder, Goethe, and Lenz had challenged stagnant cultural traditions with new ideas, Büchner's experiences provided him with a broader theoretical and practical political basis for the rejection of the restoration and the social conditions in Germany. These first-hand lessons in political development in France expanded his horizons and sharpened his political judgment, but Büchner's years in Strassburg were by no means devoted exclusively to politics. He formed a number of close friendships, particularly with Eugen Boeckel, Johann Wilhelm Baum, and the Stöber brothers, August and Adolph. Although not politically radical, they were responsible for introducing Büchner to "Eugenia," a French student fraternity. On May 24, 1832, Büchner spoke to the members of Eugenia, painting, according to one member of his audience, perhaps "somewhat too garish a picture of the ruinous state of the German governments and of the boorishness of the students at many universities, including Giessen and Heidelberg."

The father and an uncle of the Stöber brothers may have also been influential in the formation of Büchner's political position. The uncle, Gottlieb Stöber, had been the secretary of the Society of Friends of the People (*Amis du peuple*), an organization in which radical members of the intelligentsia joined with the common people against the monied aristocracy. After the July Revolution, France's acute social problems became so evident that the opposition movements united for a short while. The resulting group was the Society for Human Rights (*Société des Droits de l'homme et du citoyen*), whose hero was Robespierre. One of its most active chapters was in Strassburg. Georg Büchner was open to all of these influences. He approached the cultural-political, German-oriented group with the same independence of thought as he did the French-oriented Jacobin group. As a result of this exposure, he began to see the French model as applicable to the German situation.

The years in Alsace belong without a doubt to the happiest of

Büchner's short life. He loved the Vosges landscape, for he had always had a close affinity with nature. Following in Goethe's footsteps, he got to know the German architectural monuments of the region. He enjoyed the exciting and—in contrast to Darmstadt and later Giessen experiences—the free life of Strassburg. Although "not an admirer of the style à la Schwab and Uhland, nor of the faction that always looks back to the Middle Ages," as he expressed it in one of his letters, Büchner was actively involved in the German cultural activities of his friends in Strassburg for whom such activities represented a "spiritual bond" between Alsace and Germany. In 1835 Büchner wrote in this spirit to Karl Gutzkow: "I've gotten quite accustomed to my surroundings; I love the Vosges mountains like a mother, I know every summit and every valley, and the old legends are so strange and mysterious." Shortly before his death he wrote to his fiancée in Zurich that she should learn "to sing [her native] folk songs" for him, for where he was the people did not sing, and remarked enigmatically: "I'm coming ever closer to the folk and to the Middle Ages, every day I feel more clearheaded."

Legal exigencies made it necessary for Büchner to continue his study of medicine in Giessen, a change in location which apparently sent him into a physical, spiritual, and mental decline. To his schoolmate Luck he appeared to have "fallen out with philosophy, himself, and the world," but Büchner himself described and explained his depression in letters to August Stöber, his fiancée, and his family. To the latter he blames the "memory of two happy years" for his melancholy, as well as the "longing for all that made them happy" and the "vilest circumstances" of life in Giessen. Büchner complained that "the political situation could drive me insane. The poor people patiently draw the cart upon which the princes and the liberals play their comedy of apes." Büchner cannot accustom himself to the landscape, to the separation from his fiancée, to Giessen, that "abominable city," to the "hollow mediocrity" everywhere, and to the miserable political conditions in Germany.

As of 1830, increased taxes in the Grand Duchy of Hesse exacerbated poverty particularly among the farmers and the petty bourgeoisie. The citizens of this small, backward, agricultural state clearly suffered the sort of political misery which Büchner was soon to experience personally. The wealthy bourgeoisie negotiated with the government concerning a constitution, but was interested only in its own financial gain. Patriots dreamed of a national state and an emperor of the people. The intelligentsia of the left was unsuccessful in its campaign to educate the masses, which remained largely apathetic and unenlightened.

At first, Büchner, who had no illusions concerning the revolutionary preparedness of the people, was not politically active in Giessen. He promised his family not to become embroiled in the "clandestine politics and revolutionary children's pranks in Giessen," and he described every "revolutionary movement" of the time as a "futile undertaking." While in Giessen, Büchner was forced to interrupt his studies because of what he described as an "attack of meningitis." He felt "alone, like in a grave," and he constantly spoke of his homesickness for Strassburg, particularly for "rue St. Guillaume No. 66, up the stairs to the left," where his fiancée lived. In addition, he was forced to defend himself to his parents against the criticism, apparently often applied to him at the time, that he was arrogant and haughty. Carl Vogt, a conservative, nationalistic fellow student four years younger than Büchner, reported later: "Frankly, we didn't like Georg Büchner much. He wore a top hat which always rested on his neck, constantly made a face like a cat who hears thunder, kept completely apart."

Is it not possible that this arrogance, deny it though he might, was in fact the outer expression of the secret contempt in which Büchner held his fellow man? Why did he have only one close friend, August Becker, a rather dissipated former student of theology? Were his "brusqueness and introversion" his answer to the educated but provincial bourgeois society in which he found himself? The fragmentary nature of the letters and documents which have survived make it difficult to come up with satisfactory answers to these questions. However, Büchner's personality consisted of deep-seated contradictions. In the midst of liveliness and activity there are traces of apathy and fatigue, wit and enthusiasm alternate with recurring phases of gloom and brooding and mute depression. It may well be that it was these feelings that forced him to seek contact with Friedrich Ludwig Weidig, the liberal and politically committed Butzbach pastor he had met through Becker.

Büchner's renewed political activity coincided with the establishment of relations with Weidig, whose political convictions Büchner did not share, but who had considerable experience with revolutionary activity in Hesse and who was on good terms with the various liberal opposition movements. During this period, Büchner conceived a plan for a revolution in Hesse and he wrote *The Hessian Messenger.* Originally conceived, according to Becker, as a "sermon against mammon, with examples," *The Hessian Messenger*'s title, and some of the changes introduced into the text, were the result of Weidig's influence. Its function was to test the revolutionary readiness of the Hessian people. In this vein, Büchner founded a Society for Human Rights, based on the Strassburg group, in Giessen and Darmstadt. Its members were students and manual laborers. Büchner's two immediate goals were the expansion of the Society and agitation among the rural population whom he wanted to win for his planned revolution. He had already seen in France that "only the essential needs of the masses can bring about change, that all activity and shouting by *individuals* is vain folly." Thus, at a meeting of all the Hessian revolutionary groups at the Badenburg ruins on July 3, 1834, Büchner pleaded for the application of the French revolutionary experience to the German situation, a suggestion which met with general dismay. Bitterly, Büchner told Becker that people imagined "every village as a Paris complete with guillotine." Still, an agreement was reached concerning the distribution of flyers which were intended to reach the rural and urban dwellers in the various German states.

In July of 1834 the Butzbach and Giessen conspirators began to distribute the *Messenger.* However, the plot was betrayed to the authorities by Johann Konrad Kuhl of Butzbach, a confidant of the unsuspecting Weidig. The infamous university judge Konrad Georgi took immediate action and arrested Büchner's schoolmate, Karl Minnigerode, who later emigrated to the United States. Büchner himself traveled about to warn other friends. Upon his return to Giessen, he found his papers rifled and his room sealed. Büchner went immediately to the responsible authorities and demanded satisfaction. He repeated over and over to his family his anger over "such behavior," the violation of the "most sacred family secrets." At the same time, he had to reckon with arrest, something he feared more than death. This fear of imprisonment is hardly mentioned in the letter fragments which have survived, but it was clear it pursued him throughout his life, for it recurred in the typhus-induced hallucinations he suffered in Zurich a few years later.

In the fall of 1834, Büchner's parents summoned him back to Darmstadt where, at the beginning of 1835, he feverishly began working on *Danton's Death*. A visit by his fiancée, who came to Darmstadt in order to meet his parents, was his only diversion. Otherwise, Büchner studied philosophy and history and worked in his father's laboratory, all the time anticipating with dread the court summons he thought was bound to come. According to his brother Wilhelm, he also brooded about the fate of those of his friends and conspirators who had been jailed.

Eventually Büchner was summoned to court, but he was never jailed, either because the authorities were waiting for more evidence, or because an influential friend of his father's interceded on his behalf. Still, his situation became increasingly dangerous and he could not leave the house without being followed by police agents. Three more members of the Society for Human Rights were arrested and an order for Büchner's arrest was eventually received in Darmstadt. He consequently fled to Strassburg without waiting to hear the reaction of Karl Gutzkow and the publisher J. D. Sauerländer to the manuscript of *Danton's Death* which he had sent them. Büchner left home and country without informing his father of his plans, without a passport and with only a little money which his mother had given him.

Büchner returned to Strassburg where he resumed his study of medicine and philosophy with, as he put it, "the greatest diligence." He delivered quite convincing papers on scientific topics and, in the spring of 1836, he gave a series of three lectures on the nervous system of the barbel (a kind of carp), at the *Société d'histoire naturelle* in Strassburg. He was subsequently invited to join the society and the study was published. Although the danger of extradition was ever-present, Büchner was filled with "high spirits." His future did not look so "problematic" anymore, an impression he attempted to convey in a playful letter to Gutzkow. Memories of his former life in Giessen and Darmstadt were certainly not entirely forgotten, but they receded at least for a time in the presence of Minna, his old friends Boeckel and Baum, August and Adolph Stöber, and Wilhelm Friedrich Schulz, a Darmstadt liberal with whom he would later renew contact in Zurich.

From time to time, Büchner received news of his friends in prison. It was concern for their fate, rather than the warrant for his own arrest which reached him in exile three months after its issue, that preoccupied Büchner in Strassburg. He probably still prayed "every night to the hangman's rope and to the lampposts," as he had written on December 9, 1833, to August Stöber; "the political situation" in Germany probably still made him "insane" when he discussed it with other exiles in Strassburg; but he was telling the truth when he assured his family that he had distanced himself from all political activity. He dismissed rumors of political machinations on the part of the refugees and put them down to reactionary propaganda. The disaster of the *Messenger* experiment had convinced him "that nothing is to be done and that anyone who sacrifices himself *right now* is foolishly risking his neck."

Büchner's attitude had nothing to do with the "fatalism of history," as has often been surmised. Rather, his is a mature interpretation of the political situation of his time and demonstrates the unusual ability to reach realistic conclusions from unrealistic expectations. It would nevertheless be incorrect to presume from this logical and necessary change in Büchner's life-style that he had lost all interest in politics. His interest held, as can be seen in his letters to the "Young German" Karl Gutzkow, who often received quite copious political answers to purely literary questions. The younger man rejected his patron's attempt to reform society by ideas, through the educated classes, referring to the materialism of the time and the powerlessness of the individual. Gutzkow, on the other hand, constantly sent words of encouragement to his "dear friend" not to sacrifice his "unweakened literary power." In fact, Büchner, who proudly passed on to his family Gutzkow's words, did not take on literary work just for the money, with the exception of the translation of two plays by Victor Hugo.

In 1836 he worked on *Lenz,* alternating between an informative essay and a prose sketch. At the same time, he continued his medical and zoological studies, which had led to the above-mentioned work on the nervous system of the barbel, for which in September 1836 Büchner received the degree of Doctor of Philosophy in Zurich, where he took a university post. Before leaving Strassburg he wrote in a letter of September 2, 1836, to his brother Wilhelm that "I'm quite cheerful, except when we have a steady downpour or a northwest wind, . . . I'm now concentrating totally on the study of natural sciences and philosophy, and I'll soon go to Zurich to lecture to my fellow beings in my capacity as a superfluous member of society on an equally superfluous topic, namely schools of German philosophy since Descartes and Spinoza."

Like his first stay in Strassburg (1831–33), the second one (1835–36) had provided Georg Büchner with a very pleasant atmosphere in which to live, in spite of his continual political worries. "Life is indeed really beautiful, and in any case it's not as boring as if it were twice as boring," wrote Büchner to Eugen Boeckel. Here, he had also managed to write the prose fragment *Lenz* as well as parts of the graceful but satirical comedy *Leonce and Lena,* submitted to the Cotta publishing firm as his entry in their competition. But he was very dependent for mental stability on his proximity to Minna Jaeglé, for his attacks of depression and melancholy recurred when he moved to Zurich.

Still, a visit by his mother and sister Mathilde must have been a diversion for Büchner. From them he got news of his imprisoned friends. The fact that he still did not communicate with his father probably did not bother Georg. In the late autumn he moved to Zurich where he held a successful first lecture entitled *On Cranial Nerves.* Along with regular preparation for his lectures, he also began to work on *Woyzeck,* his last play, which was never finished.

Büchner's former pupil, the physician August Luening, said of his teacher's lectures that they were "not exactly stellar, but very clear and concise. He avoided rhetorical ornament almost fearfully, believing apparently that it did not suit the subject matter." Büchner's audience of some twenty students was particularly impressed by three things: "the unusually factual, understandable demonstrations using fresh reagents, most of which Büchner had to prepare himself"; the fact that he avoided all philosophical speculation; and that he drew many comparisons between fish and amphibians and the higher animal classes. It speaks immensely for Büchner's didactic talents that the rather reserved August Luening remembered no other teacher, sixty-one years later, as clearly as he did Büchner's lectures. This eyewitness described Büchner's introverted life in Zurich and noted his occasional vacillation between speculative philosophy and empirical natural science. Luening was also able to shed some light on Büchner's character in general. He remembered Büchner not only as the well-known and imposing writer and thinker but also the "extreme decidedness in propounding his beliefs which showed a high degree of independent judgment but which sometimes overshot its goal." Luening's account paints a picture of a sometimes quite unpleasantly dogmatic and obviously self-assured yet highly talented and successful natural scientist, who, however, apparently never hesitated to admit in a lecture that he had not found the answer for a problem. At that time, his circle of friends consisted only of Schulz and his wife and a few Hessian families with whom he had a long acquaintance.

In January of 1837 Büchner began to count the days until he would see his fiancée again. In a letter written in that month he described how he was always seeing her "partially through fish tails, frog toes, etc." and he asked her in jest: "Isn't that more touching than the story of Abelard, when Heloise always came between his lips and prayer?" For his separation from his fiancée seems to have caused Büchner great depression, as it had before in Giessen, in spite of his work and new experiences. This comes through clearly in his next-to-last letter to Minna: "You're coming soon? My youthly spirit is gone, I'll get gray hair otherwise, I'll soon have to rejuvenate myself from your inner bliss and your divine innocence and your dear carefree nature and all of your wicked attributes, wicked girl. Addio, piccola mia!"

On February 2, 1837, Büchner fell seriously ill with typhus fever. His last days are more extensively described by Caroline Schulz in her diary than in the obituary her husband wrote in the *Zürcher Zeitung* of February 23, 1837. She describes how, in his fever, Büchner believed he had been extradited to Hesse, saw his fiancée and spoke with her in French, and, curiously, believed that he had contracted debts.

Georg Büchner died on February 19, 1837, at 3:30 p.m. He was twenty-three and one-half years old. On March 5, Wilhelmine Jaeglé wrote to Eugen Boeckel, describing how she had to deal with "miserable considerations" at home before she could rush to Büchner's bedside. In a similar style and staccato-like sentences she tells of his death: "He gently drifted off, I kissed his eyes closed. . . . His parents' agony is boundless. A black veil has been thrown over the rest of my days." The burial took place on February 21, 1837. On July 6, 1875, his grave was moved to the "Hochbuck" at Zürichberg and a monument was erected to his memory.

The Aesthetic Foundations of Büchner's Works

During the nineteenth century in Germany, it was commonly held that there were primarily two stylistic models available to the dramatic poet: one represented by the works of Schiller and the other by Shakespeare and Goethe. Like Otto Ludwig, Friedrich Theodor Vischer, Karl Marx, and Friedrich Engels after him, Georg Büchner decided emphatically against the Schillerian concept of idealistic drama. Büchner believed that idealism in art amounted to an aesthetic equivalent of the same elitism fostered by the educated bourgeoisie, a snobbery he vehemently condemned as "the most despicable contempt for the holy spirit in human nature." In his short prose work *Lenz,* Büchner therefore described this "idealism" as "the most disgraceful mockery of human nature." With the advantage of hindsight and historical distance, however, we may observe that such notions as the "possibility of existence," the "holy spirit in human nature," are not completely without relevance to Schiller's aesthetic program. In his tract *On Grace and Dignity*, for example, Schiller speaks of the "god within us" and in the essay *On Pathos* he clearly stakes out the potential of human existence and designates "the entirety of human nature" as literature's proper sphere of influence. Furthermore, Schiller's mediating position between Kant's critical philosophy and Sensualism approximately parallels Büchner's integrating stance between stoicism and epicureanism.

In a well-known letter to his family, Büchner complains bitterly about "the so-called idealistic poets . . . [who have] produced hardly anything else besides marionettes with sky-blue noses and affected pathos, but not human beings of flesh and blood, whose sorrow and joy I share." Here, as well as in the brief remarks made in *Danton's Death* (II,3) and *Lenz,* we encounter Büchner's demand that the playwright should depict the world as it really is, rather than as it should ideally be. In *Danton's Death,* Camille is referring to all forms of classicism in theater, music, and art when he disparages the "wooden copies," the "marionettes whose joints crack at every step in iambic pentameter." Although mere embodied ideas are portrayed, not vivid human beings, the audience forgets its "Creator because of His poor imitators" and feels after the performance that reality pales in comparison with the illusion of theater.

Even as a schoolboy Büchner had defined *development* as the sole "purpose of life," and this philosophical notion is also reflected in his aesthetic views. The idealistic poet takes "a little bit of feeling, an aphorism, a concept, and clothe[s] it in a coat and pants," and thereby distorts reality and misrepresents human nature. Like the young Schiller, Büchner followed the aesthetic tenets formulated during the Storm and Stress period. Characteristically, both young poets were particularly interested in Jakob Michael Reinhold Lenz, who had preferred the "caricaturist" to the "idealist." For it is "ten times as difficult to depict a character with the felicity and truth with which genius perceives it than to work for ten years on an ideal of beauty that after all only exists in the mind of the artist who created it" (*Notes on the Theater*).

Lenz, like Büchner, wrote sympathetically of "suffering man" and condemned every form of elitism. In his fragment *The Little Ones,* Lenz, making reference to Matthew 18:10 ("Take heed that ye despise not one of these little ones"), distanced himself from "the great men, the geniuses, the idealists." He pronounced that he would not "participate in your soaring flights of fancy any more; you only singe your wings and imagination, think you are a God and are really a fool." Lenz rejected the elitist belief in genius and espoused humility in its place. A direct path can be traced from here to Büchner's Lenz, who claims: "One must love humanity in order to penetrate into the unique essence of each individual, no one can be too low or too ugly."

Lenz's and Büchner's understanding of pathos, the depiction of suffering, differs, however, from Schiller's conception in that the latter seeks to portray a superhuman affect that will overcome suffering and thus celebrate man's "moral [i.e., intellectual] independence from the laws of nature," thereby demonstrating the "supersensual" in man. In his early dramas, Schiller is preoccupied with proving the existence of "moral freedom," or the autonomy of the individual. Büchner, on the other hand, depicts pain and suffering in order to demonstrate not only the discrepancies within creation, but also, and most importantly, to illuminate human nature against the background of social conditions. Büchner transforms Schiller's belief in the "God within us" into the question, "what is it within us that lies, murders, steals?" He is therefore completely in accord with Schiller's goal of attaining human dignity and self-determination, but Büchner wished to achieve this goal by removing the economic and social barriers that stood in the way of free, individual development.

In *Danton's Death* Büchner parodies, and thus implicitly criticizes, the classical style he associates with a false presentation of reality. Here, the discrepancy between idealized fiction and banal reality is an intended aspect of the play which is a further trait that links Büchner with Lenz. Through this radical shift in perspective, Büchner makes clear his distance from the classical period of German literature and moves in a direction which, after 1830, led contemporary writers to a new aesthetic program. Just as Ludwig Börne and Heinrich Heine, as well as other less illustrious members of the Young Germany movement, championed the cause of reality against the traditional, idealistic conception of art, Büchner insists on the primacy of historical fact and unadulterated nature. Thus, in *Danton's Death,* he has Camille say: "The Greeks knew what they were saying when they declared that Pygmalion's statue did indeed come to life but never had any children."

This renunciation of German classical literature corresponded to the aesthetic revolt against classicism that was then taking place in France. It was therefore not entirely coincidental that Büchner translated Victor Hugo's dramas, for Hugo's *Préface de Cromwell* was hailed as the beginning of the French aesthetic campaign for European modernism. In Büchner's works, too, the sublime, as an aesthetic category, is dismantled through the use of the comic, and the high pathos of classical tragedy is stripped of its veil, corresponding to Hugo's demand for the "mélange du sublime et du grotesque."

Yet the most striking difference between Heine and the Young Germany movement and Büchner is that he, like Lenz, was a spokesman of the "little ones," the unimportant people. As already indicated, his aesthetic viewpoint is a logical extension of his political and philosophical positions. He thus rejected pure reproductions of reality that lacked human sympathy just as vigorously as the abstract falseness of idealized art. Within this context, the remark concerning the "coldbloodedness" and inhumanity of the works by the revolutionary painter Jacques Louis David fits so well into the conversation about art and literature in *Danton's Death* that, although borrowed from a historical document, the source itself seems to become an original.

In the letter to his family cited above, Büchner defines the dramatic poet as an exalted historian who "creates history a second time for us," produces "characters instead of characteristics" and creates "figures instead of descriptions." Büchner views the poet as "history's angel of resurrection" (Friedrich Hebbel), but while he advocates precision and fidelity to reality, he is not making a plea for the mere reflection of historical events in art. Rather, he dialectically combines mimesis with creative license or, in other words, he employs simultaneously both the reproductive and the productive principles of fiction. As he writes, "the poet is not a teacher of morality, he invents and creates figures, he brings past times to life."

Büchner resisted the temptation of dramatists who wished to "scrawl out anything better" and relieve reality of its inherent contradictions. According to him, aesthetic representation should not contain a moral bias or attempt to force reality into an easy formula by wrapping it in an idealistic veil, but should instead preserve its true complexity. As Camille says of the "wooden copies": "They see and hear nothing of Creation, which renews itself every moment in and around them, glowing, rushing, luminous." Paradoxically, Büchner's Lenz notes that reality is in perpetual flux, yet that precisely this change itself is a constant: "an endless beauty moving from one form to another, eternally unfolding, changing, one surely cannot always hold it fast and put it into museums and write it out in notes." The reader responds more strongly and directly to what is true and natural than to ideas or ideals, and this response alone is meaningful. "I most prefer the poet or painter," we read in *Lenz,* "who makes nature most real to me, so that I respond emotionally to his portrayal, everything else disturbs me." Thus, Büchner's aesthetic conception is deliberately aimed at emotional effect, for "the vein of sensitivity is alike in nearly all human beings, all that varies is the thickness of the crust through which it must break." Without living feeling—which, for Büchner, means the "soul"—man would be precisely that machine or marionette to which he is degraded by both materialistic and idealistic philosophy. The ideological role and the aesthetic function of the theme of suffering in *Lenz* and

Woyzeck are thus to be understood in opposition to such a philosophy. In this sense, Büchner's notion of suffering acts, on the one hand, as a sort of axe to break "the frozen sea within us" (to borrow Kafka's phrase) and, on the other hand, as an expression of the paradox that is human existence, of its insoluble contradictions and man's loss of true identity.

Büchner's Plays and Novella

Danton's Death

Since *Danton's Death* is the first German revolutionary drama and was written by an active revolutionary, there is a strong temptation to draw biographical parallels between the poet himself and his characters. Indeed, Büchner draws straight from his own letters for some of Danton's lines and it is not difficult to identify the despairing sensualist and epicurean with the author. Yet Büchner is just as critical of Danton as he is of Robespierre. The young author uses these two competitors and their parties as examples to demonstrate various aspects of the French Revolution in 1793–94. He makes extensive use of historical sources and discloses the "time-honored disguises and the borrowed language" that they contain. In his essay *The Eighteenth Brumaire of Louis Bonaparte,* Karl Marx comments on the fact that the gladiators of the French Revolution found in the Roman republic "the ideals and the art forms, the self-deceptions that they needed in order to conceal from themselves the bourgeois limitations of the content of their struggles and to keep their passion at the height of the great historical tragedy." Büchner employed the baroque model of world theater to depict this deceit, differing from his model in substituting comedy and parody for historical tragedy.

Büchner could study the meshing of existence and political role and its attendant conflicts, of being and appearance, in Schiller's dramas as well, particularly in *Fiesco,* which, like *Danton's Death,* dramatizes with the heroes the imagined Roman world of virtue and vice, of stoicism and epicureanism. In both plays, the first scene stresses the character of the action on the stage with the difference, however, that Fiesco creates a role for himself that he can potentially shed again in order to take on another, while Danton appears to have been given a role from which he may never be able to extricate himself.

In spite of a similar configuration and some parallels in motif, Büchner's emphasis is different from Schiller's. Fiesco denies his true existence because of his desire for power: he allows his political role to define his existence. Danton, however, would like to leave the Revolution, but he cannot identify himself with any new role or function. The virtuous republican Verrina allows Schiller to criticize the dogmatism of the ascetic idealist. Similarly, Robespierre's "despotism of liberty" provides Büchner with the opportunity to divulge the secret strategies of power. The sensualist Danton denounces the "righteous face," Robespierre's virtue, as a lie, and Robespierre, the stoic, sees Danton's epicureanism as a vice. Yet Robespierre, for whom virtue is an absolute, sometimes sees himself as a "sleepwalker," at the mercy of his subconscious while Danton, for whom pleasure and sensuality are the origin of all things, believes himself to be the victim of conscious thought, of reflection.

In his dialogue with Julie (I,1), Danton refuses to participate in interpersonal communication. Although he trusts his senses before he trusts his thoughts, someone like Marion must tell him: "Your lips have eyes" (I,5). Lacroix says of him that he searches "for the Venus de Medici piece by piece among all the grisettes of the Palais Royal" (I,4). Yet he admits to himself that he has difficulty "completely containing [Marion's] beauty" in himself. He wishes he could "break on every wave of [her] beautiful body" (I,5), but he cannot shut off his consciousness, cannot forget himself. Lonely in physical (Marion) as well as spiritual (Julie) love, Danton experiences only the loss of his own identity. The phenomenon of alienation in interpersonal relationships is reflected in Danton's speeches and in the way he sidesteps the questions put to him by Julie and by his friends. Hérault remarks that everything seems to Danton to be "a pastime," he can take nothing seriously anymore, neither the revolution, nor life, nor death.

In this respect and in contrast to the active, goal-oriented, and decisive Robespierre, Danton appears fragmented. However, closer examination reveals that Robespierre, too, is a victim of "fragmentation," a characteristic syndrome in Büchner's time. The "upright" Robespierre ridicules this, saying his "thoughts watch over each other," but, like Danton, he admits: "I can't tell what part of me is deceiving the other" (I,6). As Danton puts it, "What is it in us that whores, lies, steals, and murders?" (II,5). Just as Danton is continually being goaded into action because hesitation on his part would lead him and his friends to destruction (II,1), St. Just must warn Robespierre: "We will lose the advantage of the attack. How much longer are you going to hesitate?" (I,6). Robespierre speaks of his "sensitivity" (I,6), Danton of his fatigue, and of boredom (II,1).

The "principle of equivalence" (Roman Jakobson) shows up not only the differences between the two showmen of the Revolution but also their many similarities. Genius, represented by Danton, and dogma, by Robespierre, are actually but chess figures on the board of history. Danton, who later declares smugly before the revolutionary tribunal (III,4) that he is an individual chosen by fate, on whose brow "the spirit of liberty" hovers, admits, in a more private moment, that he is a product of history. "We haven't made the Revolution; the Revolution has made us," he says (II,1), and it is this insight into his own impotence that motivates his yearning for peace and quiet. Robespierre wants to see his dogma—the concept of virtue—brought to fruition at all costs, but Danton "would rather be guillotined than guillotine others," for he has discovered the senselessness of action as well as of reflection. The "bloodhound with dove's wings," as he is named by Mercier, appears infected with "sickness unto death." For Danton, "life isn't worth the effort we make to maintain it" (II,1).

Danton and Robespierre both discover that sin is rooted in thought: for Robespierre, that thought is the terror inherent in the ideology of virtue; for Danton, it is the memory of the September murders. Both of them draw parallels with Christ: Danton calls him, in no way derisively, the most refined epicurean (I,6), but for Robespierre, pain is "the agony of the executioner," by far greater than Christ's "ecstasy of pain." Both share the conviction that, as Danton puts it, "the Man on the Cross made it easy for Himself" (II,5). Robespierre accepts the accusation that he is a Messiah of Blood and formulates the difference between himself and Christ as follows: "He redeemed them with His blood and I redeem them with their own. He allowed them to sin and I take the sin upon myself" (I,6). Danton, on the other hand, brings his conscience into play. He sees himself as the victim of an "iron law," of a "must" that has destined him to be a troublemaker. While Robespierre perceives himself as an active man, Danton says of himself that he is "pulled by unknown forces" and, in a dream, he is dragged along by the globe. Yet it is Robespierre who says, "Truly the Son of Man is crucified in each of us, we all struggle in bloody sweat in the Garden of Gethsemane, but not one of us redeems the other with his wounds" (I,6).

Corresponding to the moral opposition of the stoic and the epicurean is the political difference between the dogmatist and the skeptic. Robespierre is primarily concerned with ideological purity, and St. Just with the practical deployment of ideology. Danton and his friends, however, plead for the unrepressed realization of their desires. Indeed, Robespierre is correct when he accuses them of parodying "the exalted drama of the Revolution in order to compromise it through premeditated excesses" (I,3). For Robespierre, now that the Hébertists have been liquidated, it is the Dantonists who are obstructing the work of the Revolution. If one ignores the theatricality of Robespierre's speech in which, for example, he condemns the same "sensitivity" from which he himself suffers, it is clear that he sets the Jacobin program against that of the Dantonists.

Lacroix, the most realistic of the Dantonists in Büchner's play, described the French situation in 1794, saying "the people are miserably lacking in material things. It is a terrible catalyst." For Büchner this description applied as well to the German situation of 1834, and it is this misery that he depicts in several scenes of *Danton's Death*. Through the character of Simon, he also mocks the borrowed phraseology of classical republicanism. It is in the language of *The Hessian Messenger* that one citizen complains: "A knife for those who buy the flesh of our wives and daughters! Down with those who prostitute the daughters of the people! You have hunger pains and they have stomach cramps, you have holes in your jackets and they have warm coats, you have calluses and they have velvet hands" (I,2). The uneven relationship between work and pleasure, attacked primarily by Babeuf in the name of the sansculottes, is formulated by another citizen: "Our life is murder by work; we hang on the rope for sixty years and twitch, but we'll cut ourselves loose" (I,2).

A comparison of these statements with those of the Dantonists exposes their elitist, ideological opposition and reveals the reason for Robespierre's victory through his choice of revolutionary strategy. According to his rivals, the reason for Robespierre's virtue is his impotence, while the people are virtuous only because they have no opportunity to pursue pleasure. Lacroix gives the Dantonist perspective as follows: "the people are virtuous, that is, they don't enjoy themselves, because work deadens their organs of pleasure. They don't get drunk because they don't have any money, and they don't go to whorehouses because their breath stinks of cheese and herring and that disgusts the girls" (I,5). The Dantonists confront terror with pleasure, mass murder with mercy, duty with privilege, virtue with contentment, punishment with self-defense (I,1), asceticism with sensuality—but without in any way providing a solution to social misery. "The divine Epicurus and Venus with the beautiful ass," says Camille, explaining the Dantonist position (I,1), "must replace Saints Marat and Chalier as doorkeepers of the Republic." Although Danton believes that "our whores could still compete with the pious Sisters of the Guillotine" (II,1), public opinion has already turned against his party.

In *Danton's Death,* Büchner confronts the positions of the two most important revolutionary parties, the radicals and the moderates, with the material needs of the people. He takes neither the side of the Dantonists, nor of their opponents, but points out their differences and the reasons behind the changes in critical opinion and reflects on the paradoxes of the Revolution on the basis of historical sources. The Dantonists' belief in democracy and republic satisfied only the wishes of the bourgeoisie, but Robespierre, with his dogmatic ideology of virtue, went no further toward satisfying the needs of the masses. Thus, in Büchner's version, Danton is almost successful in bringing about a change in public opinion when he speaks before the revolutionary tribunal, accusing Robespierre, St. Just, and their followers of treason, proclaiming: "You want bread and they throw you heads. You are thirsty and they make you lick the blood from the steps of the guillotine" (III,9). The people, however, choose Robespierre, with his virtue, over Danton and his good life (III,10). But after Danton's death, they demand Robespierre's head as well, proving what Büchner gives Danton to say: "the Revolution is like Saturn, it devours its own children."

The rivalry between factions lays bare the paradoxes within the Revolution. For the Dantonists, freedom and emancipation represent the ultimate realization of pleasure—really just a variation of the old aristocracy—and Robespierre's despotism is merely a new form of the old despotism and tyranny. Danton and Robespierre both believe that the role they play in history is a decisive one, and one they have created for themselves. But in reality, history made possible their roles and decided how long they would play them. "Hurry, Danton, we have no time to lose," says Camille (II,1), and Danton replies: "But time loses us." Behind all the words, costumes, and roles, the "same age-old, numberless, indestructible mutton-head" appears (IV,5), "nothing more, nothing less." People are not so very different, they're all "villains and angels, fools and geniuses," as Camille puts it, reflecting Büchner's belief that the differences between people have less to do with their natures than with the conditions in which they live.

Danton's radical skepticism leads not only to occasional nihilistic proclamations, but also to the spiritual sickness which, as Büchner wrote in a school essay, "leads to death." To that extent, *Danton's Death* is to be understood in an existential as well as a historical-political context. Danton despairs of life. He is dead to himself before Robespierre brings him to the guillotine. Unlike Robespierre and St. Just, Danton cannot identify with a single ideology, a fixed idea. He cannot bring himself to believe in a change in mankind, a "new man," or a new order of things. Danton's passivity and ennui are the expression of a despair that he attempts to hide behind the facade of epicureanism. Danton's case demonstrates that human development is not only limited materially, but also spiritually. Büchner's Robespierre is a victim of this barrier as well, but for him it is represented by isolation and alienation.

The fifth scene of the first act of *Danton's Death* illustrates that Danton's love for Marion is just as goal-oriented as his love for Julie. Camille wants to share Lucile's madness, but Danton only desires Julie's company when he is dying and fears loneliness. An enthusiast of biographical parallels finds a greater one in the relationship between Camille and Lucile and Büchner and Jaeglé than between Danton and Julie and the playwright and his fiancée. Yet Julie and Camille, in contrast to Lucile, whose worry about her lover has driven her mad, play out a classical feast at the end: they "lie in [their] places and shed a little blood as a libation" (IV,7). The life and death of the characters in *Danton's Death* is characterized well by Hérault: "Greeks and gods cry out, Romans and Stoics put on a heroic front" (IV,5).

In their clichés and the heroic roles they play, all of the parties' members, even Barère, Collot d'Herbois, and Billaud-Varennes, who eventually overthrow Robespierre, show themselves to be a part of the society that they originally rebelled against and tried to change. Mercier accuses the Dantonists and the showmen of the Revolution, with their speeches and ideas, of conjuring up a system that, as Danton himself says, "[works] everything . . . in human flesh" (III,3). The "curse of our times" of which Danton speaks is not least of all a curse of words. Mercier recommends, therefore, that this curse be carried out to the point "where it becomes flesh and blood." In this context, the parodistic elements that occur throughout the play are explained: they expose the *theatrum mundi* aspect of the Revolution. The use of foolishness, how the roles are conceived, the arrogant egotism of the revolutionaries—these are anthropologic criticisms in the form of radical satire of fundamental aspects of human society. Büchner's philosophy of critical negation corresponds to the political and existential cul-de-sac at the end of the artistic period in which he wrote more than to the epicurean philosophy of the pursuit of happiness and of pleasure that experienced a renaissance in the eighteenth century.

Lenz

Just as the factual details in *Danton's Death* and *Woyzeck* were culled from various sources by Büchner for use in his plays, *Lenz,* too, is based largely on the memoirs of Pastor Johann Friedrich Oberlin (1740–1826), which Büchner had been given by his friend August Stöber. A comparison of the Oberlin diary (the pastor commends the "pitiable patient to the compassion" of the reader) with Büchner's novella, however, reveals fundamental differences in content and structure. Oberlin's explanation for Lenz's melancholy, for his "unhappy soul," a common phenomenon in the eighteenth and nineteenth century, includes the influence of contemporary literature, Lenz's disobedience of his father, and his unordered life—in other words, his departure from the bourgeois norm. Büchner, on the other hand, wrote a scenic description of the experience of pain that goes well beyond the pastor's account. For example, Oberlin does not mention the central scene in Büchner's story in which Lenz delivers a sermon on the experience of pain to Oberlin's congregation. Lenz says that it "was a comfort to him when he could bring sleep to several eyes tired from crying, bring peace to tortured hearts, direct toward Heaven this existence tormented by material needs, these weighty afflictions." Having delivered his sermon, Lenz experiences a mystical ecstasy that permits him insight into his situation. "He felt as if he must dissolve, he could find no end to his ecstasy; finally his mind cleared, he felt a quiet, deep pity for himself, he cried over himself . . . ."

The next morning Lenz draws Oberlin into a serious conversation for the first time, but the pastor interrupts it, for "it led too far from his simple ways." Oberlin and Lenz appear here as opposites: on the one hand, the quiet, active, philanthropic, simple, balanced citizen; on the other, the unsettled, idle, introverted, complicated, and manic-depressive poet, who seems to feel at home nowhere. Without question, Oberlin represents to Lenz the potential of his own existence. He awakens in him "old, dead hopes" which are dashed again by Christoph Kaufmann (1753–95). Although the sermon reawakened the theologian in him, the meeting with Kaufmann represented a turning point for him in many ways: by releasing old memories and reminding him of his calling as a poet. At first, he talks himself into such a frenzy in the conversation about art that he forgets himself completely, until Kaufmann accuses him of "throwing away his life here, wasting it fruitlessly" and recommends that he return home. Lenz's reply reveals one cause for his sickness: "Away from here, away! Go home? Go mad there?" For Lenz, idealism in art reduces the "possibility of existence," and his father's role expectations represent to him a dangerous limitation of his existence. One psychological correlate of Lenz's lack of autonomy is the loss of identity he experiences, the various phases of which Büchner describes at the beginning of the story and after Kaufmann's visit. Lenz's condition becomes increasingly wretched, visited as he is by religious torments and strange obsessions. "The world that he had wished to serve had a gigantic crack, he felt no hate, no love, no hope, a terrible void and yet a tormenting anxiety to fill it. He had *nothing*."

Büchner unfolds Lenz's story between the two extremes represented by the sermon and the protagonist's dismal condition. The first extreme climactically represents devotion through pain, as the pietistic hymn quoted by Lenz in his sermon signals. "For him there were wounds in the universe," and he imagined mystically "another existence, divine, twitching lips bent over him." The second extreme, Lenz's nadir, shows him at a similar stage as Danton, for he feels like a living dead man. Goethe's Werther, too, was aware of this condition: "And this heart is now dead, no more delight flows from it . . . I suffer much; for I have lost that which was my life's only delight, the holy power that gives life and with which I created worlds around myself; this power is gone!" In Büchner's account, even Lenz's suicide attempts were meant to "bring himself to his senses through physical pain." Büchner's descriptions of the "feeling of having died," "an intolerable situation," were based on his own experience. In his *Anthropology for a Pragmatic Point of View,* Kant defined this *horror vacui* as "a lack of feelings, perceived in oneself, [which] gives rise to a terror (*horror vacui*) and to the presentiment of a lingering death which is held to be more painful than when destiny cuts life's thread suddenly."

The relevance of this concept for Werther and Lenz is obvious. The sermon, described in detail by Büchner, though not by Oberlin, reads like a variation on Lenz's homily entitled *On the Nature of Our Spirit.* In this essay, Lenz warns thinkers and philosophers of the danger of a "feeling of emptiness," for "to think does not mean to become deaf." Speaking of philosophers, the poet Lenz says: "They sense that they cannot escape from their uncomfortable feelings without experiencing a desert and an emptiness in their souls, and this condition, this strife is more torturous than the uncomfortable feelings themselves." Our entire autonomy and existence, Lenz continues, are based "on the amount, the extent, the truth of our feelings and experiences and on the strength with which we endure them . . . [and] *become aware* of them."

In the novella, Lenz's conversation with Oberlin the morning after the sermon seems to echo these thoughts, for, as he says to Oberlin, "the more sophisticated a person's intellectual feelings and life, the duller is this elemental sense." This elemental sense is not an elevated state of being, according to Lenz, but it must be a "boundless ecstasy to be touched in this way by the unique life of every form; to commune with rocks, metals, water, and plants; to assimilate each being in nature as in a dream . . . ." The reader glimpses in these words a yearning for identification that Lenz shares with Danton. Like Marion, Oberlin possesses the "elemental sense," but Lenz and Danton are excluded from this natural unity. Danton desires to dissolve himself in Marion's unity, just as Lenz wishes to do in nature, in God, and in his fellow man. His attempts fail in the end, however, and he sees himself as "Satan," as "the eternally damned." He feels as if he were "existing alone as if the world were merely in his imagination, as if there were nothing besides him."

At one point, Lenz's "religious torments" lead him to wish that he could "grind up the world in his teeth and spit it into the Creator's face; . . . ." Another time he complains to Oberlin: "if I were almighty, you see . . . I couldn't bear this suffering, I would save, save, I just want nothing but peace." With this lament, Lenz continues, at least initially, the problems raised in the conversation in *Danton's Death* concerning the "rock of atheism." But Lenz does not come to the same conclusions. In his crisis, self-accusation and revolt intertwine and alternate until, at the end, a complete petrification of the entire person takes place. "He seemed quite rational, spoke with people; he acted like everyone else, yet there was a terrible void within him, he no longer felt any fear, any desire; his existence was a necessary burden." Only indifference remained: he felt neither hate, nor love, nor hope.

At the beginning of the story, Lenz's unbalanced phantasies seem to be the result of a loss of identity. When he begins to share Oberlin's simple, active life, however, he appears to show signs of improvement. The experience of a sort of *unio mystica* leads to identification and communication and to freedom from mental duress. Only upon Kaufmann's appearance does the turning point occur. Lenz feels that he has been denied access to the world, where he had almost found a foothold, and his crisis begins anew, and continuing until it temporarily culminates in utter torpor. In the story, the reasons for Lenz's existential crisis remain somewhat obscure. The most important appear to be the demands and expectations of his parents, his experience with Friederike, and particularly the fear of the loss of the "vein of sensitivity," which the poet Lenz, like Büchner, sees as a sort of "central sun" in human nature. More removed, yet still important, causes are his departure from the so-called Genius period (ca. 1770–85), the criticism of its attendant dangers of self-adulation, and the subsequent return to humility, for these are things which Lenz mentioned in the fragment *The Little Ones* and which the fictional Lenz expresses in the novella in his discussion of art.

In the story, Büchner does not elaborate on the causes of the crisis, choosing instead to demonstrate how it manifests itself mentally and spiritually. He depicts how reality and personality alternately dissolve in Lenz's insane phantasies. Lenz's case, like Danton's and Woyzeck's, is exemplary to the extent that it shows the dissolution of an existence that failed to achieve self-determination and the fulfillment of its inherent potential. This "spiritual illness" leads Lenz not to suicide, but to a sort of catatonia, a theme the author returns to by exposing the robot-like nature of the role apparatus in *Leonce and Lena.*

Leonce and Lena

This comedy, which Büchner wrote as his entry in a competition, does not adhere to the traditional poetic rule of the division of genre according to social class, but plays at the highest social level. Motifs and moods from *Danton's Death,* from *Lenz,* from Büchner's letters, and from the works of Brentano, Tieck, Musset, E. T. A. Hoffmann, Jean Paul, Shakespeare, Gozzi, and Calderon are here ironically and satirically transformed. The names of the kingdoms Popo and Peepee anticipate Heine's characterization of the old Germany in *A Winter's Tale* but also carry on themes from Wieland's fairy tales, from Prince Biribinker, and from Goethe's poem "The New Amadis" in which a world-traveler named Prince Peepee is mentioned. The satire is aimed at politics, philosophies, ideologies, and faddish beliefs, and yet tragicomic undercurrents cannot be ignored.

Like Danton and sometimes Büchner himself, Prince Leonce suffers from a melancholy with a spiritual cause: disillusionment about life and its meaning. Thus, Lena herself characterizes him as follows: "I think there are people who are unhappy, incurable, just because they *exist*" (II,3). She thinks him old "under his blond curls," diagnoses "spring on his cheeks and winter in his heart," while Leonce himself says to Valerio: "I'm so young and the world is so old" (II,2).

In Leonce, idealism and skepticism are so closely bound together that he suffers "from ideals" but at the same time suffers because they are unreal and groundless. Yet his skepticism is not serious enough that he takes arsenic; indeed, he explains: "I have the ideal woman in my mind and I must search for her. She's infinitely beautiful and infinitely stupid" (II,1). With this statement, Büchner satirizes a favorite motif of the eighteenth-century novel and, indeed, the classical ideal of woman. "Those gloriously stupid eyes, that divinely simple mouth, that mutton-headed Greek profile, that spiritual death in that spiritual body" (II,1). Leonce finds, instead of this ironic ideal, a congenial idealist without skepticism who is moved by a similar romantic darker side.

The meeting between Leonce and Lena is the climax of the second act, already signaled in advance by the motto borrowed from Chamisso. Like Anselmus in E. T. A. Hoffmann's *The Golden Pot,* the melancholy, world-weary prince, who is completely resigned to idleness, is moved by a voice "deep within him" that fills his entire consciousness. When he kisses Lena, he feels "his whole being . . . in one moment" and wants to take his own life—without, however, having made a pact with the devil, like Faust. Valerio dismisses this suicide attempt and its literary tradition (Goethe's *Werther*) as "lieutenant's romanticism" and Leonce admits that he's "not in the mood anymore." Nonetheless, this short scene with its moonlight romanticism forms the center of the comedy.

There is a marked contrast between Leonce's love for Lena and for Rosetta (I,3). While he identifies Rosetta with his boredom and wants to give himself time before falling in love with her, Lena is the embodiment of his death wish and he suddenly finds life much too short to be able to really love (II,4; III,1). Like Marion and Julie in *Danton's Death,* Rosetta and Lena embody two kinds of love, whereby Danton's relationship with Julie, like Leonce's with Lena, is informed by death. Danton calls Julie a "sweet grave," and Lena is a "beautiful corpse" for Leonce. In addition, Lena sees herself as a sacrificial lamb over which a priest is holding a knife, and the world as "a crucified Savior" (I,4). Lena asks, much like Robespierre and Lenz, "My God, my God, is it true that we must redeem ourselves through pain?" Lena's religious melancholy and Leonce's philosophical dejection meet in a longing for death and their mutual desire for redemption. In their love, life and death concur or, as Lena puts it, "Death is the most blessed dream" (II,4).

In the third act, Leonce and Lena are presented at court as "the two world-famous automatons" and the "mechanism of love" is hinted at with words such as "faith, love, and hope," but this does not ironize the two main characters, but rather the empty role-playing at court from which the two had fled. For Büchner, automatons were beings without souls. Seen in a socio-political light, all the playacting indulged in at the court leads to the development of these automatic beings. In the comedy Büchner characterizes such role-playing, for example, in the affected speech of the tutor and the president, or through the attributes King Peter assumes in order to appear to be a person of distinction (I,2).

Behind this puppet play is the political belief of *The Hessian Messenger* that an honest man can only be a "puppet on strings pulled by the princely puppet" even if he is a German minister of state. King Peter must tax his brain to remember that he actually had wanted to think of his people (I,2). In the last act, this does occur after a fashion when the wind wafts from the direction of the kitchen so that the people are able to smell a roast at least once in their lives (III,2). In this scene, an ironic refraction shows the aristocratic attitude that Büchner denounced as contempt for the holy spirit in mankind. The commentary delivered by the master of ceremonies (III,3) entrenches the situation even more in the comic and grotesque.

The official control of one's emotions at court is indeed so perfect that the people really move like automatons or puppets. Leonce's behavior—obvious yawning, boredom, idleness, melancholy—can be understood as rebellion against the expectations of the court. The motto from *As You Like It* is therefore addressed to him, and Valerio calls him, too, a fool. But Leonce is no ordinary court jester. Rather, he is someone with obsessions, suffering from a life that is so calculated, so devoid of surprises, that the Prince cries out: "My life yawns at me like a large white sheet of paper that I have to fill, but I can't write a single letter" (I,3). Later, Valerio describes him as "a book without letters, with nothing but dashes."

Leonce wants to believe and cannot, he wants to identify himself with something or someone, but he is unable to do so. Together with his companion Valerio, a witty embodiment of eudaemonism, he rehearses all the ways to spend one's life: science, heroism, genius, literature, and rejects them all. When Valerio suggests that they should at least "become useful members of human society," Leonce replies that he would rather "resign from the human race" (I,3). Here and at the end of the comedy, the redeeming thought is that of Italy and the lifestyle of the professional vagabonds, the lazzaroni.

The divine idlers Leonce and Valerio follow in the tradition established by Goethe and Friedrich Schlegel. Leonce even speaks of the fact that a "horrible idleness" prevails and that all action has its inception in boredom. Like Camille in *Danton's Death,* he says: "All these heroes, these geniuses, these idiots, these saints, these sinners, these fathers of families are basically nothing but refined idlers" (I,1). Valerio is proud of his virginity in work, of being an idler, but Leonce seems to suffer from the vice of idleness, for he says: "Why can't I take myself seriously and dress this poor puppet in tails and put an umbrella in its hand so that it will become very proper and very useful and very moral?" Like the beggar in *Danton's Death,* Valerio thinks poorly of the subtle suicide called work, and for him idleness does not contain the slightest existential danger. On the contrary, as minister of state his first official act will be to declare work a punishable offense. He possesses a truly "incredible skill in doing nothing," but Leonce complains that he knows himself inside and out "like a glove" (I,3) and only experiences variations on a familiar theme.

The idealist Leonce and the materialist or realist Valerio obviously differ in their feeling for nature. For the one the evening seems "uncanny," for the other it appears as an "Inn of the Golden Sun" (II,2), which only proves that a landscape reflects one's own perspective or mood. While one speaks of romantic feelings and ideals, the other expresses his feelings for nature in the following way: "The grass looks so beautiful that I wish I were an ox so I could eat it, and then a human being again to eat the ox that has eaten such grass" (I,1). Valerio's philosophy of life corresponds to this materialistic interpretation of nature: why should he work hard just in order to be able to put on a clean shirt in the evening? Why not lay down his burden and enjoy life as long as possible (II,1)? This is a radicalization of Büchner's belief that life should not be exhausted in work. He takes this warning from a way of life that is used up by work and false morality: "out of sheer modesty we shall now clothe the inner man and put on a coat and pants internally." Valerio counters Leonce's enthusiasm and ideas with his bottle (II,2) and opposes his secret desire for fame with material needs. The preface to the comedy, the word play "E la fama?"/"E la fame?" introduces this difference, but it also suggests the connection between ideology and society.

The ironic-comic refraction softens the anti-court tendency in the play, but it is by no means completely eliminated. On the other hand, existential problems that appear in a less developed form in *Danton's Death* and *Lenz* turn up here. Like Lenz and Danton, Leonce suffers from loss of identity. He would rather be someone else. With his troubled identity, Leonce is the opposite of the elemental Valerio and also of King Peter, the comical embodiment of the philosophy of identity. Leonce is no more successful than Lenz in reaching his elemental being. And, like Danton, he cannot identify with the political and social role dictated to him by society. He ends in utopia, just as Lenz ends in insanity. Leonce shares the obsession with Lena and Valerio of importing Italy without winter, an ironic transposition of a natural condition into the political realm. What the more realistic governess believes to be impossible in the "horrible world" is shown at least in effigy in the play: a "stray prince" (II,1; III,3). And "faith, love, and hope," are reconstituted in the literary fiction and the play, in effigy as it were; and, in the end, even the eternal return of the same appears to be a game that Leonce wishes to begin again the following day "in peace and comfort." That means of course that Leonce will also resume his "ideal" preoccupations and consider "how he could manage to see the top of [his] head" (I,1). At the end of the play he has apparently landed on his feet, which nevertheless seem to still rest on rather unsteady ground.

Woyzeck

Since Büchner believed that idealism in art and philosophy was bound to lead to the mechanization of poetic representation and thought, he consciously attempted to appeal to the "vein of sensitivity . . . alike in nearly all human beings." He felt the need to engage other aesthetic methods in order to break through the more or less thick shell, as he puts it in *Lenz*. To accomplish this, Büchner returned to Storm and Stress and folk-poetry aesthetics. Rather than idealize man, Büchner preferred to view him, to quote Prince Tandi in Lenz's *The New Menoza,* "as [he is], without gracefulness, rather than as if [he] emerged from the pointed quill of a pen." Human nature seemed to emerge only in its simple, elemental, and original form, without ideological dressing, but not in "genteel society." That is why, as Büchner wrote to Gutzkow in 1836, he wanted to "strive for the formation of a new mentality among the *people.*" In *Woyzeck,* Büchner follows the same aesthetic he had used in his novella *Lenz.* He immerses himself "in the life of the most insignificant person and reproduce[s] it, in the palpitations, intimations, the most subtle, scarcely perceptible gestures."

Here, too, Büchner further develops Lenz's technique of quoting verse to achieve a differentiated, balladesque dramatic form. Although the historical basis for *Woyzeck* is provided by the testimony in the well-documented case given by the physician Johann Christian August Clarus, a civil servant (*Hofrat*) of the kingdom of Saxony, Büchner enriched Dr. Clarus's account with folk songs, verse quotations, and biblical references, which not only add a new dimension and perspective to the story, but also lend the case a representative quality. A comparison of the various stages of Büchner's play, however, reveals that the author only gradually became fully aware of the effectiveness the use of folk songs and biblical quotations possessed. They serve not just to enhance the commentary or merely to provide a thematic summary of the action, but to intensify the tragedy. It is astonishing to what extent the young playwright was able to achieve a maximum of expression with a minimum of vocabulary and with only the simplest aesthetic techniques. While *Woyzeck* exists only as a fragment and there are several rather problematic versions of the text, it has exerted a greater influence on later poets than any other of Büchner's works.

Büchner immediately indicates his attitude towards his material by giving names only to the poor people: Woyzeck, Marie, Andres, Margret, and the fool Karl, while the other characters only appear to be embodied functions: the captain, the doctor, and the drum major are the most important of these. Büchner reserves the most acerbic criticism for the two representatives of "higher" society. He mocks their "absurd superficiality called education" and the "dead stuff, learning," as he expresses it in a letter. He exposes their emptiness by pitting "arrogance against arrogance, ridicule against ridicule." Indirectly, Büchner's play refutes the materialistic-positivistic and idealistic theories that appropriated Woyzeck's case and submitted it to a scientific examination, but this was only a secondary effect. It was certainly Büchner's primary intention to depict the "suffering, oppressed being" who was powerless "not to become a criminal."

Woyzeck becomes an example, a representative case of human suffering. Like Danton, Lenz, and also Leonce, Woyzeck experiences modern man's complete isolation from the world and even from himself. This experience of such extreme self-alienation for religious and social reasons is expressed in the fairy tale told by the grandmother, which is as succinct as it is powerful: "Once upon a time there was a poor child with no father and no mother, everything was dead and no one was left in the whole world. Everything was dead, and it went and wept day and night. And since nobody was left on the earth, it wanted to go up to the heavens, and the moon was looking at it so friendly, and when it finally got to the moon, the moon was a piece of rotten wood and then it went to the sun and when it got there, the sun was a wilted sunflower and when it got to the stars, they were little golden flies stuck up there like the shrike sticks 'em on the blackthorn and when it wanted to go back down to the earth, the earth was an overturned pot and was all alone and it sat down and cried and there it sits to this day, all alone."

Although it cannot be said with certainty that Büchner intended to use the fairy tale in the final version, its content does illustrate at least one perspective of Marie's murder by Woyzeck: his increasing loneliness. When the drum major steals Marie from him, Woyzeck loses the last support the world could lend him. He despairs for Marie, himself, and the world, a process that, in the first version, Woyzeck gives voice to by saying: "Everyone's an abyss—you get dizzy when you look down into it." With this statement, Woyzeck anticipates modern self-perception as did not occur again until Franz Kafka, and like the metaphysical question of the connection between no and yes, which Büchner did not plan to use in the final version, for such thought would be above and beyond the horizon of the simple soldier. Thus, for similar reasons Büchner transposes the entire theme into a religious-apocalyptic vision: Woyzeck—and Marie—see their own destiny again and again as part of a world catastrophe. Woyzeck cries to the people dancing before him: "Why doesn't God blow out the sun so that everything can roll around in lust, man and woman, man and beast."

The first scene of the final version of *Woyzeck* establishes the referential nexus of "Sodom and Gomorrah, the whore of Babylon." The lines: "There's fire raging around the sky, and a noise is coming down like trumpets. It's coming closer! Let's go! Don't look back!" refer to Revelation 8:7 and Genesis 19:23–26. As Dr. Clarus noted, Woyzeck's vision anticipates his private fate with Marie, which, at that time, he could not have known and which assumes a metaphysical meaning through its apocalyptic undertone. But Marie, too, who scoffs at Woyzeck's visions and fears he's "going crazy with those thoughts of his," seems to have her own premonitions. For example, she tries to fend off an attack of remorse with the words: "Oh, what a world! Everything goes to hell anyhow, man and woman alike." To the drum major's question as to whether she has the devil in her eyes, Marie answers defiantly: "For all I care. What does it matter?"

Marie's infidelity, which Woyzeck declares a "mortal sin," leads him to despair. But she, too, is finally tormented by her guilt and the thought of her child's father. While the biblical quotations about Maria Magdalena allude to Marie's situation, Woyzeck's state of being is characterized by the verses, already quoted in part in *Lenz*, about suffering as devotion and an imitation of Christ. In both passages, the general situation is individualized, differentiated, and intensified by additional commentary. Marie beats her breast, as the stage directions read, and cries in despair: "It's all dead! Savior, Savior, I wish I could anoint your feet." Woyzeck, who pointedly gives away his few personal belongings to Andres, comments on the verses about "suffering," saying: "My mother can only feel the sun shining on her hands now. That doesn't matter." In both cases, the same extreme feeling of abandonment that the grandmother's fairy tale expresses is predominant.

In spite of the religious conceptual framework, neither Marie nor Woyzeck is to be understood as religious in the ecclesiastical sense. Like Danton, Robespierre, and Lenz, they refer to Christ as a model of suffering, yet without sharing the others' rebellious attitude toward God. In contrast to Marie, the "haunted" and "insane" Woyzeck is driven by the idea of plumbing the depth of things. "The toadstools," he fantasizes in the scene with the doctor. "There—that's where it is. Have you seen how they grow in patterns? If only someone could read that." Woyzeck's fixed ideas are just as much projections of his own insecurity and despair as are those of Lucile and Lenz. Woyzeck reflects, whereas Marie gives her senses free rein. For this reason, he appears broken, hunted, and persecuted, whereas she, with the exception of her moral scruples, seems at one with herself, like Marion.

The characters of Marie and Woyzeck repeat the structural configuration of Marion and Danton, sounding the familiar opposition of spirituality and sensuality. As Marie stands before the mirror judging herself in a sort of erotic competition with the "great ladies," the only difference she is able to acknowledge between rich and poor are her little room, her little piece of mirror—and the fact that the "handsome lords . . . kiss their hands." Woyzeck, however, perceives that the difference between the "common people" and the members of higher society is money. In his simple way, he sees how all notions of virtue and morality—in Marxian terms, the superstructure—derive from economic conditions, or the base. With hidden irony, he tells the captain, "Virtue must be nice, Cap'n. But I'm just a poor guy."

In this famous scene, Büchner confronts the two socially and economically determined ways of thinking and of life of the time, issues with which he had grappled before in *The Hessian Messenger*. The captain prattles on about virtue and morality and feigns respect for the "Reverend Chaplain." Woyzeck, on the other hand, speaks with remarkable accuracy about money, nature, flesh and blood, and defends his "poor little kid," who did not have the blessing of the church, with a corresponding reference to Christ's words. It is important to note that the scene is not dominated by the representative of educated society, who so effectively controls his drives that he automatically suppresses his desire for the owners of the "white stockings as they go tripping down the street." Instead, it is the representative of the poor people who dominates the scene, who, according to the Captain, thinks "too much"—and thought "upsets" one.

The antinomies of bourgeois society that were evident in Büchner's day are all included in his portrait of the Captain, which is a composite of melancholy, boredom, hypochondria, existential fear, and *Weltschmerz*. In his bourgeois way, the Captain also senses the abyss that Woyzeck traces back at one point to the Freemasons, at another to the imminent judgment day. The vertigo that grips the Captain becomes grotesque in the scene with the doctor, whereas for Woyzeck it is apocalyptic. Woyzeck is forced to run himself into the ground in order to provide the bare minimum necessary for the survival of Marie, the child, and himself, but the blissfully ignorant Captain always feels obliged to try to calm and slow him down. Ironically, the Captain, who apparently has all the leisure time in the world at his disposal, recommends that Woyzeck try "activity," although he already has more to do than he can bear. This indicates precisely that essential difference in whether one seeks something to do, like the Captain, in order to avoid the thought of eternity, or if, like Woyzeck, one must sell oneself at the doctor's to earn a couple of extra pennies just in order to eke out a scanty livelihood.

In the scene between the doctor and Woyzeck, where Büchner makes use of his memories of his former teacher, Professor Wilbrand of Giessen, the opposition of bourgeois virtue or morality and nature comes to the fore, this time, though, with a different emphasis. Philosophical-scientific idealism is called in question here by Woyzeck's nature, or more precisely, by the *musculus constrictor vesicae*. This evidently violates Woyzeck's agreement with the doctor who is paying the soldier to be a guinea pig so that he can prove that "in man alone is individuality exalted to freedom." The lapses in the Captain's and the doctor's ability to control their own emotions prove how shallow this autonomy of the individual and of the will really is. The Captain insists on morality and virtue, the doctor on health and science. When Woyzeck mentions his visions and begins to philosophize about "double nature," the doctor diagnoses "a marvelous *aberratio mentalis partialis*," an "obsession with a generally rational condition." The Captain is "quite worn out" by the end of his conversation with Woyzeck, but the doctor still maintains rational control, which he achieves by encompassing Woyzeck's interpretation and perspective of the world in established concepts and thus minimizing them.

During this scene, a sentence from Büchner's first lecture (*On Cranial Nerves*) comes unbidden to mind: "The question begins for the philosophical school where the teleological school claims to have found an answer." While the doctor transforms Woyzeck into a "complicated machine," or a mere abstraction (*aberratio mentalis partialis*), which for Büchner were the same thing, in an earlier version Woyzeck represents the "unspoiled nature" that shames "human society." What the doctor and the Captain take to be the human *specifica differentia* is nothing more than the product of social conditioning, roles that are imposed and sanctioned by society, but which Büchner divulges in all their empty functionality through the anonymity of those who play them. In the first version, the Barker derides the "progress of civilization. Everything progresses," he cries, "—a horse, a monkey, a cannery-bird. The monkey is already a soldier—that's not much, it's the lowest level of the human race!" This sentiment overlaps with the drunken apprentice's sermon in the eleventh scene of the last version, in which he asks: "Why does man exist? Why does man exist?" The reply ridicules the materialistic viewpoint in the same way that the scene with the doctor satirizes the idealistic perspective. Man exists so that the farmer, the cooper, the shoemaker, and the doctor have work and can make a living. Woyzeck identifies money as the root of his material and psychological destitution and the apprentice proves the vanity of money by indulging in the enjoyment of its exchange value: "My soul, my soul it stinks of booze.—Even money eventually decays."

Here, too, as in his other plays, Büchner differentiates the themes by mirroring them from various perspectives. Thus, the frivolous *memento mori* of the apprentice is set in contrast to Woyzeck's "terrible" presentiments and his almost sectarian philosophical-metaphysical questions; the sensualistic, vital world view shared by Marie and the Drum Major are juxtaposed to the morality and virtue of the educated bourgeoisie, and the conceptual apparatus of the scholar clashes with the contradictions of human nature. But all of these perspectives meet at a single point: the example of Woyzeck. He appears as the damned, exiled man, fallen into a veritable state of servitude. He tells the melancholic Captain that "the likes of us [poor people] are wretched in this world and in the next; I guess if we ever got to Heaven, we'd have to help with the thunder." He pursues this damning judgment and discovers the abysses in society, in mankind, in himself. Certainly, he is persecuted by voices and he is sometimes a victim of his own visions, but in the last version the possibility of a choice does occur. Woyzeck asks before the murder: "Should I? Must I?" Thematically, this points to the connection between freedom and historical necessity that Büchner had treated in *Danton's Death*. In *Woyzeck*, however, historical necessity has become eschatological necessity. Like Robespierre, who saw the original of all evil in the excesses of the

Dantonists and sought to purge all evil by liquidating them, when Woyzeck murders Marie, he is simultaneously aiming at the more general promiscuity of "man and woman, man and beast."

At the end of the play the question of redemption remains unresolved. In a way, Robespierre had already answered it representatively for Lucile, Lenz, Marie, and Woyzeck when he said: "Why do we always look only toward Him? Truly the Son of Man is crucified in each of us, we all struggle in bloody sweat in the Garden of Gethsemane, but not one of us redeems the other with his wounds." Redemption does not occur in Woyzeck's case either, only suffering, pain, and loneliness remain. Thus, a parallel can undoubtedly be drawn between *Woyzeck* and the tragedy of the German baroque which, as martyr drama, reveals history as a reenactment of the Passion. The significant difference exists in that it is not a sovereign who represents "human nature" and history, but rather what is embodied is "the life of the most insignificant person," a representative of the "poor people," and of "unspoiled nature."

W.H.

Chronology

1813 October 17: Karl Georg Büchner born in Goddelau, a small town in the Grand Duchy of Hesse-Darmstadt; to Ernst Karl Büchner (1786–1861), medical doctor, and Caroline Büchner, née Reuss (1791–1858). Other children: Mathilde (1815–1888); Wilhelm (1817–1892), pharmacologist, owner of a dye factory, member of the Hessian legislature; Louise (1821–1877), writer, campaigner for women's rights; Ludwig (1824–1899), physician, author of *Power and Matter,* a landmark of materialist philosophy; Alexander (1827–1904), writer, activist in the Revolution of 1848, eventually professor of literature in France.

1816 Family moves to Darmstadt, capital of Hesse-Darmstadt.

1825 Georg enrolls in the Ludwig-Georgs-Gymnasium in Darmstadt.

1830 Delivers a speech in defense of Cato's suicide during a ceremony at the Gymnasium.

1831 Enrolls in the medical school of the University of Strassburg. Resides with Pastor Johann Jakob Jaeglé.

1832 Delivers a speech to the student organization "Eugenia" on political conditions in Germany. Spends vacation (August–October) in Darmstadt.

1833 Becomes secretly engaged to Wilhelmine (Minna) Jaeglé (1810–1880), daughter of Pastor Jaeglé. Leaves Strassburg and enrolls at the University of Giessen, continuing his medical studies. Returns to Darmstadt in November to recover from an attack of meningitis.

1834 Returns to Giessen. Becomes acquainted with Pastor Friedrich Ludwig Weidig (1791–1837). Büchner founds a "Society for Human Rights," based on French model, in both Giessen and Darmstadt. Visits his fiancée in Strassburg, then returns to Giessen. Writes *The Hessian Messenger,* with Weidig as coauthor and editor. While being distributed, the pamphlet is seized by the authorities; Büchner goes on foot to Offenbach and Frankfurt to warn his friends. Returning to Giessen, he is interrogated by the local authorities, but, unlike numerous of his accomplices, he is not arrested. A second version of *The Hessian Messenger* is published in November. Büchner remains in Darmstadt after vacations are over.

1835 Writes *Danton's Death,* which he sends to the writer/editor Karl Gutzkow (1811–1878) and to the publisher Sauerländer. Flees to Strassburg at the beginning of March; in June the authorities issue a warrant for his arrest. A censored version of *Danton's Death* is published. He translates Victor Hugo's dramas *Lucrèce Borgia* and *Marie Tudor* for Gutzkow. Writes the prose fragment *Lenz* and begins his dissertation on the nervous system of fish.

1836 Completes dissertation, which he reads before the Society of Natural History in Strassburg. He is accepted as a Corresponding Member, and the Society publishes his thesis. Writes *Leonce and Lena* for a competition announced by the Cotta publishing house, but he misses the deadline and the comedy is returned unread. In September the University of Zurich grants him a doctorate and invites him to join the faculty, which he does in November after giving an inaugural lecture on the cranial nerves of fish. Begins lecturing on the comparative anatomy of fish and amphibians. Begins *Woyzeck*.

1837 February 2: contracts typhus. Dies on February 19. Weidig commits suicide in his cell on February 23.

1838 Gutzkow publishes scenes from *Leonce and Lena* in *Telegraph für Deutschland.*

1839 *Lenz* appears in the same periodical.

1850 Publication of Büchner's works (excluding *Woyzeck*), edited by his brother Ludwig.

1875 Karl Emil Franzos's reconstruction of *Wozzeck* [sic] appears in the Viennese newspaper *Neue Freie Presse.*

1879 Publication of Franzos's edition of Büchner's collected works.

1885 Premiere of *Leonce and Lena* in an outdoor performance by Munich's Intimes Theater.

1886 First American publication of *Danton's Death* (in German) in the Socialistic Library series.

1902 Premiere of *Danton's Death* by the Freie Volksbühne in Berlin.

1913 Premiere of *Woyzeck* by the Munich Residenztheater.

1925 Premiere of Alban Berg's opera *Wozzeck* in Berlin.

The Hessian Messenger

by Georg Büchner and Friedrich Ludwig Weidig

First Message

Darmstadt, July 1834

Preface

This paper intends to reveal the truth to the State of Hesse, but he who speaks the truth will be hanged; yes, even he who reads the truth might be punished by corrupt judges. Therefore anyone receiving this paper must take note of the following:

1) He must hide this paper carefully outside his house from the police;
2) he may only pass it on to trusted friends;
3) he may only pass it on anonymously to those who cannot be trusted as one trusts one's own self;
4) if this paper is found in the possession of anyone who has read it, he must confess he was just about to bring it to the District Council;
5) if this paper is found with anyone who has not read it, then he is of course innocent.

* * *

Peace to the huts! War on the palaces!

In the year 1834 it looks as if the Bible had been lying. It looks as if God had created peasants and laborers on the fifth day and princes and aristocrats on the sixth, saying to the latter: have dominion over every creeping thing that creepeth upon the earth—and had included peasants and the middle classes among the creeping things. The life of aristocrats is a long Sunday; they live in beautiful houses, they wear elegant clothing, they have well-fed faces, and they speak their own language, while the people lie before them like manure on the field. The peasant walks behind his plow, but behind him walks the aristocrat, driving him on with the oxen, taking the grain and leaving the stubble to the peasant. The life of the peasant is a long workday; strangers devour his land in his presence, his body is a callus, his sweat is the salt on the aristocrat's table.

The Grand Duchy of Hesse has 718,373 inhabitants who pay the state 6,363,364 florins [*sic*] every year as follows:

1) Direct taxes	2,128,131 fl.
2) Indirect taxes	2,478,264 fl.
3) Rent (for use of royal lands)	1,547,394 fl.
4) Royal prerogatives	46,938 fl.
5) Fines	98,511 fl.
6) Various sources	64,198 fl.
	6,363,363 fl. [*sic*]
	[6,363,436 fl.]

This money is the blood-tithe taken from the body of the people. Some seven hundred thousand human beings sweat, moan, and starve because of it. It is extorted in the name of the state, the extortionists claim to be authorized by the government, and the government says this is necessary to preserve order in the state. Now what kind of powerful thing is this: the state? If a number of people live in a country and regulations or laws exist to which everyone must conform, this is called a state. The state is therefore *everyone;* the regulators within the state are the laws which secure the well-being of *all,* and which should arise from the well-being of *all.*—Now see what has become of the state in the Grand Duchy; see what it means to preserve order in the state! Seven hundred thousand people pay six million for it, that means they are transformed into plowhorses and oxen so that they live in order. Living in order means starving and being oppressed.

Who are they who have created this order and who watch over its preservation? The Grand Ducal government. The government consists of the Grand Duke and his highest officials. The other officials are men appointed by the government to maintain order. Their number is legion: state and government officials, county and district officials, church and school officials, treasury and forestry officials, etc., all with their armies of secretaries, etc. The people are their flock, they are its shepherds, milkers, and fleecers; they wear the peasants' skins, the spoil of the poor is in their houses; the tears of widows and orphans are the grease on their faces; they rule freely and exhort the people to servitude. To them you pay your 6,000,000 florins in fees; for that they have the task of governing you; that is, to be fed by you and to rob you of your human and civil rights. Now see the harvest of your sweat.

The Ministries of the Interior and Justice are paid 1,110,607 florins. For that you have a chaos of laws accumulated from arbitrary ordinances of all centuries, written mostly in a foreign language. You have thereby inherited the nonsense of all previous generations; the burden that crushed them is pressing upon you. The law is the property of an insignificant class of aristocrats and intellectuals who grant themselves authority through their own machinations. This justice is merely a means to keep you under control, so that you can be more easily oppressed; it acts according to laws that you do not understand, principles about which you know nothing, judgments that you cannot comprehend. It is incorruptible, for it lets itself be paid just dearly enough not to need any bribes. But most of its servants have sold body and soul to the government. Their armchairs stand on a pile of 461,373 florins (total expenses for the courts and penal institutions). The frock coats, canes, and sabers of their inviolable servants are lined with the silver of 197,502 florins (total cost of the police force, constabulary, etc.). In Germany justice has been for centuries the whore of the German princes. You must pave each step toward her with silver and pay for her verdict with poverty and humiliation. Think of the stamp taxes, think of cringing in offices and standing sentry duty before them. Think of the fees for scribes and bailiffs. You may sue your neighbor for stealing a potato, but just try to sue for the larceny committed on your property every day on behalf of the state in the form of fees and taxes, so that a legion of useless officials may fatten themselves on your sweat; try to sue because you are subject to the whims of a few potbellies and because these whims are called law; sue because you are the plowhorses of the state; sue for your lost human rights: where are the courts that will hear your suit, where are the judges who will administer justice?—The chains of your fellow citizens of Vogelsberg who were dragged off to Rokkenburg[1] will give you an answer.

And if at last one of those few judges or other officials who holds justice and the common good dearer than his belly and Mammon wants to aid instead of persecute the people, then he himself will be persecuted by the prince's highest officials.

For the Finance Ministry 1,551,502 florins.

This pays the salaries of the treasury officials, chief revenue officials, tax collectors, and their subordinates. For this they calculate the yield of your fields and count your heads. The ground beneath your feet, the bite of food between your teeth is taxed. For this the lords sit together in frock coats and the people stand naked and cringing before them, the lords lay their hands on the people's thighs and shoulders and calculate how much they still can carry, and if the lords are merciful, it is like sparing an animal that should not be overly fatigued.

For the military 914,820 florins.

For that your sons get a colorful coat for their bodies, a gun or a drum on their shoulders, and every autumn they may shoot blanks, and they tell you how the lords of the royal court and the misbegotten sons of nobility take precedence over all children of honest people, and they march around with them on broad city streets with drums and trumpets. For those 900,000 florins your sons must swear allegiance to the tyrants and stand guard at their palaces. With their drums they drown out your groans, with their clubs they smash your skulls when you dare to think you are free men. They are legal murderers protecting legal thieves, think of Södel! There your brothers, your children were killers of brothers and fathers.

For pensions 480,000 florins.

For that the officials are put in easy-chairs after they have served the state loyally for a certain time, that means after they have been

1. They were arrested for their presumed complicity in a peasants' revolt, which ended in the "bloodbath at Södel," during which two people were shot.

zealous hacks serving in that organized oppression called law and order.

For the Ministry of State and the State Council 174,600 florins.

Just about everywhere now in Germany the biggest rascals stand closest to the princes, at least in the Grand Duchy. If an honest man were to appear in a State Council, he would be thrown out. But if an honest man could indeed become and remain a minister, as matters now stand in Germany he would merely be a puppet on strings pulled by a princely puppet, and the princely dummy is being manipulated by a valet or a coachman or his wife and her favorite, or his half-brother—or all together. The situation in Germany is now as the Prophet Micah writes, Chapter 7, Verses 3 and 4: "The great man, he uttereth his mischievous desire: so they wrap it up. The best of them is as a brier: the most upright is sharper than a thorn hedge." You must pay dearly for the briers and thorn hedges, for in addition you must pay 827,772 florins for the Grand Ducal house and royal court.

The institutions, the people of which I have spoken up to now are merely tools, merely servants. They do nothing in their own name; under their appointment to office stands an "L.," that means *Ludwig* by the Grace of God, and they say with reverence: "in the name of the Grand Duke." This is their battle cry when they auction off your equipment, drive off your cattle, throw you in jail. In the name of the Grand Duke, they say, and this man is called: inviolable, holy, sovereign, Royal Highness. Yet approach this child of man and look through his princely cloak. He eats when he is hungry and sleeps when his eyes grow heavy. Behold, like you he crept naked and soft into the world and like you he will be carried from it hard and stiff, and yet his foot is on your neck, seven hundred thousand human beings are hitched to his plow, his ministers are responsible for his actions, he controls your property through the taxes he decrees, he controls your lives through the laws he makes, around him are noblemen and women known as the royal court, and his divine power is passed on to his children through women of equally superhuman stock.

Woe unto you idolaters!—You are like the heathens who pray to the crocodile that tears them apart. You place a crown on his head, but it is a crown of thorns that you are pressing onto your own heads; you place a scepter in his hand, but it is a rod that flogs you; you place him on your throne, but it is a rack of torture for you and your children. The prince is the head of the bloodsucker that crawls over you, the ministers are its teeth and the officials its tail. The hungry bellies of all highborn gentlemen to whom he gives high positions are the cupping glasses which he applies to the body of the land. That "L." on his decrees is the mark of the beast worshiped by the idolaters of our time. The princely cloak is the carpet on which the lords and ladies of nobility and the court roll over each other in their lust—they cover their abscesses with medals and ribbons, and they cover their leprous bodies with costly garments. The daughters of the people are their maids and whores, the sons of the people their lackeys and soldiers. Go to Darmstadt once and see how the lords are amusing themselves there with your money, and then tell your starving wives and children that strangers' bellies are thriving marvelously on their bread, tell them about the beautiful clothes dyed in their sweat and the dainty ribbons cut from the calluses on their hands, tell about the stately houses built from the bones of the people; and then crawl into your smoky huts and bend over your stony fields, so that for once your children can go there too when a royal heir and a royal heiress want advice and counsel on the production of another royal heir, and your children can look through the open glass doors and see the tablecloth on which the lords dine and smell the lamps that burn from the fat of the peasants. You endure all that because rascals tell you: "This government is ordained of God." This government is ordained not of God but of the Father of Lies. These German princes have no legitimate power; to the contrary, for centuries they have scorned and finally betrayed legitimate power, namely the German Emperor, who was formerly freely chosen by the people. The power of the German princes is based on treason and perjury, not on the people's choice, and therefore their ways and doings are cursed by God; their wisdom is illusion, their justice is oppression. They beat down the land and grind the faces of the poor. You blaspheme against God if you call one of these princes the Lord's anointed, this means God has anointed devils and made them rulers over German soil. These princes have torn apart Germany, our dear Fatherland, they have betrayed the Emperor elected by our free forefathers, and now these traitors and torturers demand your loyalty!—But the kingdom of darkness is coming to an end. Now oppressed by the princes,

Germany will soon arise again as a free state with a government elected by the people. The Scriptures say: "Render unto Caesar the things which are Caesar's." But what things belong to the princes, to the traitors?—*Judas's share!*

For the legislatures 16,000 florins.

In 1789 the people of France were tired of being their king's whipping boy. They rose up and nominated trustworthy men who came together and said: a king is a man like any other, he is merely the first servant of the state, he must be accountable to the people, and if he does his job poorly, he should be punished. They then defined the rights of man: "No one shall inherit by birth any rights or titles over another, no one shall gain rights over another through property. Supreme power lies in the will of all or of the majority. This will is law, it manifests itself through legislatures or through the people's representatives, elected by all, and anyone may be elected; the elected express the will of their constituents, and the will of the elected majority thus corresponds to the will of the majority of the people; the king is merely responsible for the execution of the laws they enact." The king swore to uphold this constitution, but he perjured himself before the people, and the people sentenced him to die as is proper for a traitor. The French then abolished hereditary monarchy and freely elected a new government, to which every nation is entitled according to reason and Holy Writ. The men who were to supervise the execution of the laws were elected by the assembly of people's representatives, they formed the new government. Executive and legislative government was thus elected by the people and France was a free state.

But the remaining monarchs were terrified of the power of the French people; they thought they might all break their necks on that first royal corpse, and their mistreated subjects might awaken at the French call to freedom. With giant war machines and cavalry they descended upon France from all sides, and a large number of nobles and aristocrats bestirred themselves and joined the enemy. Then the people grew angry and arose in their strength. They crushed the traitors and annihilated the monarchs' mercenaries. This newborn freedom thrived in the blood of tyrants, and thrones trembled and nations exulted in its voice. But the French sold even their newborn freedom for the glory offered them by Napoleon, and they crowned him Emperor.—Thereupon the Almighty allowed the Emperor's army to freeze to death in Russia and lashed France with cossacks' whips and gave the French potbellied Bourbon kings again, so that France would convert from idolizing hereditary monarchy to serving the god who had created men free and equal. But when France had paid its penalty and brave men chased the corrupt Charles the Tenth out of the country in July 1830, liberated France nevertheless turned once again to *semi-hereditary* monarchy and set a new scourge on its back in the person of the hypocrite Louis Philippe. There was great joy in Germany and all of Europe, however, when Charles the Tenth was deposed, and the suppressed German states prepared to fight for freedom. Then the princes deliberated how to avoid the wrath of the people, and the cunning ones among them said: let us give up part of our power to save the rest. And they appeared before the people and spoke: we shall grant you the freedom you mean to fight for.—And trembling with fear they threw down a few scraps and spoke of their charity. Unfortunately the people trusted them and were pacified.—And thus was Germany deceived like France.

What in fact are these constitutions in Germany? Nothing but empty straw from which the princes have threshed the grain for themselves. What are our legislatures? Nothing but slow-moving vehicles which can perhaps be used once or twice to block the rapacity of the princes and their ministers, but which can never be used to build a mighty fortress for German freedom. What are our election laws? Nothing but violations of most Germans' civil and human rights. Think of the election laws in the Grand Duchy, where no one may be elected who is not well-to-do, no matter how upright and well-intentioned he may be, yet Grolmann, who wanted to steal two million from you,[2] is elected. Think of the constitution of the Grand Duchy.—According to its articles, the Grand Duke is inviolable, holy, and accountable to no one. His high position is hereditary, he has the right to wage war and has exclusive control over the military. He convenes, adjourns, or dissolves the legislatures. The legislatures may not originate laws but must request them, and it is left completely up to the prince's discretion to grant or deny them. He retains possession of nearly unlimited power,

2. Representative Friedrich von Grolmann and others proposed that the State Treasury assume the personal debts of Ludwig II. The motion was defeated (see below).

except that he may not enact new laws and impose new taxes without the approval of the legislatures. Yet often he does not adhere to this approval, often he is satisfied with the old laws deriving from princely power, and he therefore needs no new laws. Such a constitution is a miserable, deplorable thing. What can be expected from legislatures restricted by such a constitution? Even if there were no betrayers of the people nor craven cowards among the elected, even if they consisted only of determined friends of the people?! What can be expected from legislatures hardly able to defend the miserable tatters of a wretched constitution!—The only opposition they were able to muster was the denial of the two million florins the Grand Duke wanted as a gift from the heavily indebted nation for the payment of his debts. But even if the Grand Duchy's legislatures had sufficient rights, and the Grand Duchy—but the Grand Duchy alone—had a true constitution, this marvel would soon come to an end. The vultures in Vienna and Berlin would stretch their hangmen's claws and destroy this little freedom root and branch. The entire German nation must win this freedom. And this time, dear fellow citizens, is not far off.—The Lord has delivered the beautiful land of Germany—for many centuries the most glorious empire on earth—into the hands of foreign and native oppressors, because in their hearts the German people had forsaken the freedom and equality of their ancestors and forsaken the fear of the Lord, because you devoted yourselves to idolizing those many petty lords, dukes, and kinglets.

The Lord who smashed the rod of the foreign oppressor Napoleon shall also destroy the images of our native tyrants through the hands of the people. These images may glitter with gold and jewels, medals and decorations, but inside them *the worm does not die, and their feet are of clay.*—God will give you strength to smite their feet as soon as you repent the error of your ways and know the truth: "that there is only one God and no other gods before him who let themselves be called Highness and Most High, divine and accountable to no one; that God created all men free and equal in their rights; that no government has God's blessing unless it is based on the people's trust and is expressly or tacitly elected by them; but that a government with power but no rights over a nation is ordained of God only as the Devil is ordained of God; that obedience to such a devil's government is only valid until its devil's might can be broken; that God, who united a nation into one body through a common language, shall punish in this life and eternally hereafter as murderers of the people and tyrants those rulers who draw and quarter the nation or even tear it into thirty pieces, for the Scriptures say: what God hath joined together, let not man put asunder; and that the Almighty, who can create a paradise from a desert, can also transform a land of distress and misery into a paradise, like our treasured Germany before its princes tore it apart and flayed it."

Since the German Empire was decayed and rotten, and the Germans had forsaken God and freedom, God let the Empire go to ruin in order to regenerate it as a free state. For a time He gave "Satan's angels" the power to beat Germany with their fists, He gave "principalities and powers, the rulers of the darkness of this world, spiritual wickedness in high places" (Ephesians 6:12), power to torment citizens and peasants and suck their blood and do mischief to all who love justice and freedom more than injustice and servitude.—But their cup is full!

Look at that monster branded by God, King Ludwig of Bavaria,[3] the blasphemer who forces honest men to kneel before his image and allows corrupt judges to imprison those who speak the truth; the swine who rolled in every puddle of vice in Italy, the wolf who makes corrupt legislatures allot five million every year to his Baal-court, and then ask: "Is this a government with God's blessing?"

> Ha! you'd be a governor of God?
> God bestows on us his grace;
> You rob, oppress, imprison us,
> You're not of God, tyrant![4]

I say to you: the cup of the prince and his like is full. God, who has used these princes to punish Germany for its sins, shall heal it again. "He shall go through the briers and thorns and burn them together" (Isaiah 27:4).

3. Ludwig (1786–1868) was an energetic patron of the arts. His enlightened political views became increasingly reactionary after the Revolution of 1830. He abdicated in 1848.

4. Altered final stanza of "The Peasant: To His Serene Highness, the Tyrant," by the Storm and Stress poet Gottfried August Bürger (1747–1794).

Just as the hunchback with which God has branded this King Ludwig can grow no larger, so can the atrocities of these princes no longer increase. Their cup is full. God will smash their fortresses, and life and strength, the blessing of freedom, shall then bloom again in Germany. The princes have transformed German soil into a great field of corpses, as Ezekiel writes in Chapter 37: "The Lord set me down in the midst of the valley which was full of bones, and lo, they were very dry." But what is God's Word about these dry bones: "Behold, I will lay sinews upon you, and will bring up flesh upon you, and cover you with skin, and put breath in you, and ye shall live; and ye shall know that I am the Lord." And God's Word shall truly come to pass in Germany as well, as the Prophet says: "There was a noise, and behold a shaking, and the bones came together, bone to his bone.—And the breath came into them, and they lived, and stood up upon their feet, an exceeding great army."

As the Prophet writes, so it was until now in Germany: your bones are dry, for the order in which you live is sheer oppression. In the Grand Duchy you pay six million to a handful of people whose whims govern your life and property, and it is the same for others in fragmented Germany. You are nothing, you have nothing! You are without rights. You must give whatever your insatiable oppressors demand and carry whatever they load upon you. As far as a tyrant can see—and Germany has about thirty of them—land and people wither. But as the Prophet writes, so shall it soon be in Germany: the Day of Resurrection is at hand. On the field of corpses there shall be a noise and a shaking, and there will be a great army of the resurrected.

Lift up your eyes and count the little band of your oppressors, who are strong only through the blood they suck from you and through your arms which you lend them against your will. There are about ten thousand of them and seven hundred thousand of you in the Grand Duchy, and that is the ratio of people to their oppressors in the rest of Germany as well. They may threaten with royal armaments and cavalry, but I say to you: all they that take the sword against the people shall perish with the sword of the people. Germany is now a field of corpses, soon it shall be a paradise. The German nation is one body, you are a limb of that body. It makes no difference where the apparently dead body begins to twitch. When the Lord gives you his signs through the men through whom he shall lead nations from bondage to freedom, then arise, and the whole body will rise up with you.

You cringed for long years in the thorny fields of servitude, then you will sweat for one summer in the vineyard of freedom and shall be free unto the thousandth generation.

Throughout a long life you dug up the earth, then you shall dig your tyrants' grave. You built the fortresses, then you shall destroy them and build the house of freedom. Then you shall be able to baptize your children freely with the water of life. And until the Lord calls you through his messengers and signs, be watchful, prepare yourselves in spirit, pray, and teach your children to pray: "Lord, break the rod of our oppressors and let Thy kingdom come, the kingdom of righteousness. Amen."

Notes

Georg Büchner's birthplace, the Grand Duchy of Hesse-Darmstadt, was far less imposing than its name would suggest. It was a small agrarian country with a virtually stagnant economy and a feudal social structure. Its inhabitants were mostly peasants and laborers who, despite the abolition of serfdom in 1820, still adhered to the practices of their medieval ancestors. Plagued by persistent crop failure, the peasants were taxed both by their landowners and by the state; whatever they managed to produce for export was subject to high tariffs, which effectively strangled Hesse's domestic industry. While the Industrial Revolution flourished in the centralized societies of England and France, Hesse remained a European backwater. Like their colleagues elsewhere in the German Confederation, Hesse's rulers lived in splendor, draining the financial resources of their already impoverished subjects and leaving administrative matters to their ministers. The bourgeoisie, as a whole, did not threaten their dominance. Thus, while France was crowning Louis Philippe, its "citizen king," the states within the German Confederation remained in the grip of the aristocracy.

Yet even the aristocrats could not afford to ignore the liberal sentiment sweeping Europe in the wake of the American and French Revolutions. Napoleon's defeat had raised German hopes for political and cultural unification, for greater equality and individual liberties. As a consequence, the Hessian government was one of several that grudgingly agreed to establish a constitution and a representative legislature—a "reform" that in fact still left most Hessians without any voice whatsoever in government affairs. Only highly propertied individuals could be elected to the legislative assembly; in 1820 only 985 citizens from a population of 700,000 could qualify, and consequently two-thirds of the legislature consisted of high government officials. The legislature could approve but not deny taxation measures, and it could be dissolved at any time by the Grand Duke.

When Georg Büchner arrived in Strassburg in 1831 to study medicine, he left Hessian provincialism behind and entered a rich intellectual climate, a melting pot of French and German culture.

He met regularly with fellow students to discuss current conditions in France and Germany; his letters dating from this period express his outrage against the social inequity and injustice prevailing in the German states. After two years in Strassburg, he was obliged by law to continue his studies at a Hessian university, and he transferred to the University of Giessen. In January 1834, Georg Büchner met Friedrich Ludwig Weidig, a school principal and pastor, who had been involved in illegal political activities since approximately 1814 and had established extensive contacts to Hessian radicals and liberals. At the time Büchner met him, he stood at the vortex of all conspiratorial activity in Hesse. In early 1834, Büchner organized a small number of students and laborers into a "Society for Human Rights," a training group for subversive action against the government. In March he collected statistics about the economic conditions prevailing in the Grand Duchy of Hesse-Darmstadt and drafted a polemical essay, which he sent to Weidig. Weidig edited and expanded the text in order to increase its effectiveness among Hessian peasants and members of the middle-class liberal opposition. He eliminated Büchner's attacks against the bourgeoisie, focusing on the nobility as the sole perpetrator of social injustice. Thus Büchner's references to "the rich" were altered to "the aristocrats" (literally: "the elegant ones"). Weidig added numerous quotations from the Bible and provided a preface and a title: *The Hessian Messenger.*

Since the original manuscripts are lost, it is impossible to distinguish Weidig's words from Büchner's with absolute certainty, but their differing philosophies and styles are relatively easy to detect. Büchner's analytical argumentation, based on socioeconomic fact, is vivid, mercilessly logical, and devastatingly sarcastic. He focuses upon the enormous material discrepancies among social classes; as he maintained in a letter to Gutzkow a year later, "the relationship between poor and rich is the only revolutionary element in the world, hunger alone can become the goddess of freedom." Weidig, the theologian, interprets historical development in terms of divine intervention and sermonizes about the resurrection of the German Empire as a "paradise." He defends an idealized concept of human rights based on a synthesis of eighteenth-century liberalism and Holy Writ.

Despite his objections to the final version, Büchner agreed to help publish and distribute the *Messenger*. He brought the manuscript to the town of Offenbach, where approximately three hundred copies were printed on a press hidden in a cellar. On July 31, Karl Minnigerode and two other friends of Büchner's picked up the pamphlets, but Minnigerode was arrested as he returned to Giessen. The enterprise had been betrayed by a man from Weidig's circle. Hearing of the arrest, Büchner went off to warn his friends. Meanwhile in Giessen, his papers and belongings were searched by the police, but no incriminating evidence was found. Weidig was transferred to a remote village, but otherwise the authorities left the two authors of the treasonous pamphlet alone. Weidig was not to be stopped by a mere transfer; in the following months he published another number of his ongoing *Illuminator for Hesse* and a second edition of *The Hessian Messenger,* to which he added passages concerning the upcoming legislative elections. That a second edition was published seems to speak for the effectiveness of the first. True, many copies had been turned over to the police, but Weidig knew of peasants who claimed that the *Messenger* had impressed them deeply.

Eventually a second informer provided the police with enough information to proceed against Weidig and Büchner. Büchner left Darmstadt for Strassburg in March 1835; Weidig, who could not bring himself to flee, was "detained for interrogation" for two years. An acquaintance of Büchner's named Carl Vogt recalled in his memoirs the methods and consequences of such detention:

> I have known people who were driven from their houses and from thriving businesses, compelled to struggle for their bread in a foreign country, only because a spy had found a package of the hated journal [not the *Messenger*] under their front gate, placed there by a stranger. I have known others who were held in the most bitter solitary confinement for years, where any activity, even manual work, was prohibited with clever cruelty, and who were then released from detention, which had brought absolutely nothing to light, and were pardoned from that time on, broken in spirit.

Weidig's interrogator was State Commissioner Konrad Georgi, a brutal alcoholic, who had earlier ordered an illegal search of Büchner's quarters in Giessen. Weidig was subjected to torture, but he confessed to nothing. On February 23, 1837, he slashed his wrists and wrote in blood on his cell wall: "Since my enemy denies me any defense, I freely choose a shameful death." Prison officials delayed sending for a doctor, and Weidig bled to death. Soon thereafter, the regime was able to gain a ruling majority in the legislature, stifling the voice of opposition for more than a decade.

DANTON'S DEATH

CHARACTERS

GEORGE DANTON LEGENDRE CAMILLE DESMOULINS HÉRAULT-SÉCHELLES LACROIX PHILIPPEAU FABRE D'ÉGLANTINE MERCIER THOMAS PAINE	*deputies of the National Convention*
ROBESPIERRE ST. JUST BARÈRE COLLOT D'HERBOIS BILLAUD-VARENNES	*members of the Committee of Public Safety*

CHAUMETTE, *procurator of the Commune*
DILLON, *a general*
FOUQUIER-TINVILLE, *public prosecutor*

AMAR VOULAND	*members of the Committee of General Security*
HERMAN DUMAS	*presidents of the Revolutionary Tribunal*

PARIS, *a friend of Danton*
SIMON, *a prompter*
SIMON'S WIFE
LAFLOTTE
JULIE, *Danton's wife*
LUCILE, *wife of Camille Desmoulins*

ROSALIE ADELAIDE MARION	*grisettes*

LADIES *at card tables,* GENTLEMEN *and* LADIES *as well as a* YOUNG GENTLEMAN *and* EUGÉNIE *on a promenade,* CITIZENS, CITIZEN-SOLDIERS, DEPUTIES FROM LYONS *and other* DEPUTIES, JACOBINS, PRESIDENTS OF THE JACOBIN CLUB *and the* NATIONAL CONVENTION, JAILERS, EXECUTIONERS, *and* DRIVERS, MEN *and* WOMEN *of the people,* GRISETTES, BALLADEER, BEGGAR, *etc.*

Act One

1

HÉRAULT-SÉCHELLES, *a few women at a card table.* DANTON, JULIE *somewhat farther off,* DANTON *on a footstool at* JULIE'*s feet.*

DANTON. Look at the pretty lady—how neatly she plays her cards. She knows how, all right—they say she always gives her husband a heart and others a diamond. You women could even make us fall in love with a lie.

JULIE. Do you believe in me?

DANTON. How do I know? We know little about each other. We're all thick-skinned, we reach for each other, but it's all in vain, we just rub the rough leather off . . . we are very lonely.

JULIE. You know me, Danton.

DANTON. Yes, whatever "knowing" means. You have dark eyes and curly hair and a nice complexion and you always say to me: dear George. But (*He points to her forehead and eyes.*) there—there: what's behind that? No, our senses are coarse. Know each other? We'd have to break open our skulls and pull each other's thoughts out of the brain fibers.

A WOMAN. (*To* HÉRAULT.) What are you doing with your fingers?

HÉRAULT. Nothing!

WOMAN. Don't twist your thumb under like that! I can't stand it.

HÉRAULT. Just look, it has a very peculiar physiognomy.

DANTON. No, Julie, I love you like the grave.

JULIE. (*Turning away.*) Oh!

DANTON. No, listen! They say in the grave there is peace, and grave and peace are one. If that's so, then in your lap I'm already lying under the earth. You sweet grave—your lips are funeral bells, your voice my death knell, your breasts my burial mound, and your heart my coffin.

WOMAN. You lose!

HÉRAULT. That was an adventure of love. It costs money as they all do.

WOMAN. Then you made your declarations of love with your fingers, like a deaf-mute.

HÉRAULT. And why not? Some say that fingers are the easiest to understand. I plotted an affair with a queen, my fingers were princes changed into spiders, you, Madame, were the good fairy, but it didn't work: the queen was always with child, bearing jacks by the minute. I wouldn't let my daughter play games like that. The kings and queens fall on top of each other so indecently and the jacks pop up right after.

(CAMILLE DESMOULINS *and* PHILIPPEAU *enter.*)

HÉRAULT. Philippeau, what sad eyes! Did you rip a hole in your red cap, did Saint Jacob look angry, did it rain during the guillotining or did you get a bad seat and not see anything?

CAMILLE. You're parodying Socrates. Do you know what the divine man asked Alcibiades when he found him gloomy and depressed one day? "Did you lose your shield in battle, did you lose a race or a sword fight? Did someone else sing better or play the zither better than you?" What classic republicans! Just compare that to our guillotine-romanticism!

PHILIPPEAU. Another twenty victims today. We were wrong: the Hébertists were sent to the scaffold because they weren't systematic enough. Maybe also because the decemvirs thought they'd be lost if just for a week there were men who were more feared than they.

HÉRAULT. They want to change us into cavemen. St. Just would be happy to see us crawling around on all fours so that the lawyer from Arras[1] could invent beanies, school benches, and a God according to the formulas of the watchmaker from Geneva.[2]

PHILIPPEAU. They wouldn't be afraid to add a few more zeros to Marat's calculations. How much longer should we be dirty and bloody like newborn children, having coffins as cradles and playing with human heads? We must act. The Committee of Clemency must be established and the expelled deputies reinstated.

HÉRAULT. The Revolution has reached the stage of reorganization. The Revolution must stop and the Republic must begin. In our

1. Robespierre.

2. Jean-Jacques Rousseau.

constitution, right must prevail over duty, well-being over virtue, and self-defense over punishment. Everyone must be able to assert himself and live according to his nature. Be he reasonable or unreasonable, educated or uneducated, good or evil—that's not the state's business. We are all fools: no one has the right to impose his own folly on anyone else. Everyone must be allowed to enjoy himself as he likes, but not at the expense of others nor by disturbing their personal enjoyment.

CAMILLE. The government must be a transparent gown that clings closely to the body of the people. Every pulsing vein, flexing muscle, twitching sinew must leave its imprint. Its appearance may be beautiful or ugly—it has the right to be as it is. We don't have the right to cut a dress for it as we see fit. We will rap the knuckles of those who wish to throw a nun's veil over the naked shoulders of that dearest sinner, France. We want naked gods and bacchantes, Olympic games, and from melodic lips the words: "Ah, uninhibiting wicked love!" We won't prevent the Romans from sitting in a corner and cooking their turnips, but they are not to give us any more gladiatorial games. The divine Epicurus and Venus with the beautiful ass must replace Saints Marat and Chalier as doorkeepers of the Republic.

Danton, you will lead the attack in the Convention.

DANTON. I will, you will, he will. If you live that long, as the old women say. In an hour sixty minutes will have gone by. Right, my boy?

CAMILLE. What's all that for? That's obvious.

DANTON. Oh, everything is obvious. Who's going to accomplish all these beautiful things?

PHILIPPEAU. We and the respectable people.

DANTON. That "and" there is a long word, it holds us pretty far apart. The road is long and respectability runs out of breath before we come together. And what if we do!—to those respectable people you can lend money, be their godfather, give them your daughters in marriage, but that's all!

CAMILLE. If you know all that, why did you begin the fight?

DANTON. Because I loathed those people. I could never look at such pompous Catonians without giving them a kick. That's the way I am. (*He rises.*)

JULIE. You're going?

DANTON. (*To* JULIE.) I have to, their politics are getting on my nerves. (*While leaving.*) A final prophecy: the statue of freedom is not yet cast, the furnace is glowing, we can all still burn our fingers. (*Exits.*)

CAMILLE. Let him go, do you really think he could stay away once the action starts?

HÉRAULT. Yes, but just to pass the time, like playing chess.

2

A street.

SIMON. *His* WIFE.

SIMON. (*Beats his* WIFE.) Thou panderer, thou wrinkled contraceptive, thou worm-eaten apple of sin!

WIFE. Hey, help! Help!

PEOPLE. (*Running in.*) Get them apart! Get them apart!

SIMON. No—let me be, Romans! I will smite this skeleton to the earth! Thou vestal virgin!

WIFE. Me a vestal virgin? We'll see about that!

SIMON. Thus I tear thy raiment from thy shoulders,
Thy naked carcass I cast into the sun.
Thou bed of prostitution, in every wrinkle of thy body lurketh lechery.

(*They are separated.*)

FIRST CITIZEN. What's going on?

SIMON. Where is the virgin? Speak! No, I cannot call her that. The maid! No, not that either. The woman, the wife! Not that, not that either. Only one name is left. Oh, it chokes me! I have no breath for it.

SECOND CITIZEN. That's good, otherwise the name would stink from brandy.

SIMON. Old Virginius, cover thy bare pate. The raven of shame perches upon it and stabs at thine eyes. Give me a knife, Romans! (*He collapses.*)

WIFE. Oh, usually he's a good man, but when he drinks too much, brandy sticks out a leg and trips him up.

SECOND CITIZEN. Then he walks on three legs.

WIFE. No, he falls.

SECOND CITIZEN. Right. First he walks on three and then he falls on the third until the third falls too.

SIMON. Thou art the vampire's tongue that drinketh the warmest blood of my heart.

WIFE. Leave him be—about this time he always gets sentimental. He'll get over it.

FIRST CITIZEN. What happened?

WIFE. You see, I was sitting in the sun on a rock, keeping warm, you see, 'cause we don't have any wood, you see . . .

SECOND CITIZEN. So use your husband's nose.

WIFE. . . . and my daughter had gone around the corner—she's a good girl and supports her parents.

SIMON. Ha, she confesses!

WIFE. You Judas, would you have a pair of pants to pull *up* if the young gentlemen didn't pull theirs *down* with her? You barrel of brandy, do you want to die of thirst when the little spring stops running, hey? We have to work with all our limbs—why not with *that* too? Her mother worked with it when she was born, and it hurt. Can't she work for her mother with it, too, hey? And does it hurt her, hey? You idiot!

SIMON. Ha, Lucretia! A knife, give me a knife, Romans! Ha, Appius Claudius!

FIRST CITIZEN. Yes, a knife, but not for the poor whore. What did she do wrong? Nothing! It's her hunger that goes whoring and begging. A knife for those who buy the flesh of our wives and daughters! Down with those who prostitute the daughters of the people! You have hunger pains and they have gas pains, you have holes in your jackets and they have warm coats, you have calluses and they have velvet hands. Ergo: you work and they do nothing; ergo: you earn it and they steal it; ergo: if you want to get a few cents back from your stolen property, you have to go whoring and begging; ergo: they are thieves and must be killed.

THIRD CITIZEN. All the blood they have in their veins they sucked out of ours. They told us: kill the aristocrats, they are wolves!

We strung up the aristocrats on the lampposts. They said the Veto eats up your bread; we killed the Veto. They said the Girondists are starving you out; we guillotined the Girondists. But they took the clothes off the dead and we go barefoot and freeze, the same as before. We want to pull the skin off their thighs and make pants out of it, we want to melt off their fat and blend it into our soups. Let's go! Kill anyone without a hole in his coat!

FIRST CITIZEN. Kill anyone who can read and write!

SECOND CITIZEN. Kill anyone who turns up his toes when he walks!

ALL. (*Screaming.*) Kill them, kill them!

(*A* YOUNG MAN *is dragged in.*)

A FEW VOICES. He's got a handkerchief! An aristocrat! String him up! String him up!

SECOND CITIZEN. What? He doesn't blow his nose with his fingers? String him up on the lamppost!

YOUNG MAN. Oh, gentlemen!

SECOND CITIZEN. There aren't any gentlemen here. String him up!

A FEW. (*Sing.*)

If you lie within the earth,
The worms will soon invade your berth.
Hanging is a better lot,
Than lying in a grave to rot.

YOUNG MAN. Mercy!

THIRD CITIZEN. It's only a little game with a bit of hemp around your neck. It'll only take a second—we're more merciful than the likes of you. Our life is murder by work; we hang on the ropes for sixty years and twitch, but we'll cut ourselves loose. String him up on the lamppost!

YOUNG MAN. All right, but that won't make things any brighter.

THE OTHERS. Bravo, bravo!

A FEW VOICES. Let him go! (*He escapes.*)

(ROBESPIERRE *enters, accompanied by women and sansculottes.*)

ROBESPIERRE. What's the matter, citizen?

THIRD CITIZEN. What's the next step? Those few drops of blood from August and September haven't reddened the cheeks of the people. The guillotine is too slow. We need a downpour.

FIRST CITIZEN. Our wives and children cry out for bread, we want to feed them with the flesh of the aristocrats. Hey! Kill anyone without a hole in his coat!

ALL. Kill them! Kill them!

ROBESPIERRE. In the name of the law!

FIRST CITIZEN. What's the law?

ROBESPIERRE. The will of the people.

FIRST CITIZEN. We are the people, and we don't want any law, ergo: this will is law, ergo: in the name of the law there is no more law, ergo: kill them!

SEVERAL VOICES. Listen to Aristides! Listen to the Incorruptible!

A WOMAN. Listen to the Messiah, who has been sent to choose and to judge. He will destroy the wicked with his sharp sword. His eyes are the eyes of selection, his hands are the hands of judgment.

ROBESPIERRE. Poor, virtuous people! You do your duty, you sacrifice your enemies. People, you are mighty. You reveal yourselves in lightning and thunder. But you must not be wounded by your own blows; you kill yourselves in your own wrath. You can fall only through your own strength. Your enemies know that. Your lawmakers are watchful, they will guide your hands. Their eyes are infallible, your hands are inescapable. Come with me to the Jacobins. Your comrades will open their arms to you, we will hold a bloody judgment over our enemies.

MANY VOICES. To the Jacobins! Long live Robespierre! (*They all exit.*)

SIMON. Woe is me, abandoned! (*He tries to get up.*)

HIS WIFE. There! (*She helps him.*)

SIMON. Oh, my Baucis, thou heapest coals of fire on my head.

WIFE. There—stand up.

SIMON. Thou turnest away? Ha, canst thou forgive me, Portia? Did I smite thee? 'Twas not my hand, 'twas not my arm, 'twas my madness.

His madness is poor Hamlet's enemy.
Then Hamlet does it not, Hamlet denies it.

Where is our daughter, where is my Susie?

WIFE. There—around the corner.

SIMON. Let's go to her. Come, my virtuous spouse. (*Both exit.*)

3

The Jacobin Club.

A MAN FROM LYONS. Our brothers in Lyons have sent us to pour their bitter indignation in your ears. We do not know whether or not the cart on which Ronsin rode to the guillotine was the hearse of liberty, but we do know that since that day Chalier's murderers again walk the earth as if there were no grave for them. Have you forgotten that Lyons is a blot on French soil, which we must cover with the corpses of traitors? Have you forgotten that this whore of kings[3] can wash away her leprosy only in the waters of the Rhone? Have you forgotten that this revolutionary torrent must make Pitt's Mediterranean fleets run aground upon the corpses of the aristocrats? Your clemency is murdering the Revolution. The breath of an aristocrat is the death rattle of liberty. Only a coward dies for the Republic; a Jacobin kills for it. We tell you this: if we no longer find in you the vigor of the men of the 10th of August, of September, and of the 31st of May, then, like the patriot Gaillard, we can turn only to Cato's dagger. (*Applause and confused cries.*)

A JACOBIN. We will drink the cup of Socrates with you!

LEGENDRE. (*Jumps onto the tribune.*) We do not need to turn our eyes to Lyons. For several days now those who wear silk clothes, ride in carriages, sit in theater loges, and speak according to the Dictionary of the Academy have felt their heads to be secure on their shoulders. They make clever remarks, saying that Marat and Chalier should be helped to a double martyrdom by guillotining them in effigy. (*Violent commotion in the assembly.*)

SEVERAL VOICES. They are dead men. Their tongues guillotine them.

LEGENDRE. May the blood of these saints come over them! I ask you members of the Committee of Public Safety: since when have your ears become so deaf . . .

COLLOT D'HERBOIS. (*Interrupts him.*) And I ask you, Legendre: whose voice has given breath to such thoughts so that they come to life and dare to speak? It is time to tear off masks. Listen! The cause accuses its effect, the shout its echo, and the premise its

3. Lyons.

conclusion. The Committee of Public Safety is more logical than that, Legendre! Be quiet. The busts of the saints will remain untouched, like Medusa-heads they will turn the traitors into stone.

ROBESPIERRE. I wish to speak.

THE JACOBINS. Listen! Listen to the Incorruptible!

ROBESPIERRE. We were waiting only for the cry of discontent to ring out from all sides before we speak. Our eyes were open, we watched the enemy arming himself and rising up, but we did not sound the alarm. We let the people be their own guard; they have not slept, they have taken up arms. We let the enemy emerge from his cover, we let him advance; now he stands exposed in broad daylight, every blow will strike him, he is dead as soon as you have caught sight of him.

I have told you once before that the internal enemies of the Republic are split into two factions, like two armies. Under banners of various colors and on quite different paths they all rush toward the same goal. One of these factions no longer exists.[4] In its presumptuous madness it tried to cast aside the most proven patriots, branding them worn-out weaklings in order to rob the Republic of its strongest arms. It declared war on the Deity and on property in order to create a diversion on behalf of the kings. It parodied the exalted drama of the Revolution in order to compromise it through premeditated excesses. Hébert's triumph would have turned the Republic into chaos, and despotism would have been satisfied. The sword of judgment has struck the traitor down. But what does it matter to our foreign enemies when criminals of another sort remain to accomplish the same purpose? We have achieved nothing so long as another faction remains to be destroyed. This one is the opposite of the first. It leads us to weakness; its battle cry is: mercy! It intends to rob the people of their weapons and of their strength to fight in order to deliver them up to the kings, naked and unnerved.

The weapon of the Republic is terror, the strength of the Republic is virtue. Virtue: for without it, terror is corruptible; terror: for without it, virtue is powerless. Terror is an outgrowth of virtue; it is nothing more than swift, rigorous, and inflexible

4. The Hébertists.

justice. Some say terror is the weapon of a despotic government, therefore ours resembles despotism. True, but in the way a sword in the hand of a hero of liberty resembles a saber in the hand of a tyrant's minion. If a tyrant rules his brutish subjects through terror, that is his right as a despot; if you destroy through terror the enemies of liberty, you, the founders of the Republic, are no less right. The Revolutionary government is the despotism of liberty against tyranny.

Mercy to the royalists! certain people cry. Mercy to the wicked? No! Mercy to the innocent, mercy to the weak, mercy to the unfortunate, mercy to humanity! Only the peaceful citizen deserves the protection of society. In a republic only republicans are citizens, royalists and foreigners are enemies. To punish the oppressors of mankind is charity, to pardon them is barbarity. I regard all traces of false sentimentality as sighs that fly to England or Austria.

Yet not content to disarm the people, some try to poison the most sacred sources of its strength through vice. This is the most subtle, most dangerous, and most deplorable attack against liberty. Vice is the mark of Cain on the aristocracy. Within a republic it is not only a moral but a political crime; the vice-ridden are the political enemies of liberty; the more they seem to accomplish in its service, the more dangerous they are. The most dangerous citizen is the one who wears out a dozen red caps more easily than doing one good deed.

You will understand me readily when you think about those who used to live in a garret and now ride in a carriage and fornicate with former marchionesses and baronesses. We may well ask: have the people been robbed or have we grasped the golden hands of the kings when we, the people's lawmakers, display all the vices and luxuries of former courtiers, when we see these marquises and barons of the Revolution marrying rich wives, giving sumptuous banquets, gambling, keeping servants and wearing expensive clothes? We may well be surprised when we hear them being witty, playing the snob, and adopting elegant manners. Lately someone shamelessly parodied Tacitus—I could answer like Sallust, and travesty Catiline; but no more brushstrokes are necessary, the portraits are complete.

Let there be no compromise, no truce with those who were

only set on robbing the people, who hoped to rob them unpunished, for whom the Republic was business speculation and the Revolution a trade. Frightened by the rushing torrent of the examples we have set, they now very quietly seek to cool down our justice. We are to believe that they say to themselves: "We are not virtuous enough to be so terrible. Philosophic lawmakers, have mercy on our weakness! I don't dare to tell you that I am so wicked, so I'd rather tell you, don't be inhuman!"

Calm yourselves, virtuous people, calm yourselves, patriots: tell your brothers in Lyons that the sword of justice will not rust in the hands of those to whom you have entrusted it.—We will set a great example for the Republic. (*General applause.*)

MANY VOICES. Long live the Republic, long live Robespierre!

PRESIDENT. The meeting is adjourned.

4

A street.

LACROIX. LEGENDRE.

LACROIX. What have you done, Legendre? Do you realize whose head you're knocking off with those busts of yours?

LEGENDRE. The heads of a few playboys and elegant women, that's all.

LACROIX. You're suicidal, a shadow that murders its origin and thereby itself.

LEGENDRE. I don't understand.

LACROIX. I thought Collot had made himself clear.

LEGENDRE. What difference does it make? He was drunk, as usual.

LACROIX. Fools, children, and—well?—drunks speak the truth. Who do you think Robespierre was talking about with his Catiline?

LEGENDRE. Well?

LACROIX. It's very simple: the atheists and the ultrarevolutionaries have been sent to the scaffold, but the people haven't been helped; they still go barefoot in the streets and want to make shoes out of aristocratic leather. The guillotine thermometer must not drop—

a few degrees lower and the Committee of Public Safety can seek its bed on the Square of the Revolution.[5]

LEGENDRE. What do my busts have to do with that?

LACROIX. Don't you see it yet? You have officially announced the counterrevolution; you have forced the decemvirs to act; you have led their hand. The people are a Minotaur that must have a weekly supply of corpses if it is not to devour its leaders.

LEGENDRE. Where is Danton?

LACROIX. How should I know? He's searching for the Venus de Medici piece by piece among all the grisettes of the Palais Royal. He's making a mosaic, as he says; heaven knows what limb he's at right now. It's a shame that nature has cut up beauty into pieces, like Medea her brother, and has put the fragments into our bodies.

Let's go to the Palais Royal. (*Both exit.*)

5

A room.

DANTON, MARION.

MARION. No, let me be. Here at your feet. I want to tell you a story.

DANTON. You could use your lips in better ways.

MARION. No, let me stay like this. My mother was a smart woman, she always said chastity was a fine virtue—when people came to the house and started talking about certain things, she told me to leave the room; when I asked what they wanted, she said I ought to be ashamed of myself; when she gave me a book to read, I almost always had to skip a few pages. But I read the Bible whenever I liked—there everything was holy; but there were things in there that I didn't understand, and I didn't want to ask anyone; I brooded about them by myself. Then spring came, and all around me things were going on that I didn't take

5. The location of the guillotine.

part in. I found myself in a strange atmosphere, it almost choked me; I looked at my body, sometimes I felt I was double and then melted again into one. At that time a young man came to our house—he was good-looking and often said crazy things; I wasn't sure what he wanted, but I had to laugh. My mother invited him often—both he and I liked that. Finally we couldn't see why we might not just as well lie together between two sheets as sit next to each other in two chairs. I enjoyed that more than our conversations, and I didn't understand why one would allow the smaller pleasure and deny the greater one. We did it secretly. It went on like that. But I became like an ocean, consuming everything and swirling deeper and deeper. For me there was only one opposite: all men melted into one body. That was my nature—who can escape it? Finally he realized it. He came one morning and kissed me as if he wanted to choke me, his arms wrapped tight around my neck. I was terribly afraid. Then he let me go and laughed and said he had almost done a foolish thing, I ought to keep my dress and use it, it would wear out by itself, he didn't want to spoil my fun just yet, it was all I had. Then he left, and again I didn't know what he wanted. That evening I was sitting at the window; I'm very sensitive, and I relate to everything around me only through feeling. I became absorbed in the waves of the sunset. Then a group of people came down the street, children in front, women looking out of their windows. I looked down—they were carrying him by in a basket, the moon shone on his pale forehead, his hair was damp, he had drowned himself. I had to cry. That was the only break in my being. Other people have Sundays and working days, they work for six days and pray on the seventh; once a year, on their birthdays, they get sentimental, and every year on New Year's Day they reflect. I don't understand all that. For me there is no stopping, no changing. I'm always the same, an endless longing and grasping, a fire, a torrent. My mother died of grief, people point at me. That's silly. It's all the same, whatever we enjoy: bodies, icons, flowers, or toys, it's all the same feeling; whoever enjoys the most prays the most.

DANTON. Why can't I contain your beauty in me completely, surround it entirely?

MARION. Danton, your lips have eyes.

DANTON. I wish I were a part of the ether so that I could bathe you in my flood and break on every wave of your beautiful body.

(LACROIX, ADELAIDE, ROSALIE *enter.*)

LACROIX. (*Remains at the door.*) Oh, that was funny!

DANTON. (*Indignantly.*) Well?

LACROIX. The street!

DANTON. And?

LACROIX. There were dogs on the street, a Great Dane and an Italian lapdog—they were trying to have a go at it.

DANTON. So what?

LACROIX. I just thought of that and I had to laugh. That was edifying! Girls were looking out of the windows—one ought to be careful and not let them sit in the sun or the flies will do it on their hands—that's food for thought.

Legendre and I went through almost every cell—the little Sisters of the Revelation Through the Flesh were hanging on our coattails and wanted a blessing. Legendre is making one do penance, but he'll have to abstain for a month for that. Here are two priestesses of the body.

MARION. Hello, Miss Adelaide, hello, Miss Rosalie.

ROSALIE. We haven't seen you for a long time.

MARION. Yes, I'm sorry.

ADELAIDE. Oh God, we're busy night and day.

DANTON. (*To* ROSALIE.) Say, little one, your hips are getting softer.

ROSALIE. Oh yes, every day we get more perfect.

LACROIX. What's the difference between an antique and a modern Adonis?

DANTON. And Adelaide has gotten virtuous—how interesting! A fascinating change. Her face looks like a fig leaf which she holds in front of her whole body. A fig tree like that on such a frequented street throws a refreshing shadow.

ADELAIDE. I'd be a cowpath, if Monsieur . . .

DANTON. I understand, just don't get angry, my dear.

LACROIX. Listen! A modern Adonis isn't torn to pieces by a boar but by sows, he isn't wounded in the thigh but in the groin, and it's not roses that sprout from his blood but buds of mercury.

DANTON. Miss Rosalie is a restored torso, only her hips and feet are antique. She's a magnetized needle: what the headpole repels, the footpole attracts; her middle is an equator where everyone who crosses the line gets a sublimate baptism.

LACROIX. Two Sisters of Mercy—each serves in her own hospital, that is, in her own body.

ROSALIE. You ought to be ashamed! You're making our ears red.

ADELAIDE. You should have better manners.

(ADELAIDE *and* ROSALIE *exit.*)

DANTON. Good night, you beautiful children!

LACROIX. Good night, you pits of mercury!

DANTON. I'm sorry for them, they'll miss dinner.

LACROIX. Listen, Danton, I just came from the Jacobins.

DANTON. Is that all?

LACROIX. The Lyonists read a proclamation, saying that all they could do was to wrap themselves in a toga. Everybody made a face as if he wanted to say to his neighbor: Paetus, it doesn't hurt! Legendre cried that some want to shatter the busts of Chalier and Marat. I think he wants to redden his face again, he's completely turned away from the Terror—on the street children tug at his coat.

DANTON. And Robespierre?

LACROIX. Drummed on the tribune and said, "Virtue must rule through terror." That phrase made my neck hurt.

DANTON. It's planing boards for the guillotine.

LACROIX. And Collot yelled like a madman that it's time to tear off masks.

DANTON. The faces will come off with them.

(PARIS *enters.*)

LACROIX. What's new, Fabricius?

PARIS. From the Jacobins I went to Robespierre. I demanded an explanation. He tried to make a face like Brutus sacrificing his sons. He spoke in generalities about duty, said that concerning liberty he makes no compromises, he would sacrifice anyone—himself, his brother, his friends.

DANTON. That was clear. If you reverse the order, he'll stand below and hold the ladder for his friends. We owe Legendre thanks, he made them talk.

LACROIX. The Hébertists aren't dead yet and the people are impoverished—that's a terrible lever. The scale of blood must not rise lest it become a lamppost for the Committee of Public Safety. It needs ballast, it needs a weighty head.

DANTON. I know that—the Revolution is like Saturn, it devours its own children. (*After some thought.*) But they won't dare.

LACROIX. Danton, you are a dead saint, but the Revolution is not interested in relics; it has thrown the bones of kings out into the street and all the statues out of the churches. Do you think they'd let you stand as a monument?

DANTON. My name! The people!

LACROIX. Your name! You are a moderate, I am one. Camille, Philippeau, Hérault. For the masses weakness and moderation are the same. They kill the stragglers. The tailors of the red-cap faction will feel all of Roman history in their needles if the Man of September[6] appears as a moderate to them.

DANTON. Very true, and besides—the people are like children, they have to break everything open to see what's inside.

LACROIX. And besides, Danton, we are vice-ridden, as Robespierre says, that is, we enjoy ourselves; and the people are virtuous, that is, they don't enjoy themselves, because work deadens their organs of pleasure. They don't get drunk because they don't have any money, and they don't go to whorehouses because their breath stinks of cheese and herring and that disgusts the girls.

DANTON. They hate the pleasure seekers as a eunuch hates men.

LACROIX. They call us scoundrels, and (*Leaning toward* DANTON'S *ear.*) between us, there's a grain of truth to that. Robespierre and the people will be virtuous, St. Just will write a novel, and Barère will tailor a carmagnole and hang a mantle of blood over the Convention and . . . I see it all.

DANTON. You're dreaming. They never had courage without me, they won't have any against me. The Revolution isn't over yet, they might still need me—they'll keep me in the arsenal.

LACROIX. We must act.

DANTON. We'll see.

LACROIX. You'll see when we're lost.

MARION. (*To* DANTON.) Your lips have grown cold, your words have stifled your kisses.

6. Danton.

DANTON. (*To* MARION.) To have lost so much time! As if it were worth it! (*To* LACROIX.) Tomorrow I'll go to Robespierre—I'll provoke him, then he can't remain silent. Until tomorrow! Good night, my friends, good night, I thank you.

LACROIX. Out, my good friends, out! Good night, Danton, the thighs of that woman will guillotine you, the mons veneris will be your Tarpeian Rock. (*Exit.*)

6

A room.

ROBESPIERRE. DANTON. PARIS.

ROBESPIERRE. I tell you, whoever tries to stop me when I pull my sword is my enemy, his intention is of no concern. Whoever prevents me from defending myself kills me as surely as if he attacked me.

DANTON. Murder begins where self-defense stops; I see no reason to continue the executions.

ROBESPIERRE. The social revolution is not yet achieved; whoever carries out a revolution only halfway, digs his own grave. The privileged are not dead yet, the healthy strength of the people must replace this class, decadent in all respects. Vice must be punished, virtue must rule through terror.

DANTON. I don't understand the word "punishment."

You and your "virtue," Robespierre! You've never taken money, you've never been in debt, you've never slept with a woman, you've always worn a decent coat, and you've never gotten drunk. Robespierre, you are appallingly upright. I'd be ashamed to walk around between heaven and earth for thirty years with that righteous face just for the miserable pleasure of finding others worse than I.

Isn't there something in you that sometimes whispers secretly: you lie, you lie!

ROBESPIERRE. My conscience is clean.

DANTON. Conscience is a mirror before which an ape torments itself;

we preen ourselves as best we can, and we go looking for pleasure each in our own way. As if it were worth the trouble to get in each other's hair. Everyone can defend himself when someone else spoils his fun. Do you have the right to make the guillotine a basket for other people's dirty laundry and to make their decapitated heads into scrubbing balls for their dirty clothes, just because you always wear a cleanly brushed coat? Yes, you can defend yourself when they spit on it or tear holes in it, but what difference does it make to you as long as they leave you alone? If they don't mind walking around as they do, do you have the right to lock them up in a grave? Are you the military policeman of heaven? And if you can't stand the sight of it, as God can, then put a handkerchief over your eyes.

ROBESPIERRE. You deny virtue?

DANTON. And vice. There are only epicureans, either crude or refined, Christ was the most refined of all; that's the only difference I can discern among human beings. Everyone acts according to his nature, that means he does what is good for him.

Isn't it cruel, Mr. Incorruptible, to pull the rug out from under you like this?

ROBESPIERRE. Danton, at certain times vice can be high treason.

DANTON. You can't outlaw it, for heaven's sake—that would be ungrateful; you owe vice too much for providing a contrast to you.

By the way, in keeping with your terminology, our blows must serve the Republic: the innocent must not be struck down with the guilty.

ROBESPIERRE. Whoever said that an innocent person was struck down?

DANTON. Do you hear that, Fabricius? No innocent person was killed! (*Leaving, to* PARIS.) We don't have a moment to lose, we must show ourselves! (DANTON *and* PARIS *exit.*)

ROBESPIERRE. (*Alone.*) Go ahead! He wants to stop the horses of the Revolution at the whorehouse, like a coachman his trained nags; they'll have enough strength to drag him to the Square of the Revolution.

"To pull the rug out from under me!" "In keeping with your terminology!" Wait! Wait! Is it really that? They will say his gigantic figure threw too much of a shadow on me, and for that I ordered him out of the sunlight.

And if they're right?

Is it really that necessary? Yes, yes! The Republic! He must go.

It's ridiculous how my thoughts watch over each other. He must go. Whoever stands still in a mass moving forward opposes it as much as if he were moving against it; he'll be trampled.

We will not let the ship of the Revolution be stranded on the shallow calculations and the mudbanks of these people; we must cut off the hand that tries to stop it, and even if he seized it with his teeth!

Down with a society that took the clothes away from the dead aristocracy and inherited its leprosy!

"No virtue!" "Virtue: a rug under me!" "In keeping with my terminology!"

How that keeps coming back.

Why can't I escape that thought? It's always pointing there, there! with a bloody finger. No matter how many rags I wrap around it, the blood keeps seeping through. (*After a pause.*) I can't tell what part of me is deceiving the other.

(*He steps to the window.*) Night snores over the earth and wallows in wild dreams. Thoughts, hardly perceived wishes, confused and formless, having crept shyly from daylight, now take shape and steal into the silent house of dreams. They open doors, they look out of windows, they become almost flesh, their limbs stretch out in sleep, their lips murmur.—And isn't our waking a more lucid dream, aren't we sleepwalkers, aren't our actions dreamlike, only clearer, more precise, more complete? Who can reproach us for that? The mind accomplishes in one hour more acts of thought than the sluggish organism of our body can carry out in years. The sin is in our thoughts. Whether thought becomes action, whether the body carries it out—that is pure chance.

(ST. JUST *enters.*)

ROBESPIERRE. Hey—who's there, in the dark? Hey—lights, lights!

ST. JUST. Do you know my voice?

ROBESPIERRE. Oh, it's you, St. Just! (*A maid brings a light.*)

ST. JUST. Were you alone?

ROBESPIERRE. Danton just left.

ST. JUST. I met him on the way in the Palais Royal. He made his revolutionary face and spoke in epigrams; he spoke familiarly with the sansculottes, the grisettes were at his heels, and people were standing around whispering in each other's ears what he had said.

We will lose the advantage of the attack. How much longer are you going to hesitate? We will act without you. We are resolved.

ROBESPIERRE. What do you want to do?

ST. JUST. We will call a formal session of the Committees of Legislation, General Security, and Public Safety.

ROBESPIERRE. Quite a bother.

ST. JUST. We must bury the great corpse with proper decorum, like priests, not murderers. We dare not chop it up; all its limbs must fall with it.

ROBESPIERRE. Speak more clearly.

ST. JUST. We must bury him in full armor and slaughter his horses and slaves on his burial mound: Lacroix . . .

ROBESPIERRE. A confirmed scoundrel, formerly a law clerk, presently Lieutenant General of France. Go on.

ST. JUST. Hérault-Séchelles.

ROBESPIERRE. A handsome head.

ST. JUST. He was the beautifully painted first letter of the Constitution; we have no further need of such ornaments, he will be erased. Philippeau, Camille . . .

ROBESPIERRE. He too?

ST. JUST. (*Hands him a piece of paper.*) I thought so. Read that!

ROBESPIERRE. Aha, *The Old Franciscan,* is that all? He's a child, he was laughing at you.

ST. JUST. Read it, here, here! (*He points to a passage.*)

ROBESPIERRE. (*Reads.*) "Robespierre, this Messiah of Blood on his Calvary between the two thieves Couthon and Collot, upon which he sacrifices and is not sacrificed. The worshipful Sisters of the Guillotine stand below like Mary and Magdalene. St. Just lies at his heart like St. John and reveals to the Convention the apocalyptic revelations of the Master. He carries his head like a monstrance."

ST. JUST. I will make him carry his like St. Denis.

ROBESPIERRE. *(Reads on.)* "Are we to believe that the clean shirt of the Messiah is the shroud of France and that his thin fingers, fidgeting on the tribune, are guillotine blades?

And you, Barère, who said our coinage is being minted on the Square of the Revolution. Yet—I don't want to dig up that old sack again.[7] He is a widow who had half a dozen husbands and helped bury them all. Who can help that? That is his talent: he sees a death's head on people half a year before they die. Who would want to sit with corpses and smell the stench?"

You too, then, Camille?

Away with them! Quickly! Only the dead do not return. Have you prepared the indictment?

ST. JUST. It will be easy. You made allusions to it at the Jacobins.

ROBESPIERRE. I wanted to scare them.

ST. JUST. I merely have to carry out your threats; the Forgers are the appetizer and the Foreigners the dessert. They will die from the meal, I promise you.

ROBESPIERRE. Then quickly, tomorrow. No long death agony! I've become sensitive lately. Quickly!

(ST. JUST *exits.*)

ROBESPIERRE. *(Alone.)* That's true, Messiah of Blood who sacrifices and is not sacrificed—He redeemed them with His blood and I redeem them with their own. He allowed them to sin and I take the sin upon myself. He had the ecstasy of pain, and I the agony of the executioner.

Who renounced more, I or He?

And yet there is something foolish in that thought.

Why do we always look only toward Him? Truly the Son of Man is crucified in each of us, we all struggle in bloody sweat in the Garden of Gethsemane, but not one of us redeems the other with his wounds.—My Camille!—They're all leaving me—all is desolate and empty—I am alone.

7. A pun on Barère de Vieuzac.

Act Two

1

A room.

DANTON. LACROIX. PHILIPPEAU. PARIS. CAMILLE DESMOULINS.

CAMILLE. Hurry, Danton, we have no time to lose.

DANTON. (*Getting dressed.*) But time loses us.

It's very boring, always putting on the shirt first and the pants over it and going to bed at night and crawling out again in the morning and always putting one foot before the other—there's no hope that it will ever be any different. It's very sad; and that millions have done it this way and millions will keep on doing it—and, above all, that we're made up of two halves which do the same thing so that everything happens twice—that's very sad.

CAMILLE. You're talking like a child.

DANTON. The dying often become childish.

LACROIX. Your hesitation is dragging you down to destruction, you're taking all your friends with you. Let the cowards know that it's time to rally around you; summon them from the Plain and from the Mountain. Cry out against the tyranny of the decemvirs, speak of daggers, call on Brutus—then you will frighten the tribunes and even gather up those who are denounced as accomplices of Hébert. You must give way to your anger! At least don't let us die defenseless and humiliated like the disgraceful Hébert.

DANTON. You have a poor memory, you called me a dead saint. You were right, even more than you realized. I was at the Section meetings—they were respectful but like undertakers. I am a relic and relics are thrown into the street, you were right.

LACROIX. Why did you let it come to that?

DANTON. To that? Yes, that's true, I was finally bored with it all. Always walking around in the same coat and making the same face! That's pitiful. To be such a wretched instrument, on which one string always sounds just one note.

I can't bear it. I wanted to make it easy for myself. I was

successful: the Revolution is letting me retire, but not in the way I expected.

Besides, what can we rely on? Our whores could still compete with the worshipful Sisters of the Guillotine; that's all I can think of. I can count it all off on my fingers: the Jacobins have announced that virtue is now the order of the day, the Cordeliers call me Hébert's executioner, the Commune does penance, the Convention—that might still be a way! But there'd be a 31st of May, they wouldn't withdraw without a fight. Robespierre is the dogma of the Revolution, it cannot be erased. That wouldn't work either. We haven't made the Revolution; the Revolution has made us.

And even if it worked—I would rather be guillotined than guillotine others. I'm sick of it—why should we human beings fight each other? We should sit down with each other in peace. A mistake was made when we were created—something is missing. I have no name for it. We won't rip it out of each other's intestines, so why should we break open each other's bodies? Oh, we are miserable alchemists.

CAMILLE. To say it in a more sublime way: how long should humanity devour its own limbs in eternal hunger? Or: how long should we, stranded on a wreck, suck blood out of each other's veins with unquenchable thirst? Or: how long should we algebraists of the flesh write our calculations with mangled limbs while searching for the unknown, eternally withheld X?

DANTON. You are a strong echo.

CAMILLE. Yes, a pistol shot resounds as loudly as a thunderclap, doesn't it? So much the better for you, you should always have me with you.

PHILIPPEAU. And France is left with her executioners?

DANTON. What's the difference? The people are very comfortable with them. They aren't well off; can one ask for more in order to be moved, noble, virtuous, or witty, or never to be bored?

What's the difference if they die under the guillotine or from a fever or from old age? As long as they can walk offstage nimbly and can make nice gestures and hear the audience clap as they exit. That's very proper and suits us well—we're always on stage, even if we're finally stabbed to death in earnest.

It's a good thing that our life span is being shortened a little;

the coat was too long, our bodies couldn't fill it out. Life becomes an epigram—that's not so bad; whoever has enough breath and spirit for an epic poem in fifty or sixty cantos? It's time that we drink that little bit of essence not out of tubs but out of liqueur glasses, that will still fill our mouths; before, we could hardly get a few drops to run together in that bulky container.

Finally—I ought to cry out, but that's too much trouble; life isn't worth the effort we make to maintain it.

PARIS. Then escape, Danton!

DANTON. Do we take our homeland along on the soles of our shoes?

And finally—and that's the main point: they won't dare. (*To* CAMILLE.) Come, my boy, I tell you, they won't dare. Adieu. Adieu!

(DANTON *and* CAMILLE *exit.*)

PHILIPPEAU. There he goes.

LACROIX. And he doesn't believe a word he's said. Nothing but laziness! He would rather let himself be guillotined than make a speech.

PARIS. What do we do now?

LACROIX. We'll go home and think like Lucretia about an honorable death.

2

A promenade.

PASSERSBY.

A CITIZEN. My good Jacqueline—I mean, Corn . . . uh, Cor . . .

SIMON. Cornelia, citizen, Cornelia.

CITIZEN. My good Cornelia has blessed me with a little boy.

SIMON. Has borne a son for the Republic.

CITIZEN. . . . for the Republic—that's too general, one might say . . .

SIMON. That's just it, the part must succumb to the whole . . .

CITIZEN. Oh, yes, my wife says the same thing.

BALLADEER. Tell me, tell me everyone,
What's man's joy, what's his fun?

CITIZEN. Oh, but his name, I just can't think of anything.

SIMON. Call him Pike, Marat.

BALLADEER.

With sorrow and with care he's worn,
Working from the early morn,
Till the day is done.

CITIZEN. Three'd be better, there's something about the number three—and then something useful and something just. I've got it: Plow, Robespierre. And then the third?

SIMON. Pike.

CITIZEN. Thank you, neighbor. Pike, Plow, Robespierre, those are pretty names, that'll be nice.

SIMON. I tell you, the breast of your Cornelia will be like the udder of the Roman she-wolf—no, that won't do—Romulus was a tyrant, that won't do. (*They pass on.*)

A BEGGAR. A handful of earth
And a little bit of moss . . .

Dear sirs, kind ladies!

FIRST GENTLEMAN. Go and work, you dog, you look very well fed.

SECOND GENTLEMAN. There! (*He gives him money.*) His hand's like velvet. What impudence!

BEGGAR. Sir, how did you get that coat of yours?

SECOND GENTLEMAN. Work, work! You could have one just like it. I'll give you a job. Call on me—I live at . . .

BEGGAR. Sir, why did you work?

SECOND GENTLEMAN. So I could have the coat, idiot.

BEGGAR. You tortured yourself for a piece of pleasure. A coat like that's a pleasure, so's a rag.

SECOND GENTLEMAN. Certainly, there's no other way.

BEGGAR. If I were such a fool! It all balances out.

The sun's shining warm on the corner and that's easy to enjoy.

(*Sings.*) A handful of earth
And a little bit of moss . . .

ROSALIE. (*To* ADELAIDE.) Hurry up, there come the soldiers, we haven't had anything warm in our bodies since yesterday.

BEGGAR. . . . Is all I'll have left
When I lie beneath the cross!

Gentlemen, ladies!

SOLDIER. Wait! Where are you off to, my dears? (*To* ROSALIE.) How old are you?

ROSALIE. As old as my pinkie.

SOLDIER. You're very sharp.

ROSALIE. You're very blunt.

SOLDIER. So I'll have to whet myself on you. (*He sings.*)

Christina, O Christina dear,
Does the pain make you sore, make you sore,
Make you sore, make you sore?

ROSALIE. (*Sings.*)

Oh no, dear soldiers,
All I say is: give me more, give me more,
Give me more, give me more!

(DANTON *and* CAMILLE *enter.*)

DANTON. Isn't that amusing!

I sense something in the atmosphere—it's as if the sun were breeding lechery.

Don't you feel like jumping into the middle of it, tearing off your pants and copulating from the rear like dogs in the street? (*They go past.*)

YOUNG GENTLEMAN. Ah, Madame, the tolling of a bell, twilight on the treetops, a twinkling star . . .

MADAME. A flower's scent! These natural pleasures, this pure enjoyment of nature! (*To her daughter.*) You see, Eugénie, only virtue has eyes for such things.

EUGÉNIE. (*Kisses her mother's hand.*) Oh, Mama, I see only you!

MADAME. Good girl!

YOUNG GENTLEMAN. (*Whispers into* EUGÉNIE's *ear.*) Do you see that pretty lady over there with the old gentleman?

EUGÉNIE. I know her.

YOUNG GENTLEMAN. They say her hairdresser did her hair "à l'enfant."

EUGÉNIE. (*Laughs.*) Naughty tongues.

YOUNG GENTLEMAN. The old gentleman walks with her, he sees the little bud swelling and takes it for a walk in the sun, thinking he was the thundershower that made it grow.

EUGÉNIE. How shameful! I almost feel like blushing.

YOUNG GENTLEMAN. That could make me turn pale.

DANTON. (*To* CAMILLE.) Don't expect me to be serious. I can't understand why people don't stop on the street and laugh in each other's faces. I'd think they'd have to laugh out of the windows and out of the graves, and the heavens would burst and the earth would be convulsed with laughter.

FIRST GENTLEMAN. An extraordinary discovery, I assure you. All the technical arts will acquire a new look. The human race is making giant strides toward its great destiny.

SECOND GENTLEMAN. Have you seen the new play? A Tower of Babylon! A maze of arches, stairways, halls—and it's all blown up with the greatest of ease. You get dizzy at every step.

A bizarre idea! (*He stops in embarrassment.*)

FIRST GENTLEMAN. What's the matter?

SECOND GENTLEMAN. Oh, nothing! Your arm, sir! The puddle—there! Thank you. I barely managed it—that could have been dangerous!

FIRST GENTLEMAN. You weren't afraid?

SECOND GENTLEMAN. Yes, the earth is a thin crust. I always think I'll fall through a hole like that.

You have to walk carefully—you might break through. But go to the theater—take my advice.

3

A room.

DANTON. CAMILLE. LUCILE.

CAMILLE. I tell you, if they aren't given everything in wooden copies, scattered about in theaters, concerts, and art exhibits, they'll have neither eyes nor ears for it. Let someone whittle a marionette where the strings pulling it are plainly visible and whose joints crack at every step in iambic pentameter: what a character, what consistency! Let someone take a little bit of feeling, an aphorism, a concept, and clothe it in a coat and pants, give it hands and feet, color its face and let the thing torment itself through three acts until it finally marries or shoots itself: an ideal! Let someone fiddle an opera which reflects the rising and sinking of the human spirit the way a clay pipe with water imitates a nightingale: oh, art!

Take people out of the theater and put them in the street: oh, miserable reality! They forget their Creator because of His poor imitators. They see and hear nothing of Creation, which renews itself every moment in and around them, glowing, rushing, luminous. They go to the theater, read poetry and novels, make faces like the masks they find there, and say to God's creatures: how ordinary!

The Greeks knew what they were saying when they declared that Pygmalion's statue did indeed come to life but never had any children.

DANTON. And the artists treat nature like David, who cold-bloodedly sketched those murdered in September as they were being thrown out of the Force Prison onto the streets, and said: I am capturing the last spasms of life in these villains. (DANTON *is called out.*)

CAMILLE. What do you think, Lucile?

LUCILE. Nothing, I like to watch you talk.

CAMILLE. Do you listen to what I say, too?

LUCILE. Yes, of course.

CAMILLE. Was I right? Did you understand what I said?

LUCILE. No—not at all. (DANTON *returns.*)

CAMILLE. What's the matter?

DANTON. The Committee of Public Safety has decided to arrest me. I've been warned and offered a place of refuge.

They're after my head—so what? I'm sick of all the fuss. Let them have it. What will it matter? I'll know how to die bravely—that's easier than living.

CAMILLE. Danton, there's still time.

DANTON. Impossible—but I wouldn't have thought . . .

CAMILLE. Your laziness!

DANTON. I'm not lazy, just tired. The soles of my feet are on fire.

CAMILLE. Where will you go?

DANTON. Yes, if I only knew.

CAMILLE. Seriously, where?

DANTON. For a walk, my boy, for a walk. (*He goes.*)

LUCILE. Oh, Camille!

CAMILLE. Don't worry, my dear.

LUCILE. When I think that this head—Camille! That's nonsense, right? Am I crazy to think it?

CAMILLE. Don't worry. Danton and I are not the same person.

LUCILE. The world is large and there are many things on it—why just this one? Who would take this from me? That would be awful. What good would it do them?

CAMILLE. I'm telling you, it'll be all right. Yesterday I talked to Robespierre, he was friendly. Things are a little strained, that's true—differing opinions, that's all.

LUCILE. Go look for him.

CAMILLE. We sat next to each other in school. He was always gloomy and aloof. I was the only one who went to him and made him laugh sometimes. He's always showed me great affection. I'll go.

LUCILE. Off so fast, my friend? Go ahead! Come here! Just that (*She kisses him.*) and that! Go! Go! (CAMILLE *exits.*)

These are terrible times. But that's the way it is. Who can change it? You have to live with it. (*Sings.*)

Oh, parting, oh parting, oh parting,
Whoever invented parting?

Why did I just think of that? That's not good, if it simply comes out by itself that way.

When he left it seemed as if he could never turn back and had to go farther and farther away from me, farther and farther away.

The room's so empty, the windows are open, as if a dead person had been lying here. I can't stand it up here. (*She leaves.*)

4

Open field.

DANTON. I don't want to go on. I don't want to break this silence with my clattering footsteps and my panting breath. (*He sits. After a pause.*)

I've heard of a sickness that makes one lose one's memory. Death, they say, is like that. Then I hope sometimes that death would be even stronger and make one lose *everything*. If only that were so!

Then I'd run like a Christian to save my enemy—that is, my

memory.

That place[8] is supposed to be safe; maybe for my memory, but not for me—the grave would be safer. At least it would make me *forget*. It would kill my memory. But there my memory will live on and kill me. I or it? The answer is easy. (*He rises and turns around.*)

I'm flirting with death; it's pleasant to ogle him like this through an eyeglass from a distance. Actually, the whole affair makes me laugh. There's a feeling of permanence in me which says that tomorrow will be the same as today, and the day after and all the days to come will be alike. It's all empty noise, they want to scare me, they won't dare. (*Exit.*)

5

A room. Night.

DANTON. JULIE.

DANTON. (*At the window.*) Won't it ever stop? Won't the light ever fade, the sound die away, won't it ever become quiet and dark so that we don't hear and see each other's ugly sins?—September!—

JULIE. (*Calls from inside.*) Danton! Danton!

DANTON. Yes?

JULIE. (*Enters.*) What did you shout?

DANTON. Did I shout?

JULIE. You talked of ugly sins and then you moaned, "September!"

DANTON. Did I? No, I didn't say it. I hardly thought it; those were just very quiet, secret thoughts.

JULIE. You're trembling, Danton.

DANTON. And shouldn't I tremble when the walls begin to talk? When my body is so shattered that my uncertain, wavering thoughts speak with the lips of stones? That's strange.

JULIE. George, my George!

DANTON. Yes, Julie, that's very strange. I'd like to stop thinking

8. The place to which he is fleeing.

when they speak like that. There are thoughts, Julie, for which there shouldn't be any ears. It's not good that they scream at birth like children. That's not good.

JULIE. May God keep you in your right mind, George. George, do you recognize me?

DANTON. Oh, why not? You are a human being, a woman, and finally my wife, and the earth has five continents, Europe, Asia, Africa, America, Australia; and two times two is four. I haven't lost my mind, you see. Didn't something scream "September"? Isn't that what you said?

JULIE. Yes, Danton, I heard it through all the rooms.

DANTON. As I came to the window—*(He looks out.)* the city is quiet, the lights are out . . .

JULIE. A child is crying nearby.

DANTON. As I came to the window—through all the streets it cried and shrieked—"September!"

JULIE. You were dreaming, Danton. Get hold of yourself.

DANTON. Dreaming? Yes, I was dreaming—but it was different—I'll tell you right away, my poor head is weak—right away! There—now I've got it! Beneath me the earth was panting in its flight, I had seized it like a wild horse, with immense limbs I rooted in its mane and pressed its ribs, with my head bent down, my hair streaming out over the abyss. I was being dragged along. Then I screamed in fear and awoke. I went to the window—and that's when I heard it, Julie.

What does that word want from me? Why just that, what do I have to do with that? Why does it stretch out its bloody hands toward me? I didn't strike it down.

Oh, help me, Julie, my senses are dull. Wasn't it in September, Julie?

JULIE. The kings were just forty hours from Paris . . .

DANTON. The defenses had fallen, the aristocrats were in the city . . .

JULIE. The Republic was lost.

DANTON. Yes, lost. We couldn't ignore the enemy at our backs, we would have been fools—two enemies at once, we or they, the stronger strikes down the weaker, isn't that reasonable?

JULIE. Yes, yes.

DANTON. We killed them. That was not murder, that was internal warfare.

JULIE. You saved the country.

DANTON. Yes, I did. It was self-defense, we had to. The Man on the Cross made it easy for Himself: "It must needs be that offenses come, but woe to that man by whom the offense cometh."

It must—it was this "must." Who would curse the hand on which the curse of "must" has fallen? Who has spoken this "must," who? What is it in us that whores, lies, steals, and murders?

We are puppets, our strings are pulled by unknown forces, we ourselves are nothing, nothing! Swords that spirits fight with—you just don't see any hands, as in a fairy tale.

Now I'm calm.

JULIE. Quite calm, dear?

DANTON. Yes, Julie, come to bed.

6

Street in front of DANTON's *house.*

SIMON. CIVILIAN TROOPS.

SIMON. How far into the night?

FIRST CITIZEN. What into the night?

SIMON. How far are we into the night?

FIRST CITIZEN. As far as between sunset and sunrise.

SIMON. Idiot, what time is it?

FIRST CITIZEN. Look on your dial. It's the time when perpendiculars rise up under the bed sheets.

SIMON. Let's go up! Onward, citizens! We'll stake our heads on it. Dead or alive! He's very strong. I'll go first, citizens.

Make way for freedom.

Look to my wife! I'll bequeath her a wreath of oak leaves.

FIRST CITIZEN. With acorns on them? Enough acorns fall into her lap every day.

SIMON. Onward, citizens! The country will be grateful for your service!

SECOND CITIZEN. I wish the country would serve *us*; with all those holes we make in other people's bodies, not a single one in our pants has been mended.

FIRST CITIZEN. Do you want your fly sewed up? Heh, heh, heh!
THE OTHERS. Heh, heh, heh!
SIMON. Let's go, let's go! (*They force their way into* DANTON'S *house.*)

7

The National Convention.

A group of DEPUTIES.

LEGENDRE. When will this slaughtering of deputies stop? Who is safe if Danton falls?
A DEPUTY. What can we do?
ANOTHER DEPUTY. He must be heard before the Convention. It's bound to work; how can they compete against his voice?
ANOTHER DEPUTY. Impossible. A decree prohibits it.
LEGENDRE. It must be repealed or an exception must be granted. I'll make the motion. I'm counting on your support.
PRESIDENT. The session is opened.
LEGENDRE. (*Ascends the tribune.*) Four members of the National Convention were arrested last night. I know that Danton is one of them; I do not know the names of the others. Whoever they may be, I demand that they be heard here. Citizens, I declare Danton to be as innocent as myself, and I believe my record to be beyond reproach. I do not wish to accuse any member of the Committees of Public Safety or General Security, but for well-founded reasons I fear that personal enmity and emotion could deprive liberty of men who have served it well. The man whose energy saved France in 1792 deserves to be heard; he must be allowed to account for himself when he is accused of high treason. (*Great commotion.*)
SEVERAL VOICES. We support Legendre's motion.
A DEPUTY. We are here in the name of the people, we cannot be deprived of our seats without the consent of the electorate.
ANOTHER DEPUTY. Your words smell of corpses. You took them from the mouths of the Girondists. Are you asking for privileges? The ax of the law hangs over all heads.

ANOTHER DEPUTY. We cannot allow our committees to send our legislators from the immunity of the law to the guillotine.

ANOTHER DEPUTY. Crime knows no immunity, only royal crimes find it on the throne.

ANOTHER. Only scoundrels appeal to the right of immunity.

ANOTHER. Only murderers refuse to recognize it.

ROBESPIERRE. Such disorder, unknown in this assembly for a long time, proves that weighty matters are at stake. It shall be decided today whether a few men will stand as victors over the fatherland. How can you compromise your principles to such an extent that you grant a few individuals today what you refused Chabot, Delaunai, and Fabre yesterday? Why should these men be treated differently? What do I care about the eulogies one showers upon oneself and upon one's friends? Only too many experiences have shown us what to think of that. We do not ask whether a man has performed this or that patriotic act; we inquire about his entire political career.

Legendre does not appear to know the names of those who were arrested; the entire Convention knows them. His friend Lacroix is among them. Why does Legendre appear not to know that? Because he knows that only shamelessness can defend Lacroix. He named only Danton because he believes that this name demands special privileges. No, we want no privileges, we want no idols! (*Applause.*)

What distinguishes Danton from Lafayette, from Dumouriez, from Brissot, Fabre, Chabot, Hébert? What was said about them that you could not also say about him? Did you spare them? Why should he be favored above his fellow citizens? Possibly because a few deceived individuals and others who did not let themselves be deceived gathered around him as his followers in order to rush into the arms of fortune and power? The more he has deceived patriots who trusted him, the more forcefully he must feel the severity of the friends of liberty.

They want to make you fear the misuse of power which you yourselves have wielded. They cry out against the despotism of the committees, as if the trust which the people have placed in you and which you have delegated to these committees were not a certain guarantee of patriotism. They pretend to tremble. But I say that whoever trembles at this moment is guilty, for innocence never trembles before the watchful eye of the public. (*General applause.*)

They tried to intimidate me: I was led to understand that the danger which threatens Danton might extend to me.

They wrote me that Danton's friends had besieged me in the belief that a memory of old ties, a blind faith in simulated virtues could induce me to moderate my zeal and passion for liberty.

Thus I declare that nothing shall stop me, even if Danton's danger should become my own. We all need some courage and magnanimity. Only criminals and base souls fear to see their allies fall at their side, for when they are no longer hidden by a crowd of accomplices, they are exposed to the light of truth. Yet if there are such souls in this assembly, there are also heroic ones here. The number of villains is not great. We need only strike down a few heads, and the fatherland is saved. (*Applause.*)

I demand that Legendre's motion be defeated. (*The* DEPUTIES *rise together as a sign of universal approval.*)

ST. JUST. There appear to be in this assembly a number of sensitive ears that cannot endure the word "blood." May a few general observations convince them that we are no crueler than nature and time. Nature follows its laws serenely and irresistibly; man is destroyed when he comes in conflict with them. A change in the elements of the atmosphere, an eruption of tellurian fires, a fluctuation in the balance of a body of water, a plague, a volcanic eruption, a flood bury thousands. What is the result? An insignificant, barely noticeable change of physical nature that would have passed almost without a trace, were not corpses lying in its path.

I ask you now: should moral nature in its revolutions be more considerate than physical nature? Should not an idea be permitted to destroy its opposition just as well as a law of physics? Should any event whatsoever that transforms the shape of moral nature—that is, humanity—not be permitted to shed blood? The world spirit makes use of our arms in the sphere of the intellect just as in the physical sphere it generates volcanic eruptions or floods. What does it matter if men die from a plague or a revolution?

The strides of humanity are slow, they can only be counted in centuries; behind each rise the graves of generations. The achievement of the simplest inventions or principles has cost the lives of millions who died along the way. Is it then not obvious that at a time when the course of history accelerates, more people lose their breath?

We will conclude quickly and simply: since everyone was created under the same conditions, all are therefore equal, aside from the differences caused by nature itself.

Therefore everyone may enjoy advantages, yet no one may enjoy privileges, neither an individual nor a smaller nor a greater class of individuals. Every portion of our proposition, applied in reality, has killed its human beings. The 14th of July, the 10th of August, the 31st of May are its punctuation marks. It needed four years to be realized in the physical world, and under normal conditions it would have required a century and would have been punctuated with generations. Is it therefore so surprising that the flow of the revolution throws out its corpses at every dip, at every new turn?

We have yet to add several conclusions to our proposition; shall a few hundred corpses prevent us from doing so?

Moses led his people through the Red Sea and into the desert until the old corrupt generation had destroyed itself, before he founded the new state. Legislators! We have neither a Red Sea nor a desert, but we have the war and the guillotine.

The Revolution is like the daughters of Pelias: it cuts humanity in pieces to rejuvenate it. Humanity will rise up with mighty limbs out of this cauldron of blood, like the earth out of the waters of the Flood, as if it had been newly created. (*Long, sustained applause. Several* DEPUTIES *rise in enthusiasm.*)

We summon all secret enemies of tyranny, who in Europe and in the entire world carry the dagger of Brutus beneath their cloaks, to share with us this sublime hour! (*The spectators and the* DEPUTIES *begin the Marseillaise.*)

Act Three

1

The Luxembourg prison. A room with prisoners.

CHAUMETTE. PAINE. MERCIER. HÉRAULT-SÉCHELLES. *Other prisoners.*

CHAUMETTE. (*Tugs at* PAINE's *sleeve.*) Listen, Paine, it could be that way after all, something came over me a while ago. Today I have a headache; help me a little with your syllogisms, I feel very peculiar.

PAINE. Come then, philosopher Anaxagoras, I will catechize you. *There is no God,* because: either God created the world or He did not. If He did not, then the world has its cause within itself and there is no God, since God only becomes God in that He contains the cause of all existence. However, God cannot have created the world, for Creation is either eternal like God or it has a beginning. If the latter be true, then God must have created it at a specific moment. Thus, having been idle for an eternity, God must have become active at a certain point; He must therefore have experienced a change within Himself, which subjects Him to the concept of *time.* Both these points contradict the nature of God. God therefore cannot have created the world. Since we know very well, however, that the world or at least our own self exists, and, according to the above, must contain its cause within itself or within something that is not God, God therefore cannot exist. Quod erat demonstrandum.

CHAUMETTE. Yes, indeed, that makes it all very clear again, thank you, thank you.

MERCIER. Just a moment, Paine. What if Creation is eternal?

PAINE. Then it is no longer Creation, then it is one with God or an attribute of God, as Spinoza says; then God is in everything, in you, my dear friend, in the philosopher Anaxagoras here, and in me. That would not be so objectionable, but you must admit that the Heavenly Majesty wouldn't amount to much if our dear Lord could suffer a toothache, get the clap, or be buried alive along with each of us—or could at least have the very unpleasant conceptions of these miseries.

MERCIER. But a cause must exist.

PAINE. Who denies that? But who can claim that this cause is that which we imagine to be God—that is, perfection? Do you think the world is perfect?

MERCIER. No.

PAINE. Then how can you postulate a perfect cause from an imperfect effect?

Voltaire dared to offend God as little as the kings, that's why *he* did it. One who has nothing but his reason and doesn't even know or dare to use it logically is a bungler.

MERCIER. To that I ask: can a perfect cause have a perfect effect—that is, can perfection create perfection? Isn't that impossible because the created object can never have its cause within itself, which, however, as you said, is a part of perfection?

CHAUMETTE. Be quiet! Be quiet!

PAINE. Calm yourself, philosopher. You are right; but if God were once to create and could only create imperfection, He had better forget about it entirely. Isn't it very human to be able to think of God only as a Creator? Just because we always have to stretch and shake ourselves only in order to say, "we exist," do we also have to attribute this miserable necessity to God? When our spirit becomes absorbed in the essence of an everlasting bliss, harmoniously at rest within itself, must we immediately assume that it has to stretch out its fingers and knead little men of dough on the table? It's because of a boundless need of love, as we secretly whisper into each other's ears. Must we do this just to make ourselves sons of God? I am satisfied with a lesser father; at least, I won't be able to blame him for raising me beneath his station in pigsties or in galleys.

Eliminate imperfection; only then can you demonstrate God, Spinoza tried it. One may deny evil but not pain; only reason can prove the existence of God, our feelings rebel against it. Note this, Anaxagoras: why do I suffer? That is the rock of atheism. The smallest twinge of pain—and may it stir only in a single atom—makes a rent in Creation from top to bottom.

MERCIER. And what of morality?

PAINE. First you prove God from morality and then morality from God. What do you want with your morality? I don't know if in fact good or evil exist, and therefore I certainly don't need to change my way of life. I act according to my nature; whatever suits it is good for me, and I do it, and whatever is contrary to it is bad for me, and I don't do it, and I defend myself against it when it gets in my way. One can remain virtuous, as they say, and resist so-called vice without having to despise one's opponents—which is really a sad feeling.

CHAUMETTE. True, very true!

HÉRAULT. Oh, philosopher Anaxagoras, one could, however, also say that if God were to be all things, He would also have to be His own opposite—that is, perfect and imperfect, evil and good, blissful and suffering. The result would certainly equal zero, it would cancel itself out, we would come to nothing. Be happy, you'll survive; you can go on worshiping nature's masterpiece in Madame Momoro—at least she has left rosaries for it in your groin.

CHAUMETTE. I'm much obliged to you, gentlemen. (*Exits.*)

PAINE. He still doesn't believe it—in the end he'll take extreme unction, turn his feet toward Mecca, and get circumcised so he doesn't miss a chance.

(DANTON, LACROIX, CAMILLE, PHILIPPEAU *are led in.*)

HÉRAULT. (*Goes up to* DANTON *and embraces him.*) Good morning—good night, I should say. I can't ask how you've slept. How will you sleep?

DANTON. Well—one has to go to bed laughing.

MERCIER. (*To* PAINE.) This bloodhound with dove's wings! He's the evil genius of the Revolution, he ventured against his mother, but she was stronger than he.

PAINE. His life and death are equally unfortunate.

LACROIX. (*To* DANTON.) I didn't think that they would come so quickly.

DANTON. I knew it, I had been warned.

LACROIX. And you said nothing?

DANTON. What for? A stroke is the best death; would you rather be sick before it? And—I didn't believe they would dare. (*To* HÉRAULT) It's better to lie down in the earth than to get corns walking on it; I'd rather have it as a pillow than a footstool.

HÉRAULT. At least we won't stroke the cheeks of the fair Lady Decay with callused fingers.

CAMILLE. (*To* DANTON.) Don't trouble yourself. You can hang your tongue out as far as you like and you still won't be able to lick the sweat of death from your brow. Oh, Lucile! It's a great pity.

(*The prisoners crowd around the new arrivals.*)

DANTON. (*To* PAINE.) What you have done for the good of your country, I have tried to do for mine. I wasn't as lucky; they're sending me to the scaffold—so what, I won't stumble.

MERCIER. (*To* DANTON.) The blood of the twenty-two is drowning you.

A PRISONER. (*To* HÉRAULT.) "The power of the people and the power of reason are one."[9]

ANOTHER. (*To* CAMILLE.) Well, High Commissioner of the Lamp-post, your improvement of street lighting hasn't made things any brighter in France.

ANOTHER. Let him be! Those are the lips that spoke the word "mercy." (*He embraces* CAMILLE, *several prisoners follow his example.*)

PHILIPPEAU. We are priests who have prayed with the dying; we have been infected and will die of the same plague.

SEVERAL VOICES. The blow that strikes you kills us all.

CAMILLE. Gentlemen, I regret that our efforts were so fruitless. I go to the scaffold because my eyes grew moist at the fate of some unfortunates.

2

A room.

FOUQUIER-TINVILLE. HERMAN.

FOUQUIER. Is everything ready?

HERMAN. It'll be hard to make it stick; if Danton weren't among them, it would be easy.

FOUQUIER. He'll have to lead the dance.

HERMAN. He'll frighten the jury; he's the scarecrow of the Revolution.

9. The prisoner taunts Hérault with his own words.

FOUQUIER. The jury must will it.

HERMAN. I know of a way, but it would violate legal formality.

FOUQUIER. Go ahead.

HERMAN. We won't draw lots, but we'll pick out the reliable ones.

FOUQUIER. That will have to work. We'll have a nice shooting gallery. There are nineteen of them, a cleverly mixed group. The four forgers, then a few bankers and foreigners. It's a spicy meal—the people need things like that. Dependable people, then! Who, for instance?

HERMAN. Leroi—he's deaf and won't hear a word from the defendants. Danton can shout himself hoarse at him.

FOUQUIER. Very good. Go on.

HERMAN. Vilatte and Lumière. The one's always sitting in a tavern and the other's always asleep; they open their mouths only to say the word "guilty."

Girard maintains that no one who has been brought before the Tribunal may go free. Renaudin . . .

FOUQUIER. He, too? He once spared a few priests.

HERMAN. Don't worry, he came to me a few days ago demanding that all who are to be executed should be bled beforehand to weaken them, because their usually defiant attitude annoys him.

FOUQUIER. Oh, very good. Then I'll count on you.

HERMAN. Leave it up to me.

3

The Conciergerie. A corridor.

LACROIX, DANTON, MERCIER, *and other prisoners are walking up and down.*

LACROIX. (*To a prisoner.*) What, are there so many unfortunates, and in such miserable condition?

PRISONER. Didn't the guillotine carts ever tell you that Paris is a slaughterhouse?

MERCIER. That's true, Lacroix. Equality swings its sickle over all our heads, the lava of the Revolution flows, the guillotine republicanizes! The galleries clap and the Romans rub their hands, but they don't hear that each of these words is the death rattle of a victim. Try following your rhetoric to the point where it becomes flesh and blood.

Look around you: all this you have spoken; here is a visual translation of your words. These wretches, their hangmen, and the guillotine are your speeches come to life. You built your systems, like Bayezid his pyramids, out of human heads.

DANTON. You're right. These days everything is worked in human flesh. That's the curse of our times. Now my body will be used up, too.

One year ago I created the Revolutionary Tribunal. I ask God and mankind to forgive me for that; I wanted to prevent new September massacres, I hoped to save the innocent, but this gradual murder with its formalities is more horrible and just as inevitable. Gentlemen, I hoped to help you leave this place.

MERCIER. Oh, we'll leave it all right.

DANTON. Now I'm here with you. Heaven knows how this will end.

4

The Revolutionary Tribunal.

HERMAN. (*To* DANTON.) Your name, citizen.

DANTON. The Revolution calls out my name. My residence will soon be in nothingness and my name in the Pantheon of history.

HERMAN. Danton, the Convention accuses you of having conspired with Mirabeau, with Dumouriez, with Orléans, with the Girondists, with foreigners, and with the faction of Louis XVII.

DANTON. My voice, which has so often rung out on behalf of the people, will easily refute this slander. Let the wretches who accuse me appear here and I will cover them with disgrace. Let the committees appear; I will only answer before them. I need them as accusers and witnesses.

Let them show themselves.

Besides, why should I care about you or your judgment? I have already told you: nothingness will soon be my abode—life is a burden, let them tear it from me; I long to shake it off.

HERMAN. Danton, audacity suits a crime, calmness reflects innocence.

DANTON. Personal audacity certainly deserves reproach, but national audacity, which I have shown so often, with which I have so often fought for liberty, is the worthiest of all virtues. This is my audacity, I use it here for the sake of the Republic against my wretched accusers. Can I control myself when I see myself slandered so basely? One cannot expect a dispassionate defense from a revolutionary such as I. Men of my sort are invaluable in revolutions, on our brows hovers the spirit of liberty. (*Signs of applause among the spectators.*)

They accuse me of conspiring with Mirabeau, with Dumouriez, with Orléans; of crawling to the feet of wretched despots; they challenge me to answer before inescapable, unbending justice.

You, miserable St. Just, will answer to posterity for this slander!

HERMAN. I demand that you answer calmly. Remember Marat—he appeared before his judges with respect.

DANTON. They have laid hands on my whole life, so let it arise and confront them; I will bury them under the weight of my every deed.

I am not proud about this. Fate guides our arm, but only powerful natures are its instruments.

On the Field of Mars I declared war on the monarchy; I defeated it on the 10th of August, I killed it on the 21st of January and threw a king's head down as a gauntlet before all monarchs. (*Repeated signs of applause. He takes the papers of indictment.*) When I glance at these slanderous words, I feel my whole being tremble. Who are they, who had to force Danton to appear on that memorable day, the 10th of August? Who are the privileged beings, from whom he borrowed his energy? Let my accusers come forth! This is a most reasonable demand. I will unmask these base scoundrels and hurl them back into the nothingness out of which they never should have crept.

HERMAN. (*Rings a bell.*) Don't you hear the bell?

DANTON. The voice of a man who defends his honor and his life will drown out your bell.

In September I gorged the young brood of the Revolution with the dismembered corpses of the aristocrats. My voice forged weapons for the people out of the gold of the aristocrats and the rich. My voice was the typhoon that buried the minions of despotism under waves of bayonets. (*Loud applause.*)

HERMAN. Danton, your voice is worn out, you are far too emotional. At the next meeting you will conclude your defense. You are in need of rest.

The session is adjourned.

DANTON. Now you know Danton; in a few hours he will fall asleep in the arms of glory.

5

The Luxembourg prison. A cell.

DILLON. LAFLOTTE. *A* JAILER.

DILLON. Hey, stop shining your nose in my face. Heh, heh, heh!

LAFLOTTE. Keep your mouth shut—your moon has a halo. Heh, heh, heh!

JAILER. Heh, heh, heh! Sir, do you think you could read by its light? (*Points to a paper in his hand.*)

DILLON. Give it here!

JAILER. Sir, my moon's brought on a low tide.

LAFLOTTE. From the looks of your pants I'd say a high tide.

JAILER. No, my moon attracts water. (*To* DILLON.) It's hidden itself away from your sun, sir. You'll have to give me something to fire it up again if you want to read by its light.

DILLON. Here, take this! Now get out. (*He gives him money. Exit* JAILER. DILLON *reads.*) Danton has frightened the Tribunal, the jury wavers, the spectators were grumbling. The crowds were enormous. The people massed around the Palace of Justice out to the bridges. A handful of money, a willing arm—hm, hm! (*He walks back and forth, drinking out of a bottle from time to time.*) If only I had one foot in the street. I won't let myself be slaughtered like this. Yes, just one foot in the street!

LAFLOTTE. And on the guillotine cart, it's all the same.

DILLON. You think so? There'd still be a few steps in between, long enough to measure with the corpses of the decemvirs.—It's high time that the honest people raise their heads.

LAFLOTTE. (*To himself.*) So much the better, that makes it easier to cut them off. Keep it up, old man, a few more glasses and my ship will be afloat.

DILLON. The rascals, the fools—they'll end up guillotining each other. (*He walks up and down.*)

LAFLOTTE. (*Aside.*) One could really love life again, like one's own child, if one presents it to oneself. It doesn't happen often that one can commit incest with chance and become one's own father. Father and child at the same time. A pleasant Oedipus!

DILLON. The people can't be fed with corpses; Danton's and Camille's wives ought to throw money to the people, that's better than heads.

LAFLOTTE. But I wouldn't tear out my eyes afterward. I might need them to mourn for the good general.

DILLON. Laying their hands on Danton! Who is still safe? Fear will unite them.

LAFLOTTE. He's lost anyway. What does it matter if I step on a corpse in order to climb out of the grave?

DILLON. Just one foot in the street! I'll find enough people, old soldiers, Girondists, former noblemen—we'll storm the prisons; we must unite with the prisoners.

LAFLOTTE. Well, yes, it smells a little like villainy. So what? I feel like trying that for once, up to now I was too one-sided. I'll have conscience pangs, but that's a change too; it's not so unpleasant to smell one's own stench.

The prospect of the guillotine has gotten boring; to have to wait for it so long! I've experienced it in my mind twenty times already. It's not even enticing anymore; it's gotten quite ordinary.

DILLON. We must send a letter to Danton's wife.

LAFLOTTE. And then—I'm not afraid of death, but of pain. It could hurt—who is to answer for that? They say it's only for an instant, but pain measures time more finely, it splits a fraction of a second. No! Pain is the only sin and suffering the only vice; I'll remain virtuous.

DILLON. Listen, Laflotte, where did that fellow go? I've got money, that'll have to work; we must strike while the iron is hot, my plan is complete.

LAFLOTTE. Right away, right away. I know the jailer, I'll speak to him. You can count on me, general. We'll get out of this hole (*To himself as he leaves.*) and enter into another, I into the largest, the world; he into the smallest, the grave.

6

The Committee of Public Safety.

ST. JUST. BARÈRE. COLLOT D'HERBOIS. BILLAUD-VARENNES.

BARÈRE. What does Fouquier write?

ST. JUST The second hearing is over. The prisoners demand the appearance of several members of the Convention and of the Committee of Public Safety. They appeal to the people because they are being denied witnesses. The excitement among the people is said to be indescribable. Danton parodied Jupiter and shook his locks.

COLLOT. All the more easily will Samson grasp hold of them.

BARÈRE. We dare not show ourselves. The fishwives and the ragpickers might find us less impressive.

BILLAUD. The people have an instinct for letting themselves be stepped upon, be it only with a glance; they love insolent faces such as his. Such brows are worse than a noble coat of arms. The refined aristocratic scorn of humanity sits upon them. Everyone who resents being looked down on should help smash them in.

BARÈRE. He's like the horn-skinned Siegfried—the blood of the September massacres has made him invulnerable.

What does Robespierre say?

ST. JUST. He acts as if he had something to say.

The jury must declare itself to be sufficiently informed and close the debate.

BARÈRE. Impossible, that can't be done.

ST. JUST. They must be taken care of at all costs, even if we have to strangle them with our own hands. "Dare!" Let it not be said that Danton taught us this word in vain. The Revolution will not stumble over their dead bodies, but if Danton remains alive, he will catch it by the robe, and he has something about him that could ravish liberty itself. (ST. JUST *is called out.*)

(*A* JAILER *enters.*)

JAILER. In St. Pelagie prisoners are dying, they are calling for a doctor.

BILLAUD. That's unnecessary; less work for the executioner.

JAILER. There are pregnant women among them.

BILLAUD. So much the better; their children won't need a coffin.

BARÈRE. A consumptive aristocrat saves the Revolutionary Tribunal a session. Any medical help would be counterrevolutionary.

COLLOT. (*Takes a paper.*) A petition, a woman's name!

BARÈRE. Probably one of those who would like to be forced to choose between the board of the guillotine and the bed of a Jacobin. They will die like Lucretia after being dishonored, but a little later than the Roman—namely, in childbirth, or from cancer or old age. It might not be so unpleasant to drive a Tarquinius out of the virtuous republic of a virgin.

COLLOT. She is too old. Madame demands death, she knows how to express herself—the prison rests upon her like the lid of a coffin. She's been there only four weeks. The answer is easy. (*He writes and reads.*) "Citizen, you have not wished for death long enough."

BARÈRE. Well said. But Collot, it's not good if the guillotine begins to laugh; the people will no longer fear it. One shouldn't be so familiar.

(ST. JUST *returns.*)

ST. JUST. I've just received a denunciation. There's a conspiracy in the prisons; a young man named Laflotte discovered it all. He sat in the same room with Dillon, Dillon was drinking and chattering.

BARÈRE. He cuts off his head with his bottle, that's happened before.

ST. JUST. The wives of Danton and Camille are to throw money among the people, Dillon is to escape, the prisoners will be set free, the Convention blown up.

BARÈRE. Those are fairy tales.

ST. JUST. We will put them to sleep with this fairy tale. The denunciation I have right here; then the impudence of the accused, the unrest among the people, the consternation of the jury—I'll make a report.

BARÈRE. Yes, go, St. Just, and spin your phrases, where each comma is a swordstroke and each period a decapitated head.

ST. JUST. The Convention must decree that the Tribunal should continue the trial without interruption and may exclude from debate any of the accused who infringes upon the respect due to the court or creates a disturbance.

BARÈRE. You have a revolutionary instinct; that sounds very moderate, but it will have its effect. They cannot remain silent; Danton will have to shout.

ST. JUST. I will count on your support. There are people in the Convention who are as sick as Danton and are afraid of getting a similar cure. They have taken courage again, they will scream about violation of rules . . .

BARÈRE. (*Interrupting him.*) I will tell them: in Rome the consul who had discovered the Catiline conspiracy and had executed the criminals on the spot was accused of violating rules. Who were his accusers?

COLLOT. (*With pathos.*) Go, St. Just. The lava of the Revolution is flowing. Liberty will strangle in its embrace those weaklings who tried to fertilize its mighty womb; the majesty of the people will appear to them in thunder and lightning like Jupiter to Semele and reduce them to ashes. Go, St. Just, we will help you hurl the thunderbolt upon the heads of the cowards. (ST. JUST *exits.*)

BARÈRE. Did you hear the word "cure"? They'll manage to turn the guillotine into medication against venereal disease. They're not fighting the moderates, they're fighting vice.

BILLAUD. Up to now the two have followed the same path.

BARÈRE. Robespierre wants to turn the Revolution into a lecture hall for morality and the guillotine into a pulpit.

BILLAUD. Or a church pew.

COLLOT. On which he'll eventually lie rather than kneel.

BARÈRE. That will be easy. The world would have to be upside down if the so-called scoundrels are to be hanged by the so-called righteous people.

COLLOT. (*To* BARÈRE.) When will you come again to Clichy?

BARÈRE. When the doctor stops coming to me.

COLLOT. Yes, indeed, there's a comet over that place whose scorching rays dry out your spinal fluid.

BILLAUD. Soon the pretty fingers of the charming Demahy will pull it out of its case and make it hang down over his back like a braid.

BARÈRE. (*Shrugs his shoulders.*) Shh! The Incorruptible must not know about that.

BILLAUD. He is an impotent Mohammed. (BILLAUD *and* COLLOT *leave.*)

BARÈRE. (*Alone.*) The monsters! "You have not wished for death long enough!" Those words should have withered the tongue that spoke them.

And what about me?

When the September murderers forced their way into the prisons, a prisoner grabs his knife, mingles with the killers, plunges it into the breast of a priest—he is saved! Who can object to that? Now what if I mingle with the killers or join the Committee of Public Safety? What if I use a guillotine blade or a pocketknife? The situation remains the same, only with somewhat more complicated circumstances; the basic principles are the same.

And if he could murder one—what about two, or three, or more? Where does it stop? Here come the barleycorns—are two a pile, three, four—how many then? Come, conscience, come, my little chicken, come, cluck, cluck, cluck—here's food for you.

And yet—was I ever a prisoner? I was suspect, that's the same thing, my death was certain. (*Exits.*)

7

The Conciergerie.

LACROIX. DANTON. PHILIPPEAU. CAMILLE.

LACROIX. Well roared, Danton. If you had agonized about your life a little sooner, things would be different now. It's bad, isn't it, when death comes so shamefully close and its breath stinks and it becomes ever more insistent?

CAMILLE. If only it would ravish us and tear its prey from our hot bodies in a fierce fight! But with all these formalities, it's like marrying an old woman, with the contracts drawn up, the witnesses called, amen said, and then the bed sheets are raised and she crawls in with her cold limbs!

DANTON. If only it were a fight with hands and feet! But I feel as if I've fallen into a mill and my limbs were slowly, systematically being twisted off by cold physical force. To be killed so mechanically!

CAMILLE. To lie there alone, cold, stiff, in the rotting dampness; it's possible that death slowly tortures life out of our fibers, perhaps to rot away consciously.

PHILIPPEAU. Be calm, my friends. We are like the autumn crocus which only goes to seed after winter is over. We differ from transplanted flowers only in that we stink a little from the experiment. Is that so bad?

DANTON. An edifying prospect! From one dungheap to another! The divine theory of classes, right? From first grade to second, from second to third, and so on? I'm sick of school benches, I've gotten calluses on my ass like a monkey from sitting on them.

PHILIPPEAU. Then what do you want?

DANTON. Peace.

PHILIPPEAU. Peace is in God.

DANTON. In nothingness. Try to immerse yourself in something more peaceful than nothingness, and if God is the greatest peace, isn't nothingness God? But I'm an atheist. Those cursed words: something cannot become nothing! And I am something, that's the pity of it!

Creation has spread itself out so far that nothing is empty, it's all a swarm.

Nothingness has killed itself, Creation is its wound, we are its drops of blood, the world is the grave in which it rots.

That sounds crazy, but there's some truth to it.

CAMILLE. The world is the Wandering Jew, nothingness is death, but death is impossible. Oh, that I cannot die, that I cannot die, as the song says.

DANTON. We are all buried alive and entombed like kings in triple or quadruple coffins—under the sky, in our houses, in our coats and shirts.

For fifty years we scratch on the lid of the coffin. Oh, to believe in obliteration—that would help.

There's no hope in death; it's only a simpler—and life a more complicated, organized—form of decay; that's the only difference!

But I just happen to be used to this kind of decay; the devil only knows how I could adjust to another.

Oh, Julie! If I had to go *alone*! If she were to abandon me!

And if I decomposed entirely, dissolved completely—I'd be a handful of tormented dust; each of my atoms could find peace only with her.

I can't die, no, I cannot die. We must cry out; they will have to tear out every drop of life from my limbs.

8

A room.

FOUQUIER. AMAR. VOULAND.

FOUQUIER. I no longer know how to answer; they demand a commission.

AMAR. We've got the scoundrels. Here's what you need. (*He gives* FOUQUIER *a paper.*)

VOULAND. This will satisfy you.

FOUQUIER. You're right, we needed that.

AMAR. Now go to work, so all of us can get this thing off our necks.

9

The Revolutionary Tribunal.

DANTON. The Republic is in danger and he has no instructions! We appeal to the people—my voice is still strong enough to hold a funeral oration for the decemvirs. I repeat: we demand a commission; we have important revelations to make. I shall withdraw into the citadel of reason, I shall burst forth with the cannon of truth and crush my enemies. (*Signs of applause.*)

(FOUQUIER, AMAR, VOULAND *enter.*)

FOUQUIER. Silence in the name of the Republic, reverence before the law!

The Convention has resolved:

whereas signs of mutiny are evident in the prisons; whereas the wives of Danton and Camille are throwing money to the people and General Dillon is to escape and become the leader of the insurgents in order to free the accused; whereas the latter have acted in a disorderly fashion and have attempted to libel the Tribunal, the Tribunal is hereby authorized to continue the investigation without interruption and bar from debate any of the accused who neglects the respect due to the law.

DANTON. I ask those present if we have libeled the Tribunal, the people, or the National Convention?

MANY VOICES. No! No!

CAMILLE. The wretches, they want to murder my Lucile!

DANTON. Someday the truth will come to light. I see great misfortune coming over France. This is dictatorship—it has torn off its veil, it carries its head high, it strides over our dead bodies. (*Pointing to* AMAR *and* VOULAND.) Look there at the cowardly murderers, look at the scavengers of the Committee of Public Safety!

I accuse Robespierre, St. Just, and their hangmen of high treason.

They want to choke the Republic in blood. The tracks of the guillotine carts are the highways upon which the foreign powers will penetrate into the heart of the fatherland.

How much longer should the footprints of liberty be graves?

You want bread and they throw you heads. You are thirsty and they make you lick the blood from the steps of the guillotine. (*Great agitation among the spectators, shouts of approval.*)

MANY VOICES. Long live Danton, down with the decemvirs! (*The prisoners are forcibly led away.*)

10

Square before the Palace of Justice.

A crowd of people.

SEVERAL VOICES. Down with the decemvirs! Long live Danton!

FIRST CITIZEN. Yes, that's right, heads instead of bread, blood instead of wine.

SEVERAL WOMEN. The guillotine is a bad mill and Samson is a bad baker's helper—we want bread, bread!

SECOND CITIZEN. Danton gobbled up your bread; his head will give bread to all of you again, he was right.

FIRST CITIZEN. Danton was with us on the 10th of August, Danton was with us in September. Where were those who accused him?

SECOND CITIZEN. And Lafayette was with you at Versailles and was a traitor anyway.

FIRST CITIZEN. Who says Danton is a traitor?

SECOND CITIZEN. Robespierre.

FIRST CITIZEN. And Robespierre is a traitor.

SECOND CITIZEN. Who says that?

FIRST CITIZEN. Danton.

SECOND CITIZEN. Danton has fancy clothes, Danton has a nice house. Danton has a beautiful wife, he bathes in Burgundy wine, eats venison from silver plates, and sleeps with your wives and daughters when he's drunk.

Danton was poor like you. Where did he get all this?

The Veto bought it for him so he would save the crown.

The duke of Orléans gave it to him so Danton would steal the crown for him.

That foreigner[10] gave it to him so he would betray you all.

What does Robespierre have? The virtuous Robespierre. You all know him.

ALL. Long live Robespierre! Down with Danton! Down with the traitor!

10. Probably William Pitt the Younger, with whom Danton is alleged to have conspired.

Act Four

1

A room.

JULIE. *A* BOY.

JULIE. It's all over. They were trembling before him. They'll kill him out of fear. Go! I've seen him for the last time—tell him I couldn't see him this way. (*She gives the* BOY *a lock of her hair.*)

There, bring him that and tell him he won't go alone. He'll understand—and then come back quickly. I want to read his glances in your eyes.

2

A street.

DUMAS. *A* CITIZEN.

CITIZEN. How can they condemn so many unfortunate people to death after such a trial?

DUMAS. That is unusual, to be sure, but the men of the Revolution have an instinct which is lacking in other men, and this instinct never deceives them.

CITIZEN. That is the instinct of a tiger.—You have a wife.

DUMAS. I shall soon have had one.

CITIZEN. So it's true!

DUMAS. The Revolutionary Tribunal will announce our divorce, the guillotine will separate us from bed and board.

CITIZEN. You are a monster!

DUMAS. Idiot! You admire Brutus?

CITIZEN. With all my heart.

DUMAS. Must one be a Roman consul and cover his head with a toga in order to sacrifice his beloved to the fatherland? I shall wipe my eyes with the sleeve of my red coat, that's the only difference.

CITIZEN. That's horrible.
DUMAS. Go on, you don't understand me. (*They exit.*)

3

The Conciergerie.

LACROIX, HÉRAULT *on a bed.* DANTON, CAMILLE *on another.*

LACROIX. It's really shameful how one's hair and nails grow here.
HÉRAULT. Watch out—you're sneezing sand into my face.
LACROIX. And please don't step on my feet like that, friend, I've got corns.
HÉRAULT. You've got lice besides.
LACROIX. Oh, if I could only get rid of the worms.
HÉRAULT. Sleep well, now—we'll have to see how we can work this out, we've got little space.

Don't scratch me with your fingernails while you sleep. There! Don't tug at your shroud, it's cold down there.

DANTON. Yes, Camille, tomorrow we'll be worn-out shoes that are thrown into the lap of that beggar, earth.
CAMILLE. The cowhide from which, according to Plato, the angels cut out slippers to trot around on the earth. No wonder things are so bad. My Lucile!
DANTON. Calm down, my boy.
CAMILLE. Can I? Do you really think so, Danton? Can I? They cannot lay hands on her. The light of beauty that radiates from her sweet body is inextinguishable. Impossible! Look, the earth wouldn't dare cover her, it would arch around her, the mist of the grave would sparkle on her eyelashes like dew, crystals would sprout around her limbs like flowers, and bright springs would lull her to sleep.
DANTON. Sleep, my boy, sleep.
CAMILLE. Listen, Danton, between you and me—it's so miserable to have to die. It's of no use either. I want to steal the last glances from life's beautiful eyes; I want to keep my eyes open.
DANTON. They'll stay open on their own. Samson won't close them for us. Sleep is kinder. Sleep, my boy, sleep.

CAMILLE. Lucile, your kisses are floating on my lips; every kiss becomes a dream, my eyes sink down and enclose it tightly.

DANTON. Why doesn't the clock stop? With every tick it moves the walls closer around me until they're as tight as a coffin.

I once read a story like that as a child; my hair stood on end.

Yes, as a child! Was it worth the trouble to let me grow up and keep me warm? Just more work for the gravedigger!

It's as if I'm smelling already. My dear body, I'll hold my nose and imagine that you're a woman, sweating and stinking after the dance, and pay you compliments. We've often passed the time with each other already.

Tomorrow you'll be a shattered violin; the melody is played out. Tomorrow you'll be an empty bottle; the wine has been drunk, but it hasn't made me drunk and I'll go to bed sober. Happy are they who can still get drunk. Tomorrow you'll be a worn-out pair of pants; you'll be thrown into the closet and the moths will eat you, no matter how much you stink.

Oh, that doesn't help. Yes, it's so miserable to have to die. Death apes birth: dying we're just as helpless and naked as newborn children.

Indeed, our shroud is our diaper. What's the use? We can whimper in the grave as well as in the cradle.

Camille! He's asleep. (*Bending over him.*) A dream is dancing under his eyelashes. I won't brush the golden dew of sleep from his eyes.

(*He gets up and goes to the window.*) I won't go alone—thank you, Julie. And yet I'd have liked to die in another way, as effortlessly as a falling star, as an expiring tone kissing itself dead with its own lips, as a ray of light burying itself in clear waters.—

The stars are scattered over the sky like shimmering tears; there must be deep sorrow in the eye from which they trickled.

CAMILLE. Oh! (*He has gotten up and is reaching toward the ceiling.*)

DANTON. What's the matter, Camille?

CAMILLE. Oh, oh!

DANTON. (*Shakes him.*) Do you want to tear down the ceiling?

CAMILLE. Oh, you, you—oh, hold me—say something, Danton!

DANTON. You're trembling all over, there's sweat on your brow.

CAMILLE. That's you—this is me—there! This is my hand! Yes, now I remember. Oh, Danton, that was terrifying.

DANTON. What was?

CAMILLE. I was half dreaming, half awake. Then the ceiling disappeared and the moon sank down very near, very close, my hand seized it. The sky with its lights had come down, I beat against it, I touched the stars, I reeled like a man drowning under a layer of ice. That was terrifying, Danton.

DANTON. The lamp is throwing a round beam at the ceiling, that's what you saw.

CAMILLE. For all I care—you don't need much to lose the little bit of saneness you have. Insanity grabbed me by the hair. (*He gets up.*) I don't want to sleep anymore, I don't want to go mad. (*He reaches for a book.*)

DANTON. What are you reading?

CAMILLE. The *Night Thoughts.*

DANTON. Do you want to die prematurely? I'll read *La Pucelle.* I don't want to sneak out of life from a church pew but from the bed of a Sister of Mercy. Life's a whore, it fornicates with the whole world.

4

Square in front of the Conciergerie.

A JAILER. *Two* DRIVERS *with carts. Women.*

JAILER. Who called you here?

FIRST DRIVER. I'm not called Here, that's a funny name.

JAILER. Stupid, who gave you the order to come?

FIRST DRIVER. I don't get any ordure, just ten sous a head.

SECOND DRIVER. That dog wants to take the bread out of my mouth.

FIRST DRIVER. What do you mean, your bread? (*Pointing to the prison windows.*) There's food for worms.

SECOND DRIVER. My kids are worms too and they want their share. Oh, things are bad in our profession, and yet we're the best drivers.

FIRST DRIVER. How's that?

SECOND DRIVER. Who is the best driver?

FIRST DRIVER. Whoever drives farthest and fastest.

SECOND DRIVER. Now, you ass, who drives farther than a man who drives someone out of this world, and who's faster than the man who does it in fifteen minutes? It's exactly fifteen minutes from here to the Square of the Revolution.

JAILER. Hurry up, you bums! Closer to the gate! Make room, girls!

FIRST DRIVER. Stay where you are—you don't drive around a girl, but always right through the middle.

SECOND DRIVER. Yeah, I'll believe that, you can drive in with cart and horse, you'll find good tracks, but when you come out, you'll have to go into quarantine.

(*They drive up.*)

SECOND DRIVER. (*To the women.*) What are you staring at?

A WOMAN. We're waiting for old customers.

SECOND DRIVER. You think my cart is a whorehouse? It's a respectable cart—it's carried the king and all the elegant men of Paris to the table.

LUCILE. (*Enters. She sits on a rock under the prison windows.*) Camille, Camille! (CAMILLE *appears at a window.*)

Listen, Camille, you make me laugh with your long coat of stone and your iron mask over your face—can't you bend down? Where are your arms?

I want to lure you down, dear bird. (*Sings.*)

Two little stars shine in the sky
Shining brighter than the moon,
One shines at my dear love's window,
The other at her chamber door.

Come, come, my friend! Up the steps, quietly—they're all asleep. The moon helps me in my long wait. But you can't get through the gate, that's an unbearable costume you have. It's too nasty for a joke, please stop it. But you aren't moving either—why don't you say anything? You're making me afraid. Listen! People say you must die, and they make such somber faces.

Die! The faces make me laugh. Die! What kind of a word is that? Tell me, Camille. Die. I'll think about it. There—there it is. I want to run after it, come, sweet friend, help me catch it, come, come! (*She runs off.*)

CAMILLE. (*Calls out.*) Lucile! Lucile!

5

The Conciergerie.

DANTON *at a window that opens into the next room.* CAMILLE. PHILIPPEAU. LACROIX. HÉRAULT.

DANTON. You're quiet now, Fabre.

A VOICE. (*From inside.*) Dying.

DANTON. Do you know what we'll do now?

THE VOICE. Well?

DANTON. What you did all your life—*des vers.*[11]

CAMILLE. (*To himself.*) Insanity lurked behind her eyes. She isn't the first to go insane, that's the way of the world. What can we do about it? We wash our hands of it. It's better that way.

DANTON. I'm leaving everything behind in terrible confusion. No one knows how to govern. Things might still work out if I left Robespierre my whores and Couthon my legs.

LACROIX. We would have made a whore out of liberty.

DANTON. What's the difference? Whores and liberty are the most cosmopolitan things under the sun. Liberty will now respectably prostitute herself in the marital bed of the lawyer of Arras. But I imagine she'll play Clytemnestra to him; I don't give him six months, I'm dragging him down with me.

CAMILLE. (*To himself.*) May heaven help her to a comfortable delusion. The usual delusions we call sound reason are unbearably dull. The happiest of all people was the one who could imagine he was God the Father, the Son, and the Holy Ghost.

LACROIX. The asses will bray "Long live the Republic!" as we go by.

DANTON. What does it matter? The flood of the Revolution can discharge our corpses wherever it wants; they'll still be able to smash the heads of all kings with our fossilized bones.

HÉRAULT. Yes, if a Samson turns up for our jawbones.

DANTON. They are brothers of Cain.

LACROIX. There's no better proof that Robespierre is a Nero than

11. Verses or worms.

the fact that he was never friendlier to Camille than he was two days before Camille's arrest. Isn't that so, Camille?

CAMILLE. If you like—what does it matter to me?

(*To himself.*) What a beautiful child she has borne of insanity. Why must I leave now? We would have laughed with it, cradled it, kissed it.

DANTON. If history ever opens its graves, despotism can still suffocate from the stench of our dead bodies.

HÉRAULT. We stank well enough while alive.

This is all rhetoric for posterity, isn't it, Danton? It means nothing to us.

CAMILLE. He's making a face as if it should turn to stone to be dug up by posterity as an antique.

Is it worth the trouble to put on false smiles and rogue and speak with a good accent? We ought to take the masks off for once: as in a room with mirrors we would see everywhere only the same age-old, numberless, indestructible muttonhead, no more, no less. The differences aren't so great; we're all villains and angels, fools and geniuses—and all that in one. These four things find enough space in the same body, they aren't as large as one thinks.

Sleeping, digesting, making children—that's what we all do; all other things are merely variations in different keys on the same theme. Is that why we stand on tiptoe and make faces, is that why we're self-conscious in front of each other? We've all eaten ourselves sick at the same table and have a bellyache. Why are you holding your napkins in front of your faces? Just scream and whine as it suits you.

Just don't make such virtuous and witty and heroic and intelligent faces—we know each other, after all; save yourselves the trouble.

HÉRAULT. Yes, Camille, we'll sit down together and cry out; there's nothing more stupid than to press one's lips together when something hurts.

Greeks and gods cried out, Romans and Stoics put on a heroic front.

DANTON. The ones were just as good epicureans as the others. They worked out for themselves a very comfortable feeling of self-satisfaction. It's not such a bad idea to drape yourself in a toga and look around to see if you throw a long shadow. Why should we be at odds? Does it matter if we cover our shame with laurel leaves, rose wreaths, or vine leaves, or if we carry the ugly thing openly and let the dogs lick at it?

PHILIPPEAU. My friends, one needn't stand very far above the earth to blot out all this confused wavering and flickering and to have one's eyes filled with a few great, divine forms. There is an ear for which cacophony and deafening outcries are a stream of harmonies.

DANTON. But we are the poor musicians and our bodies the instruments. Are those horrible sounds they scratch out only meant to rise up higher and higher and finally die away as a sensual breath in heavenly ears?

HÉRAULT. Are we like suckling pigs that are beaten to death with rods for royal dinners so that their meat is tastier?

DANTON. Are we children who are roasted in the fiery Moloch arms of this world and are tickled with light rays so that the gods can enjoy their laughter?

CAMILLE. Is the ether with its golden eyes a bowl of golden carp, which stands at the table of the blessed gods, and the blessed gods laugh eternally and the fish die eternally and the gods eternally enjoy the iridescence of the death battle?

DANTON. The world is chaos. Nothingness is the world-god yet to be born.

(*The* JAILER *enters.*)

JAILER. Gentlemen, you may depart. The carts are at the door.

PHILIPPEAU. Good night, my friends. Let us pull the great blanket over ourselves under which all hearts stop beating and all eyes fall shut. (*They embrace each other.*)

HÉRAULT. (*Takes* CAMILLE*'s arm.*) Be happy, Camille, the night will be beautiful. The clouds hang in the quiet evening sky like a dying Olympus with fading, sinking, godlike forms. (*They exit.*)

6

A room.

JULIE. The people were running through the streets, now all is quiet. I don't want to keep him waiting for a moment.

(*She takes out a vial.*) Come, dearest priest, your amen makes us go to sleep.

(*She goes to the window.*) Parting is so pleasant; I only have to close the door behind me. (*She drinks.*)

I'd like to stand here like this forever.

The sun has set. The earth's features were so sharp in its light, but now her face is as still and serious as that of a dying person. How beautifully the evening light plays on her forehead and cheeks.

She's becoming ever paler; she's sinking like a corpse into the flood of the ether. Will no arm catch her by her golden locks and pull her from the stream and bury her?

I'll leave quietly. I won't kiss her, so that no breath, no sigh will wake her from her slumber.

Sleep, sleep. (*She dies.*)

7

The Square of the Revolution.

The carts drive up and stop before the guillotine. Men and women sing and dance the carmagnole. The prisoners sing the Marseillaise.

A WOMAN WITH CHILDREN. Make room! Make room! The children are crying, they're hungry. I have to let them look, so they'll be quiet. Make room!

A WOMAN. Hey, Danton, now you can fornicate with the worms.

ANOTHER WOMAN. Hérault, I'll have a wig made out of your pretty hair.

HÉRAULT. I don't have enough foliage for such a barren mound of Venus.

CAMILLE. Damned witches! You'll be screaming, "Fall on us, you mountains!"

A WOMAN. The mountain's already on you, or rather you fell from it.

DANTON. (*To* CAMILLE.) Easy, my boy, you've screamed yourself hoarse.

CAMILLE. (*Gives the driver money.*) There, old Charon, your cart is a good serving platter.

Gentlemen, I'll serve myself first. This is a classic meal: we'll lie in our places and shed a little blood as a libation. Adieu, Danton. (*He ascends the scaffold. The prisoners follow him one after the other.* DANTON *is the last to ascend.*)

LACROIX. (*To the people.*) You kill us on the day when you have lost your reason; you'll kill *them* on the day when you've regained it.

SEVERAL VOICES. We've heard that before! How dull!

LACROIX. The tyrants will break their necks on our graves.

HÉRAULT. (*To* DANTON.) He thinks his dead body will be a hotbed of liberty.

PHILIPPEAU. (*On the scaffold.*) I forgive you—I hope that your last hour be no more bitter than mine.

HÉRAULT. I thought so; once again he has to bare his chest to show the people down there that he has clean linen.

FABRE. Farewell, Danton. I'm dying twice.

DANTON. Adieu, my friend. The guillotine is the best doctor.

HÉRAULT. (*Tries to embrace* DANTON.) Oh, Danton, I can't even make a joke anymore. Then it's time. (*An* EXECUTIONER *pushes him back.*)

DANTON. (*To the* EXECUTIONER.) Do you want to be crueler than death?

Can you prevent our heads from kissing at the bottom of the basket?

8

A street.

LUCILE. There seems to be something serious about it. I'll have to think about that. I'm beginning to understand it. To die—to die . . .

Everything may live, everything, the little fly there, the bird. Why not he? The stream of life ought to stop short if that one drop were spilled. The earth ought to be wounded from the blow.

Everything moves, clocks tick, bells ring, people walk around, water runs—it all keeps going up to that point—no! It mustn't happen, no—I'll sit on the ground and scream so that everything will stop in fear—everything will stand still, nothing will move. (*She sits down, covers her eyes and screams. After a pause she arises.*)

It doesn't help—it's all still the same, the houses, the street, the wind blows, the clouds move.—I suppose we must bear it.

(*Several women come down the street.*)

FIRST WOMAN. A good-looking man, that Hérault.

SECOND WOMAN. When he stood at the Arch of Triumph during the Constitutional Celebration, I thought, "He'll look good next to the guillotine, he will." That was sort of a hunch.

THIRD WOMAN. Yes, you got to see people in all kinds of situations. It's good that dying has become so public now. (*They go past.*)

LUCILE. My Camille! Where should I look for you now?

9

The Square of the Revolution.

Two EXECUTIONERS *busy at the guillotine.*

FIRST EXECUTIONER. (*Stands on the guillotine and sings.*)

And when I'm off to bed,
The moon shines on my head . . .

SECOND EXECUTIONER. Hey! You! Finished soon?

FIRST EXECUTIONER. Right away, take it easy. (*Sings.*)

My grandpa says when I come,
"Been with the whores, ya bum?"

Come on! Gimme my jacket! (*They go off singing.*)

And when I'm off to bed,
The moon shines on my head.

LUCILE. (*Enters and sits on the steps of the guillotine.*) I'm sitting in your lap, you silent angel of death. (*She sings.*)

There's a reaper, Death's his name,
His might is from the Lord God's flame.

You dear cradle, who lulled my Camille to sleep, who smothered him under your roses.

You death knell, who sang him to the grave with your sweet tongue. (*She sings.*)

A hundred thousand, big and small,
His sickle always makes them fall.

(*A patrol appears.*)

A CITIZEN. Hey—who's there?

LUCILE. Long live the king!

CITIZEN. In the name of the Republic! (*She is surrounded by the watch and is led off.*)

Glossary

Adonis: figure of Greek mythology. In his *Metamorphoses,* Ovid tells of Venus's love for the young man. After he was killed by a wild boar, Venus caused a flower to spring from his blood.

Alcibiades: (c.450–404 B.C.) Athenian statesman and general, a devoted friend of Socrates.

Amar: Jean Baptiste André Amar (1755–1816), a lawyer who greatly admired Robespierre.

Anaxagoras: Chaumette called himself "Anaxagoras" after the Greek philosopher (c. 500–428 B.C.) who was forced to flee from Athens after being charged with atheism and blasphemy.

Appius Claudius: see **Virginius.**

Arch of Triumph: not the *Arc de Triomphe de l'Étoile,* which was built to commemorate Napoleon's victories, but probably an arch glorifying the achievements of the French Revolution.

Aristides: (c. 530–468 B.C.), Athenian statesman and general, known for his rectitude as "Aristides the Just."

August 10, 1792: The Tuileries were stormed, King Louis XVI was taken captive, and his Swiss Guard massacred.

bacchantes: also called "maenads," female worshipers of the god Dionysus or Bacchus. Their rites were performed in frenzied ecstasy.

Bayezid: Bayezid I (c. 1360–1403), Ottoman sultan, known as a fierce warrior and a merciless conqueror.

Barère: Bertrand Barère de Vieuzac (1755–1841), a prominent radical who turned against Robespierre soon after Danton's execution. Barère was later by turns an agent of Napoleon and a royalist. He was eventually granted a pension by Louis Philippe.

Baucis: figure of Greek mythology. She and her husband Philemon, both aged and poor, showed hospitality to the gods Zeus and Hermes. Philemon and Baucis typify marital devotion, since they wished to die together.

Billaud-Varennes: Jacques Nicolas Billaud-Varennes (1756–1819), like Barère, a radical antimonarchist who eventually denounced his former ally Robespierre, calling him a "moderate" and a Dantonist. Billaud-Varennes was subsequently arrested and deported.

Brissot: Jacques Pierre Brissot de Warville (1754–1793), editor of the Girondist paper *Patriote français* and a popular Girondist leader. The Jacobins brought about his execution.

Brutus: Lucius Junius Brutus, one of the first consuls of Rome (c. 509 B.C.). He sentenced his sons to death for conspiring against him.

carmagnole: a coat popular with the Revolutionaries; also a Revolutionary dance and song that often accompanied the executions.

Catiline: Lucius Sergius Catilina (c. 108–62 B.C.). Sallust describes Catiline's attempt to seize the Roman consulship by force. His plans were thwarted by Cicero.

Cato's dagger: Cato the Younger or Cato of Utica (95–46 B.C.) committed suicide after an unsuccessful attempt to oppose Julius Caesar.

such pompous Catonians: Cato of Utica (see above) was known as an austere, stoic politician.

Chabot: Francǫis Chabot (1757–1794), a Forger (see below).

Chalier: Joseph Chalier (1747–1793), Jacobian leader in Lyons. After an unsuccessful attempt to purge the city of royalists, he was executed by them. The Jacobins regarded him as a martyr.

Charon: in Greek mythology, the boatman who carried the souls of the dead across the river Styx to Hades.

Chaumette: Pierre Gaspard Chaumette (1763–1794), a member of the Cordeliers and procurator of the Paris Commune. He promoted with Hébert the worship of Reason. His sympathy for the Hébertists led to his arrest and execution.

Clichy: a town northwest of Paris where Jacobin leaders kept women.

Clytemnestra: murdered her husband, Agamemnon, when he returned from the Trojan War.

Collot d'Herbois: Jean Marie Collot d'Herbois (1750–1796), originally an actor and playwright. As an ally of Robespierre, he was president of the National Convention and a member of the Committee of Public Safety. His suppression of the counterrevolutionary movement in Lyons resulted in a bloodbath. After helping to overthrow Robespierre, he was deported along with Billaud-Varennes and Barère.

Committee of Clemency: proposed in December 1793 by Camille

Desmoulins as a measure to reduce the excesses of the "Reign of Terror."

Committee of General Security: established in 1792, it had unlimited powers to prosecute "crimes against the state."

Committee of Public Safety: created from the Committee of General Defense. The ten members of the Committee of Public Safety were the supreme authority in France from 1793 until Robespierre's fall. The Committee was responsible for national defense, and it was empowered to carry out whatever measures it considered necessary to protect the country.

Conciergerie: a royal palace that was converted into a prison.

Constitutional Celebration: held on August 10, 1793, in honor of the Constitution.

Convention: see **National Convention.**

Cordeliers: a political club named after its original meeting place, the monastery of the Cordeliers (Franciscan Recollects). Founded in 1790, its first leaders were Danton and Desmoulins, but it became more extremist under Marat and Hébert. After Hébert's fall it was dissolved.

Couthon: Georges Auguste Couthon (1755?–1794), partially paralyzed. He was a member of the Committee of Public Safety and a close associate of Robespierre, with whom he was guillotined.

Danton, George: Georges Jacques Danton (1759–1794). At the start of the French Revolution, Danton was active as a lawyer and as a leader of the Cordeliers club. The Cordeliers championed the cause of the lower classes, calling for radical measures against the monarchy. Danton was their most popular spokesman. A robust, impulsive man of great intelligence and energy, he was probably the most imposing orator of the entire Revolution. August 10, 1792, was a significant date in his political career: he helped to instigate the attack on the Tuileries, which resulted in the overthrow of the monarchy and the establishment of a republic. He was immediately appointed minister of justice. He was not directly responsible for the September massacres, but he did not intervene, perhaps thinking that violence might calm the panic brought about by the threat of foreign invasion. In 1793 he helped found the Revolutionary Tribunal and the Committee of Public Safety. His opposition to the Girondists was dictated by practical considerations: the revolutionary spirit in France was too strong, the dangers too great, to permit a moderate, decentralized government as the Girondists wished. On the other hand, he deplored Hébert's "anarchism" and the terror tactics of numerous Jacobins. Hoping to overcome factionalism in France and strengthen the nation, he and Camille Desmoulins called for a cessation of wanton executions. Robespierre was too powerful, however. Despite warnings, Danton did not act to strengthen his position until after his arrest. He was executed on April 5, 1794.

Danton, Julie: actually Sébastienne-Louise Danton, née Gély, Danton's second wife, whom he married six months before his death. She did not commit suicide; in fact, she remarried three years after Danton's death and outlived even Georg Büchner.

David: Jacques Louis David (1748–1825), court painter to Louis XVI. After 1789 he was an ardent Revolutionary and sat in the National Convention. He was the foremost painter of Revolutionary events and themes, which he executed in a rigidly classical style. Napoleon later appointed him as his leading artist.

decemvirs: F. A. Mignet called the Committee of Public Safety *les décemvirs* from the Latin *decemviri*—committee of ten.

Delaunai: a Forger (see below).

Demahy: a courtesan; Barère's mistress.

Desmoulins, Camille: Lucie Simplice Camille Benoît Desmoulins (1760–1794). He and Robespierre were fellow students in the Collège Louis-le-Grand in Paris. Like Danton, he began his career as a lawyer, but he was to make his mark as a radical pamphleteer and journalist. On July 12, 1789, hearing of the dismissal of the finance minister Necker, he raised an impromptu and impassioned call to arms in the streets of Paris. This agitation resulted in the storming of the Bastille two days later. Desmoulins soon acquired much notoriety and many enemies with his bitingly critical extremist publications. As Danton's secretary he began to voice more moderate views, calling in his journal *Le Vieux Cordelier* for a Committee of Clemency. He was guillotined with Danton.

Desmoulins, Lucile: née Duplessis. Camille and Lucile were married in 1790. They had one child. Lucile did not willingly surrender to the authorities; she was guillotined eight days after her husband because of Laflotte's denunciation.

Dictionary of the Academy: the standard dictionary of the French language, first published in 1694 by the French Academy.

Dillon: Arthur Dillon (1750–1794), general of the army of the

Ardennes in 1792. He was arrested for complicity with the royalists. His attempt to help Danton was used by Robespierre as proof of a Dantonist conspiracy.

Dumas: René François Dumas (1758–1794). Dumas' enthusiasm for the Revolution led Robespierre to appoint him president of the Revolutionary Tribunal. He tried to prevent Robespierre's downfall and was therefore executed with him.

Dumouriez: Charles François Dumouriez (1739–1823), French general who became commander of the army in August 1792. After initial victories he was defeated by the Austrians. He deserted, finally settling in England.

Epicurus: (341–270 B.C.), Greek philosopher who taught that pleasure is the highest good that man can achieve. Epicurus's concept of pleasure, based on self-control, implied serenity in the absence of pain. Epicureanism later came to be associated with indulgent hedonism.

Fabre d'Églantine: Philippe François Nazaire Fabre d'Églantine (1755–1794), a dramatist; arrested and executed as a Forger (see below).

Fabricius: Gaius Fabricius Luscinus (died 250 B.C.), Roman general and statesman noted for his honesty.

Field of Mars: on July 17, 1791, on the *Champs de Mars*, Danton incited Parisians to sign petitions calling for the abolition of the monarchy.

Force Prison: the building in which it was housed originally belonged to the de la Force family.

Foreigners: a group arrested for financial speculation. They and the Forgers were tried and executed together with the Dantonists to give the appearance of mutual complicity.

Forgers: a group of Jacobins, including Chabot, Delaunai, and Fabre d'Églantine, who forged for personal profit a document relating to the liquidation of the India Company.

Fouquier-Tinville: Antoine Quentin Fouquier-Tinville (1746–1795), from March 1793 to July 1794 public prosecutor of the Revolutionary Tribunal. As coldly ruthless as Robespierre, he seldom failed to secure a conviction. After Robespierre's fall he was brought to trial and executed in May 1795.

Gaillard: an actor and Hébertist who committed suicide.

Girondists: a moderate political group, so named because many of its leaders came from the Gironde department. Sometimes called Brissotins, after J. P. Brissot, they originally were allies of the Jacobins, but their allegiance to the middle classes rather than to the poor soon caused them to clash with the Jacobin radicals. When twenty-two Girondist leaders were executed in 1793, others fled to the provinces and attempted to stir up a civil war. Marat's assassination added to their unpopularity, and they were expunged from the government, only to be formally reinstated in 1795.

grisettes: working girls who usually dressed in gray (*gris*). Some supplemented their income by catering to the pleasures of the rich bourgeoisie and the aristocracy, and the term came to mean "high-class whore."

Hébert: Jacques René Hébert (1757–1794), journalist, prominent member of the Cordeliers. He and Chaumette founded the cult of the worship of Reason. As deputy procurator of the powerful Paris Commune (which was the political voice of the people of Paris), he challenged the authority of Robespierre, who seized on the opportunity to suppress the atheistic Hébertists.

Hérault-Séchelles: Marie Jean Hérault de Séchelles (1759–1794), originally a lawyer, popular for his good looks and elegant manners. He was from the beginning an ardent reformer, eventually allying himself with Danton. He served several times as president of the National Convention. He was executed with Danton.

Herman: Martial Joseph Armand Herman (1749–1795), formerly president of the criminal court of Calais, appointed by Robespierre to the presidency of the Revolutionary Tribunal. The Tribunal condemned him to death after Robespierre's fall.

Jacobins: a political club founded in 1789. Its members first assembled in the unused monastery of the Jacobins (Dominicans) in Paris. Affiliated clubs sprang up all over France. In 1791 the public was admitted to the political debates at the club. The Jacobins supported universal social equality, a welfare system for the poor, and a centralized national government. Under the leadership of Marat and Robespierre, the Jacobins became the dominant force in the National Convention, overcoming all those who disagreed with them. After Robespierre's downfall the club was closed.

January 21, 1793: date of the execution of King Louis XVI.

July 14, 1789: date of the fall of the Bastille.

Lacroix: actually Jean François Delacroix (1754–1794), a lawyer, ally of Danton. He and Danton were sent to the Netherlands in 1792 to assist the French army. He was executed with Danton.

Lafayette: Marie Joseph Paul Yves Roch Gilbert du Motier, Marquis de Lafayette (1757–1834). Of noble birth, he was attracted to the American Revolution and joined George Washington's army in 1777. He was highly respected by the reformers in the early days of the French Revolution, but when the radicals seized power he fled from France and was imprisoned in Austria. Reinstated by Napoleon, he lived to take part in the Revolution of 1830.

Legendre: Louis Legendre (1752–1797). Originally a butcher, he joined the Jacobins and helped found the Cordelier Club. He played a prominent role in the major events of the Revolution. When Danton was brought to trial, Legendre at first defended him, but he soon became intimidated and allowed events to run their course. After Robespierre's fall, Legendre became a reactionary and was elected president of the Convention.

Louis XVII: proclaimed king by the royalists after the execution of Louis XVI. It is assumed that he died in prison in 1795, aged ten.

Lucretia: Roman matron who committed suicide after being raped by Sextus Tarquinius.

Luxembourg prison: the state prison, formerly a palace.

Marat: Jean Paul Marat (1743–1793). In 1789 he founded the radical journal *L'Ami du peuple*; in 1790 he suggested "executing 500 royalists in order to save the lives of 500,000 innocent citizens." A foe of the Girondists, he was brought to trial while they were still in power, but he was acquitted. His assassination by Charlotte Corday prompted the Jacobins to take reprisals against the Girondists.

Marseillaise: French national anthem, composed in 1792 by Claude Joseph Rouget de Lisle. Originally known as *Chant de guerre pour l'armée du Rhin,* it was sung by men from Marseilles as they marched on the Tuileries on August 10, 1792.

May 31, 1793: date of the Jacobin victory over the Girondists.

Medea: in Greek mythology, princess of Colchis. When she fled from Colchis with Jason, she murdered her brother Absyrtus and scattered parts of his body, delaying her pursuing father.

Mercier: Louis-Sébastien Mercier (1740–1814), dramatist and essayist. Politically he was a moderate (Girondist), which led to his arrest in 1793. He was set free after Robespierre's execution. His *Le Nouveau Paris* (1799), a description of the Revolution, was one of Büchner's sources for *Danton's Death*.

Minotaur: born of a woman and a bull, this monster lived in King Minos's labyrinth in Crete. It devoured youths and maidens, who were sacrificed to it.

Mirabeau: Honoré Gabriel Riquetti, comte de Mirabeau (1749–1791). Although one of the most effective Revolutionary leaders in 1789, he was secretly allied to the court of Louis XVI. To avoid the excesses of the "Terror," which he foresaw, he hoped to create a constitutional kingdom like that of England. He was nevertheless still popular with the masses at the time of his death in 1791.

Moloch: Canaanitish god of fire to whom children were sacrificed.

Momoro, Madame: an actress who represented the Goddess of Reason in Chaumette's Festival of Reason in 1793.

the Mountain: see **the Plain.**

National Convention: created in September 1792, replacing the Legislative Assembly. France thereby became a republic. The Convention was dominated by the Jacobins; its power was centralized in its committees.

Night Thoughts: *Night Thoughts on Life, Death, and Immortality,* a blank-verse poem in nine books written between 1742 and 1745 by Edward Young (1683-1765). Translated into many languages, the work influenced many European sentimental and Romantic poets.

The Old Franciscan: *Le Vieux Cordelier,* edited by Camille Desmoulins. The journal voiced his and Danton's desire to bring an end to the "Reign of Terror."

Orléans: Louis Philippe Joseph, duc d'Orléans (1747–1793). Although an aristocrat, he championed the cause of the lower classes and helped the Jacobins to power. As "Citizen Égalité" he even voted for the execution of Louis XVI. He was nevertheless charged with aspiring to the crown and plotting with Dumouriez, for which he was executed. His son became King Louis Philippe.

Paetus: when Caecina Paetus was sentenced to die, his wife Arria stabbed herself, then handed him the dagger, saying, "Paete, non dolet."

Palais Royal: formerly the property of the duc d'Orléans, it contained shops, cafés, and gambling casinos. It was frequented by politicians and prostitutes.

Panthéon: named after the Pantheon in Rome, the French Panthéon was dedicated to the memory of the great men of France.

Paris: ("Fabricius"), a member of the Revolutionary Tribunal who warned Danton of his impending arrest.

Paine: Thomas Paine (1737–1809), political theorist and author. Born in England, Paine went to America in 1774 at Benjamin Franklin's urging. In 1776 he published the pamphlet *Common Sense*, calling for the establishment of a republic. During the Revolutionary War his *The American Crisis* bolstered the morale of the colonists. Returning to Europe, he countered Edmund Burke's negative appraisal of the French Revolution with *The Rights of Man* (1791, 1792). Indicted for treason, he fled from England to France, where he was elected to the National Convention. Robespierre had him arrested for opposition to the Jacobins, but after Robespierre's fall, Paine was released. In 1802 he returned to America. His religious views were expressed in *The Age of Reason* (1794, 1795); they are not those of an atheist, as Büchner indicates, but those of a deist, who rejects organized religion in favor of a moral code founded on natural religion.

Pelias: Pelias stole the kingdom Iolcus from his brother and sent his nephew Jason in search of the Golden Fleece. In revenge, Medea advised his daughters to cut their father to pieces and boil him in a cauldron to restore his youth. Contrary to St. Just's implication, Pelias was not restored to life.

Philippeau: Pierre Philippeaux (1754–1794), a lawyer and a member of the National Convention. He was a Dantonist, but he did not share the Dantonists' libertinism.

Pitt: William Pitt (1759–1806), prime minister of England who launched a blockade against the ports of France in 1793.

the Plain and the Mountain: Jacobin and Girondist delegates sat separated during meetings of the National Convention. The Jacobins took the highest seats on the left and were known as "the Mountain." The Girondists were on the right, and the other delegates sat in the middle, in "the Plain."

Portia: daughter of Cato of Utica, wife of Marcus Brutus. She killed herself when her husband, having taken part in the assassination of Julius Caesar, was defeated by Marc Antony and Octavian.

La Pucelle: *La Pucelle d'Orléans,* a satire of Joan of Arc by Voltaire.

Pygmalion: in Greek mythology, king of Cyprus. His marble sculpture of Galatea was so beautiful that he prayed to Aphrodite for a wife like it. The goddess made the statue come to life and Pygmalion married Galatea.

red caps: the symbol of the Jacobins.

Revolutionary Tribunal: created by Danton, it tried all crimes against the state without appeal. The jury voted openly.

Robespierre: Maximilien François Marie Isidore de Robespierre (1758–1794). A scholarship enabled the young and impoverished Robespierre to study law at the Collège Louis-le-Grand in Paris. Afterward he returned to his native Arras to practice. He resigned from a judgeship in Arras because he disapproved of capital punishment. He returned to Paris as a representative from his native district, soon distinguishing himself as a radical reformer. He was intensely devoted to the philosophy of Rousseau, espousing deism, utopian democracy, and a rigid moral ethos, for which he received the nickname "the Incorruptible." Unlike the Girondists, he was opposed to a war against Austria, fearing a resurgence of militarism in France. Having tried in vain to prevent the September massacres, he called for the execution of Louis XVI. The Girondists, unwilling to form a coalition with the Jacobins, were eventually defeated, and Robespierre was elected to the Committee of Public Safety. He was fundamentally opposed to the communism of the Hébertists and the libertinism of the Dantonists, and he helped eradicate both factions. On May 7, 1794, he officially inaugurated the worship of the Supreme Being. On June 10, the Revolutionary Tribunal (with Robespierre's connivance) was granted completely arbitrary powers in its sentencing, since witnesses were no longer allowed to testify. On July 26, he called for the removal of certain members of the Committees of Public Safety and of General Security in order to secure his position as absolute dictator of France, but on the following day the National Convention turned against him, ordering his arrest. That night he was freed by members of the Paris Commune; but the next day, July 28, he was guillotined with several followers.

Romulus: the legendary founder of Rome. He and his twin brother,

Remus, were abandoned at birth and suckled by a she-wolf. Romulus eventually killed his brother during a quarrel.

Ronsin: commandant of the Revolutionary army. A follower of Hébert, he was executed in 1794 with his leader.

St. Denis: first bishop of Paris, patron saint of France, who died a martyr. He is generally represented carrying his own head.

Saint Jacob: the Jacobin club, which originally met in the monastery of the Jacobins (Dominicans).

St. Just: Louis Antoine Léon de Richebourg de Saint-Just (1767–1794), a worshipful adherent of Robespierre who shared his idol's idealism. He supervised the military operations at the Rhône which drove the allies out of France. Upon his return to Paris he was appointed president of the National Convention. Robespierre arranged his appointment to the Committee of Public Safety, where he ruthlessly eliminated enemy factions. He called for the automatic execution of deserters and defeated generals and proposed a dictatorship for the sake of France's salvation. On July 27, 1794, he attempted to defend Robespierre before the Convention but was shouted down. He went to the guillotine with Robespierre on the following day.

St. Pelagie: a cloister used as a prison.

Sallust: Gaius Sallustius Crispus (86–34 B.C.), Roman historian. His major work describes the Catiline conspiracy.

Samson: actually Henri Sanson (1767–1840), chief executioner during the "Reign of Terror."

sansculottes: lower-class Frenchmen wore long trousers instead of the aristocratic knee breeches (*culottes*). Revolutionaries who wished to be identified with this class often adopted this form of dress.

Saturn: Roman equivalent of the Greek god Kronos, who swallowed his children to prevent them from overthrowing him.

Sections: Paris was divided into forty-eight sections by the Municipal Law of 1790.

Semele: figure in Greek mythology. Semele was loved by Zeus. His jealous wife, Hera, convinced her to ask Zeus to appear before her in his magnificence as a god. Zeus was bound by oath to comply, and Semele was consumed by his lightning.

September 7, 1792: the culmination of the September massacres. Armed volunteers entered Paris prisons and murdered a great number of inmates.

Siegfried: in Germanic mythology Siegfried killed a dragon and bathed in its blood, making him invulnerable except for a spot between his shoulders where a leaf had fallen.

Spinoza: Baruch Spinoza (1632–1677), Dutch philosopher. His *Ethics* reflects a radically pantheistic concept of God. Free will and chance are denied, since they are part of God's will.

sublimate baptism: corrosive sublimate or mercuric chloride was often used to treat venereal disease. Büchner creates a double pun on "sublimate" and "baptism."

Tacitus: Publius Cornelius Tacitus (c. 55–117), Roman historian. In his *Annals* he criticizes the tyranny of the emperor Tiberius and the corruption of Rome. Camille Desmoulins quoted Tacitus in his *Le Vieux Cordelier* with obvious reference to Robespierre.

Tarpeian Rock: cliff on the Capitoline Hill from which the Romans threw criminals and traitors.

Tarquin: see **Lucretia.**

the twenty-two: on October 31, 1793, twenty-two Girondists were executed.

Venus with the beautiful ass: the Callipygian Venus (Greek *kallipygos,* "beautiful buttocks").

vestal virgins: Roman girls of noble birth who tended the temple of the goddess Vesta. They swore an oath of obedience and chastity.

the Veto: King Louis XVI was called "the Veto" because he had the right of veto in the Legislative Assembly.

Virginius: a Roman centurion who stabbed his daughter Virginia to protect her from the lust of the decemvir Appius Claudius Crassus.

the Wandering Jew: according to legend, a Jew who taunted Jesus on the way to Calvary. The Jew was condemned to wander on earth until Judgment Day.

Notes

Büchner began work on *Danton's Death* at the end of January 1835 while living with his parents in Darmstadt. It was finished five weeks later shortly before he fled into exile in Strassburg, so the play was written while Büchner was in constant fear of arrest for his political activities. His brother Wilhelm described how Büchner had long had the plan in mind and "began the outline of *Danton's Death* working very quickly because he wanted to make money with it." On February 21 he sent the manuscript to Frankfurt to the publisher Sauerländer and also to Karl Gutzkow, a member of the Young Germany movement. Georg is reported to have told his brother: "I'm writing feverishly but that's not a drawback—on the contrary! Anyway, I have no choice. I can't allow myself any rest until I've gotten Danton to the guillotine, and above all I need money, money!"

Büchner's first exposure to the subject matter of *Danton's Death* may have been listening to his father read aloud to the family from *Our Times* (*Unsere Zeit*), an account of the major historical events from 1789 to 1830 (30 vols., Stuttgart, 1826–30). After graduating from high school he continued to study the French Revolution intensively. The sources he consulted for *Danton's Death* were numerous and included principally:

> Louis Adolphe Thiers, *Histoire de la Révolution Française . . .*, 10 vols., Paris, 1823–24 (especially vol. 6); Louis Sébastien Mercier, *Le nouveau Paris,* 6 vols., Paris, 1799; Honoré Riouffe, *Mémoires d'un Detênu, pour servir a l'Histoire de la Tyrannie de Robespierre*, Paris, 1794/95 and 1823; *Galerie historique des Contemporains, ou nouvelle Biographie . . .*, 8 vols., Brussels, 1817 ff.; *Almanach des prisons, ou Anecdotes sur le régime intérieur de la Conciergerie, du Luxembourg . . .*, Paris, 1794/95; and M. de Proussinalle (= Pierre-Joseph-Alex Roussel), *Histoire secrète du Tribunal révolutionnaire . . .*, 2 vols., Paris, 1815, [2]1830.

In a letter to his family of July 28, 1835, he wrote about his play: see p. 275 below.

In the magazine *The Phoenix* (*Phönix*), Karl Gutzkow outlined the historical situation of the play in the following terms:

A tragic catastrophe of the French Revolution takes place before our eyes in Büchner's *Danton's Death*. Robespierre's star is in ascendance and the second reaction against the Revolution has set in. First, the Gironde and then the moderates were overthrown. Like Saturn, the Revolution devoured its own offspring. But what a difference between the two reactions! The Girondists had not been drawn into the Revolution by political intrigue or by design: it was their own sympathies and principles and the sublime enthusiasm that gripped every heart during those turbulent times and spread like a fever. The Girondists died with their flowery speeches, their noble earnestness, and the refined contempt that often accompanied the theoretical doctrine and the Juste-milieu in practice. They died because they wanted a revolution that did not include the masses. The Dantonists had blood on their hands—the blood of the September murders, not blood that they had shed to punish their victims, but to terrorize them. The aristocrats of Paris and the kings at Versailles had driven them into a surgical ecstasy, amputating a dead limb and smiling all the while. The Dantonists sacrificed their feelings, their humanity, and nights of peace to the Revolution. Indeed, they had sacrificed so much they could not believe the Revolution would demand their sacrifice as well. Robespierre accused them of having been both too moderate and too immoral. If the Girondists were the Romans of the Revolution, the Dantonists were the Greeks. Character had been guillotined, now it thirsted for genius. Danton was Alcibiades. Camille Desmoulins could live only in Athens. All his opinions were derived from Ilissus: he called the Palais Royal the "Ceramicus"; he hoped for a republic in which men were as patriotic as Demosthenes, as wise as Socrates and as congenial as the members of Aspasia's circle. The third phase of the Revolution was Robespierre's and it was religiously fanatic. The Revolution had become a cult with its sacrificial altars, its dogmas and ceremonies. Next to Robespierre, the Messiah of Blood, as Camille called him, stood St. Just, apocalypse next to gospel.

The terms applied to the three phases of the Revolution described the respective phases remarkably aptly. The Gironde believed the Revolution was replaceable. Danton thought it finite. For Robespierre, though, it was a revelation that lay beyond the scope of human free will: it was providence and the deity himself. But they all perceived the Revolution as something complete, defined by a power above them. For the Girondists it was a burden, for the Dantonists a hindrance, for Robespierre and his band, it was a messianic idea, and they forced themselves into it, emulating Christ who adopted his nation's ideas and subjected himself to them. Men were despotized by an idea and became its henchmen. To a man

> they invoked the Revolution as if it were an invisible deity that they could nevertheless hold in their hands, as I hold my hat in mine.

In this context, see the following works:

J. E. E. D. Acton. *Lectures on the French Revolution*. London, 1910.
Hanna Arendt, *On Revolution*. New York, 1963.
Thomas Carlyle. *The French Revolution. A History*. 3 vols. London, 1837.
N. Hampson. *A Social History of the French Revolution*. London 1963 (1970).
E. J. E. Hobsbawm. *The Age of Revolution. Europe 1789–1848*. London, 1962, New York, 1964.
Albert Sorel. *Europe and the French Revolution. The Political Traditions of the Old Regime*. Trans. and ed. by Alfred Cobban and J. W. Hunt. London, 1969.
M. J. Snydenham. *The French Revolution*. London/New York, 1965.
J. M. Thompson. *The French Revolution*. Oxford 1943 (1959).

Versions

In addition to the draft which appeared in Gutzkow's *Phoenix* (J) and the first printing of 1835 (E), the following versions of *Danton's Death* are extant:

a) a complete manuscript (H; in Weimar) which some scholars believe to be a complete version, but not the source for the printed version. For others, H is the "original manuscript."

b) two copies of the published book (E) with corrections in Büchner's writing, and a dedication by the author to his friends Johann Wilhelm Baum and August Stöber. They are designated by the location of their last owners, i.e. Darmstadt (E^d) and Hamburg (E^h).

First Editions

a) First published version of parts of the work in Karl Gutzkow's *Phoenix, Frühlingszeitung für Deutschland* (published weekly by Sauerländer), appearing from March 26–April 7, 1835 (J). Contains an introduction and notes by Gutzkow.

b) *Danton's Death, Dramatic Scenes of the French Reign of Terror*. Frankfurt/Main: J. D. Sauerländer, 1835 (E). Unabridged, but the text was altered by Gutzkow and Eduard Duller, an editor for Sauerländer.

Lenz

On the 20th[1] Lenz went through the mountains. The peaks and high slopes in snow, gray rock down into the valleys, green fields, boulders, and pine trees. It was cold and damp, water trickled down the rocks and sprang over the path. Pine branches hung down heavily in the moist air. Gray clouds moved across the sky, but everything so dense, and then the fog steamed up, and trailed, oppressive and damp, through the bushes, so sluggish, so shapeless. He went on indifferently, the path did not matter to him, sometimes up, sometimes down. He felt no fatigue, but at times he was irritated that he could not walk on his head. At first he felt tension in his chest when stones jumped away, when the gray forest shivered beneath him, when at times the fog enveloped the shapes or partly revealed the powerful branches; he felt an urge, he searched for something, as though for lost dreams, but he found nothing. Everything seemed to him to be so small, so close, so wet, he would have liked to set the earth behind the stove, he could not understand why he needed so much time to climb down a steep slope, to reach a distant point; he felt he should be able to cover any distance in a few steps. Only at times when the storm hurled the clouds into the valley, and the forest steamed up, and voices awakened on the rocks, often like thunder echoing in the distance and then raging up violently, as if they wanted to celebrate the earth in their wild rejoicing, and the clouds galloped along like wild neighing horses, and sunshine pierced through them and emerged and drew its flashing sword along the snowy slopes, so that a bright, blinding light cut across the peaks down into the valleys; or when the storm forced the clouds downward and tore a light blue sea into them, and then the wind died down, humming up like a lullaby and chiming bells from deep within the ravines, from the tops of the pine trees, and

1. January 20, 1778.

when a soft red glow arose against the deep blue, and tiny clouds fled by on silver wings, and all the mountain peaks, sharp and firm, gleamed and flashed far across the countryside: then pain tore through his chest, he stood, panting, his body bent forward, eyes and mouth wide open, he thought he must draw the storm into himself, contain all within him, he stretched out and lay over the earth, he burrowed into the cosmos, it was a pleasure that hurt him; or he stood still and rested his head on the moss and half-closed his eyes, and then it all moved far away from him, the earth receded below him, it grew small like a wandering star and plunged into a rushing stream flowing limpidly beneath him. But these were only moments, and then he rose, calm, steady, quiet, as if phantoms had passed before him, he remembered nothing. Toward evening he came to the mountain ridge, to the snowfield from which one descended again to the plain in the west, he sat down at the top. It had become more peaceful toward evening: the clouds hung firm and motionless against the sky, as far as the eye could see, nothing but mountaintops, with broad slopes leading down, and all so quiet, gray, in twilight; he became terribly lonely, he was alone, all alone, he wanted to talk to himself, but he could not breathe, he hardly dared, the creak of his foot below him sounded like thunder, he had to sit down; a nameless fear seized him in this nothingness, he was in a void, he jumped up and raced down the slope. It had grown dark, heaven and earth melted together. It seemed as if something were following him, as if something horrible would overtake him, something that humans cannot endure, as if insanity were pursuing him on horseback. At last he heard voices, he saw lights, he was relieved, he was told it was another half hour to Waldbach. He went through the village, lights shone through the windows, he looked in as he passed by, children at the table, old women, girls, all calm, quiet faces, it seemed to him as if the light must be radiating from them, he felt at ease, he was soon in the parsonage at Waldbach. They were sitting at the table, he went in; his blond curls hung around his pale face, his eyes and mouth twitched, his clothes were torn. Oberlin welcomed him, he took him for a laborer. "Welcome, although I don't know you." I am a friend of + + +[2] and bring you greetings

2. Christoph Kaufmann (1753–1795), called the "Apostle of Genius" because of his friendship with many of the major authors of the Storm and Stress period. He had known Lenz for two years and had taken him into his house a few months before Lenz's visit to Oberlin.

from him. "Your name, if you please?" Lenz. "Ha, ha, ha, hasn't it appeared in print? Haven't I read several dramas ascribed to a man of that name?" Yes, but I beg you not to judge me by them. They continued talking, he searched for words and spoke rapidly but in torment; gradually he became calm, the cozy room and the quiet faces emerging from the shadows, the child's bright face, on which all light seemed to rest, looking up curiously, trustingly, finally the mother, sitting quietly back in the shadows like an angel. He began to tell of his homeland; he drew all sorts of costumes, they gathered around him with interest, he felt right at home, his pale child's face, smiling now, his lively narration; he grew calm, it seemed to him as if old shapes, forgotten faces were stepping out of the dark once again, old songs awoke, he was far, far, away. At last it was time to leave, he was led across the street, the parsonage was too small, he was given a room in the schoolhouse. He went upstairs, it was cold up there, a large room, empty, a high bed in the background, he placed the lamp on the table and walked up and down, he recalled the day just past, how he had come here, where he was, the room in the parsonage with its lights and dear faces, it was like a shadow to him, a dream, and he felt empty again like on the mountain, but he could no longer fill the void with anything, the light was out, darkness swallowed everything; an unnameable fear seized him, he jumped up, he ran through the room, down the stairs, in front of the house; but in vain, all was dark, nothing, he felt himself to be a dream, isolated thoughts flitted by, he held them fast, he felt he had to keep saying "Our Father"; he could no longer find himself, an obscure instinct urged him to save himself, he beat against the stones, he tore at himself with his fingernails, the pain began to restore him to consciousness, he threw himself into the basin of the fountain, but the water was not deep, he splashed around in it. Then people came, they had heard this, they called out to him. Oberlin came running; Lenz had come to his senses again, fully aware of his situation, he was at ease again, now he was ashamed and sorry to have frightened these good people, he told them he was used to taking cold baths, and went back up; exhaustion finally allowed him to rest.

The next day went well. With Oberlin through the valley on horseback; broad mountain slopes contracting from a great height into a narrow, winding valley that led high up into the mountains in many directions, large masses of rock, spreading out toward the base, few woods, but all in a gray, somber hue, a view toward the west into the country and to the mountain range running straight from south to north, immense, grave or silent peaks standing like a dusky dream. Huge masses of light gushing at times from the valleys like a golden river, then clouds again, hanging on the highest peak, then climbing down the forest slowly into the valley or sinking and rising in the sunbeams like a flying silvery web; not a sound, no movement, no birds, nothing but the wailing of the wind, sometimes near, sometimes far. Dots also appeared, skeletons of huts, boards covered with straw, a somber black in color. People, silent and grave, as though not daring to disturb the peace of their valley, greeted them quietly as they rode past. The huts were full of life, people crowded around Oberlin, he instructed, gave advice, consoled; everywhere trusting glances, prayer. People told of dreams, premonitions. Then quickly to practical affairs, laying roads, digging canals, visiting the school. Oberlin was tireless. Lenz his constant companion, at times conversing, attending to business, absorbed in nature. It all had a beneficial and soothing effect on him, he often had to look into Oberlin's eyes, and the immense peace that comes upon us in nature at rest, in the deep forest, in moonlit, melting summer nights seemed even nearer to him in these calm eyes, this noble, serious face. He was shy, but he made remarks, he spoke, Oberlin enjoyed his conversation and Lenz's charming child's face delighted him. But he could bear it only as long as the light remained in the valley; toward evening a strange fear came over him, he felt like chasing after the sun; as objects gradually became more shadowy, everything seemed so dreamlike, so abhorrent, he felt the fear of a child sleeping in the dark; he seemed to be going blind; now it grew, the demon of insanity sat at his feet, the hopeless thought that all was but a dream gaped before him, he clung to all objects, shapes rushed past him, he pressed up against them, they were shadows, life drained from him, and his limbs were quite rigid. He spoke, he sang, he recited passages from Shakespeare, he clutched at everything that used to make his blood run faster, he tried everything, but cold, cold. Then he had to go out into the open, when his eyes had gotten used to the dark, the weak light diffused through the night restored him, he threw himself into the fountain, the harsh effect of the water restored him, he also secretly hoped to fall ill, he now bathed with less noise. Yet the more he accustomed himself to this way of life, the calmer he became, he assisted Oberlin, drew, read the Bible; old, long gone hopes reawakened in him; the New Testament was so near to him here, and one morning he went out. When Oberlin told him how an irresistible hand had stopped him on the bridge, how a dazzling light on the heights had blinded him, how he had heard a voice, how it had spoken to him at night, and how God had entered into him so completely that he took his Bible verses[3] from his pocket like a child in order to know what to do, this faith, this eternal Heaven in life, this being in God; now for the first time he comprehended the Scriptures. How close nature came to these people, all in heavenly mystery; yet not overpoweringly majestic, but still familiar!—He went out in the morning, snow had fallen that night, bright sunshine lay in the valley, but farther off the landscape partly in fog. He soon left the path, up a gradual slope, no more sign of footprints, past a pine forest, the sun formed crystals, the snow was light and fluffy, here and there on the snow light traces of wild animals leading up into the mountains. No movement in the air except for a soft breeze, the rustle of a bird lightly dusting snowflakes from its tail. All so quiet, and into the distance, trees with swaying white feathers in the deep blue air. Gradually it all became comfortable to him, hidden were those massive, uniform planes and lines that at times seemed to be speaking to him in mighty sounds, a cozy Christmas spirit crept over him, sometimes he thought his mother would step out from behind a tree, tall, and tell him she had given all this to him as a gift; as he went down, he saw that a rainbow of rays surrounded his shadow, something seemed to have touched his forehead, the being spoke to him. He came back down. Oberlin was in the room, Lenz went up to him cheerfully, saying he would like to hold a sermon sometime. "Are you a theologian?" Yes!—"Good, then next Sunday." Lenz went happily to his room, he thought about a text for his sermon and grew pensive, and his nights became peaceful. Sunday morning came, a thaw had set in. Clouds streaming by, blue in between, the church stood on a rise on the mountainside, the churchyard around it. Lenz stood up above as the churchbell rang, and the congregation came from various directions on the narrow paths up and down among the rocks, women and girls in their somber black dresses, a folded white handkerchief on the hymnal

3. The pietistic Herrenhuter sect regularly published collections of verses from the Scriptures for each day of the year; Oberlin presumably had a devotional handbook of this sort.

and a sprig of rosemary. Patches of sunshine lay at times on the valley, the warm air moved slowly, the countryside swam in a haze, distant church bells, it seemed as if everything were dissolving into one harmonious wave.

The snow had disappeared from the little churchyard, dark moss under the black crosses, a late rosebush leaned against the churchyard wall, late flowers coming up through the moss, sometimes sunshine, then darkness again. The service began, voices joined in clear, bright sound; an effect like looking into a pure mountain spring. The singing died away, Lenz spoke, he was shy, the music had calmed his convulsions entirely, all his pain awakened now and settled in his heart. A sweet feeling of endless well-being crept over him. He spoke simply to the people, they all suffered with him, and it was a comfort to him when he could bring sleep to several eyes tired from crying, bring peace to tortured hearts, direct toward Heaven this existence tormented by material needs, these weighty afflictions. He had grown stronger toward the end, then the voices began again:

> Burst, o divine woe,
> The floodgates of my soul;
> May pain be my reward,
> Through pain I love my Lord.[4]

The urge in him, the music, the pain shattered him. For him there were wounds in the universe; he felt deep, inexpressible grief because of it. Now, another existence, divine, twitching lips bent over him and sucked on his lips; he went up to his lonely room. He was alone, alone! Then the spring rushed forth, torrents broke from his eyes, his body convulsed, his limbs twitched, he felt as if he must dissolve, he could find no end to this ecstasy; finally his mind cleared, he felt a quiet, deep pity for himself, he cried over himself, his head sank on his chest, he fell asleep, the full moon hung in the sky, his curls fell over his temples and his face, tears hung on his eyelashes and dried on his cheeks, so he lay there alone, and all was calm and silent and cold, and the moon shone all night and hung over the mountains.

4. See *Woyzeck*, Scene 4,17.

Next morning he came down, he told Oberlin quite calmly how during the night his mother had appeared to him; she had stepped out from the dark churchyard wall in a white dress, and had a white and a red rose on her breast; then she had sunk down in a corner, and the roses had slowly grown over her, she was surely dead; he was quite calm about it. Then Oberlin told him how he had been alone on a field when his father died, and he had then heard a voice, so that he knew his father was dead, and when he came home it was so. That led them further, Oberlin also spoke about the people in the mountains, about girls who sensed water and metals under the earth, about men who had been seized on certain mountaintops and had wrestled with a spirit; he told him too how in the mountains he had once fallen into a kind of somnambulism by looking into a clear, deep mountain pool. Lenz said that the spirit of the water had come over him, that he had at that moment sensed something of his unique being. He continued: the simplest, purest character was closest to elemental nature, the more sophisticated a person's intellectual feelings and life, the duller is this elemental sense; he did not consider it to be an elevated state of being, it was not independent enough, but he believed it must be boundless ecstasy to be touched in this way by the unique life of every form; to commune with rocks, metals, water, and plants; to assimilate each being in nature as in a dream, as flowers take in air with the waxing and waning of the moon.

He continued to speak his mind, how in all things there was an inexpressible harmony, a tone, a blissfulness that in higher forms of life reaches out, resounds, comprehends with more organs but was consequently far more sensitive, whereas in the lower forms everything was more repressed, limited but was therefore far more at peace with itself. He continued this further. Oberlin broke it off, it led too far from his simple ways. Another time Oberlin showed him color charts, telling him the relationship of each color to human beings, he brought out twelve Apostles, each represented by a color. Lenz understood, he carried the idea further, came to have frightening dreams and began like Stilling[5] to read the Apocalypse, and read much in the Bible.

5. Johann Heinrich Jung-Stilling (1740-1817), a Pietist, wrote an interpretation of Revelation. He was best known for his autobiographical novel *Heinrich Stilling's Youth* (1777).

Around this time Kaufmann came to the Steintal[6] with his fiancée. At first Lenz was troubled by the encounter, he had created a small place for himself, that little bit of peace was so valuable to him, and now someone was coming who reminded him of so much, with whom he had to speak, converse, who knew his situation. Oberlin knew nothing of all this; he had taken him in, cared for him; he saw this as the will of God, who had sent him this unfortunate one, he loved him dearly. Besides, it was necessary that he was there, he belonged to them as though he had been there for a long time, and no one asked where he came from and where he would go. At table Lenz was in a good mood again, they talked about literature, he was in his element; the idealistic period was beginning then, Kaufmann was one of its supporters, Lenz disagreed vehemently. He said: the poets who supposedly give us reality actually have no idea of it, yet they are still more bearable than those who wish to transfigure it. He said: the good Lord has certainly made the world as it should be, and we surely cannot scrawl out anything better, our only goal should be to imitate Him a little. In all, I demand—life, the possibility of existence, and then all is well; we must not ask whether it is beautiful or ugly, the feeling that the work of art has life stands above these two qualities and is the sole criterion of art. Moreover, we encounter it rarely, we find it in Shakespeare, and it resounds fully in folk songs, sometimes in Goethe. All the rest can be thrown in the fire. Those people cannot even draw a doghouse. They wanted idealistic figures, but all I have seen of them are wooden puppets. This idealism is the most disgraceful mockery of human nature. They ought to try immersing themselves for once in the life of the most insignificant person and reproduce it, in the palpitations, the intimations, the most subtle, scarcely perceptible gestures; he had attempted this in *The Tutor* and *The Soldiers*.[7] These are the most prosaic people under the sun; but the vein of sensitivity is alike in nearly all human beings, all that varies is the thickness of the crust through which it must break. One need only have eyes and ears for it. As I went by the valley yesterday, I saw two girls sitting on a rock, one was putting up her hair, the other was helping her; and the golden hair hung down, and a serious,

6. "Stone valley" in which Waldbach is located.

7. Dramas by J. M. R. Lenz.

pale face, and yet so young, and the black dress, and the other one working with such care. The most beautiful, most intimate paintings of the Old German School barely hint at it. At times one would like to be a Medusa's head in order to transform such a group into stone and summon everyone to see it. They stood up, the beautiful group was destroyed; but as they climbed down among the rocks they formed another picture. The most beautiful pictures, the richest sounds group together and dissolve. Only one thing remains, an endless beauty moving from one form to another, eternally unfolding, changing, one surely cannot always hold it fast and put it into museums and write it out in notes and then summon young and old and let boys and old men chatter about it and go into raptures. One must love humanity in order to penetrate into the unique essence of each individual, no one can be too low or too ugly, only then can one understand them; the most insignificant face makes a deeper impression than the mere sensation of beauty, and one can let the figures emerge without copying anything into them from the outside, where no life, no muscles, no pulse swells and beats. Kaufmann objected that he would find no prototype in reality for an Apollo of Belvedere or a Raphael Madonna. What does it matter, he answered, I must admit they make me feel quite lifeless, if I delve into myself, I may indeed feel something, but then I do most of the work. I most prefer the poet or painter who makes nature most real to me, so that I respond emotionally to his portrayal, everything else disturbs me. I prefer the Dutch painters to the Italians, they alone are accessible; I know of only two paintings, by Dutchmen, which gave me the same impression as the New Testament; one is, I don't know by whom, "Christ and the Disciples at Emmaus."[8] When you read how the disciples went forth, all nature is in those few words. It's a gloomy, dusky evening, a straight red streak on the horizon, the street half dark, a stranger comes to them, they talk, he breaks bread, then they recognize him in a simple, human way, and his divine, suffering features speak distinctly to them, and they are afraid because it has grown dark, and something incomprehensible has neared them, but it is no spectral terror; it is as though a beloved dead man had come to them in his accustomed way at twilight, that's what the painting is like, with its uniform,

8. Luke 24:13–49.

brown mood, the gloomy, quiet evening. Then another. A woman sits in her room holding a prayer book. Everything is cleaned up for Sunday, the sand strewn on the floor, so comfortably clean and warm. The woman was unable to go to church, and she performs her devotions at home, the window is open, she sits turned toward it, and it seems as if the sound of the bells from the village were floating over the wide, flat landscape into the window, and from the church the singing of the nearby congregation were drifting over to her, and the woman is following the text.—He continued in this manner, the others listened attentively, much was to the point, his face had flushed from speaking, and often smiling, often serious, he shook his blond curls. He had totally forgotten himself. After the meal Kaufmann took him aside. He had received letters from Lenz's father, his son should return, should support him. Kaufmann told him how he was throwing away his life here, wasting it fruitlessly, he should set a goal for himself, and more of the same. Lenz snapped at him: away from here, away! Go home? Go mad there? You know I can't stand it anywhere but here, in this area; if I couldn't go up a mountain and see the countryside and then back into the house, walk through the garden and look in through the window. I'd go mad! Mad! Leave me in peace! Just a little peace, now that I'm beginning to feel a little better! Away from here? I don't understand that, those three words ruin the world. Everyone needs something; if he can rest, what more could he have! Always climbing, struggling, and thereby eternally throwing away all that the moment can offer and always starving just to enjoy something for once; thirsting while bright springs leap across one's path. I can bear it now, and I want to stay here; why? Why? Because I feel comfortable here; what does my father want? What can he give me? Impossible! Leave me in peace. He became vehement, Kaufmann left, Lenz was upset.

On the following day Kaufmann wanted to leave, he convinced Oberlin to accompany him to Switzerland. He was persuaded by the desire to meet Lavater[9] in person, whom he had known for a long time through correspondence. He agreed to go. Preparations kept them waiting an extra day. Lenz was struck to the heart, he had anxiously clung to everything to be rid of his endless torment;

9. Johann Caspar Lavater (1741–1801), Swiss theologian noted for his *Physiognomic Fragments* (1775–1778), composed of investigations of human character based on facial features.

at certain moments he felt deeply how he was merely deceiving himself; he treated himself like a sick child, he rid himself of certain thoughts, powerful feelings only with the greatest fear, then he was driven back to them again with boundless force, he trembled, his hair almost stood on end, until he conquered it with incredible exertion. He found refuge in an image that always floated before his eyes, and in Oberlin; his words, his face did him a world of good. So he was apprehensive about his departure. Lenz now found it intolerable to remain in the house alone. The weather had become mild, he decided to accompany Oberlin into the mountains. On the other side where the valleys opened into a plain, they parted. He went back alone. He wandered through the mountains in various directions, broad slopes led down into the valleys, few woods, nothing but mighty lines, and farther out the broad, smoking plain, a strong wind, not a trace of people except for an occasional deserted hut resting against the slopes where shepherds spent the summer. He grew still, perhaps almost dreaming, everything seemed to melt into a single line like a rising and falling wave between heaven and earth, it seemed as though he were lying at an endless sea that gently rose and fell. Sometimes he sat, then he went on again, but slowly, dreaming. He did not look for a path. It was dark when he came to an inhabited hut on a slope toward the Steintal. The door was locked, he went to the window, through which faint light came. A lamp illuminated little more than one spot, its light fell on the pale face of a girl resting behind it, eyes half open, softly moving her lips. Farther off an old woman sat in the dark, singing from a hymnal in a droning voice. After much knocking she opened; she was partly deaf, she served Lenz some food and showed him to a place to sleep, singing her song continuously. The girl had not moved. A little later a man entered, he was tall and thin, traces of gray hair, with a restless, perplexed face. He approached the girl, she gave a start and became restless. He took a dried herb from the wall and put the leaves on her hand to calm her, and she crooned intelligible words in sustained, piercing tones. He told of hearing a voice in the mountains and then seeing sheet lightning over the valleys, it had seized him too, and he had wrestled with it like Jacob. He dropped to his knees and prayed softly with fervor while the sick girl sang in a sustained, softly lingering voice. Then he went to sleep.

Lenz fell asleep dreaming, and then he heard the clock ticking in his sleep. The rushing wind sounded sometimes near, sometimes far through the girl's soft singing and the old woman's voice, and the moon, now bright, now hidden, cast its changing light dreamlike into the room. At one point the sounds grew louder, the girl spoke intelligibly and decisively, she said that a church stood on the cliff opposite. Lenz looked up and she was sitting upright behind the table with her eyes wide open, and the moon cast its quiet light on her features, which seemed to radiate an uncanny glow, while the old woman droned on, and during this changing and sinking of light, tones, and voices, Lenz fell at last into a deep sleep.

He awoke early, everyone was asleep in the dim room, even the girl had become quiet, she was leaning back, hands folded under her left cheek; the ghostly look had vanished from her features, she now had an expression of indescribable suffering. He went to the window and opened it, the cold morning air struck him. The house lay at the end of a narrow, deep valley open toward the east, red rays shot through the gray morning sky into the half-lit valley lying in white mist, and they sparkled on gray rocks and shone through the windows of the huts. The man awoke, his eyes met an illuminated picture on the wall, he stared at it fixedly, then he began to move his lips and pray softly, then ever louder. Meanwhile people entered the hut, they sat down in silence. The girl was in convulsions, the old woman droned her song and chatted with the neighbors. The people told Lenz that the man had come into the region a long time ago, no one knew from where; he was said to be a saint, he could see water underground and conjure up spirits, and people made pilgrimages to him. At the same time Lenz discovered that he had strayed farther away from the Steintal, he left with several woodsmen going in that direction. It did him good to find company; he now felt ill at ease with that powerful man who seemed at times to be speaking in horrendous tones. Besides, he was afraid of himself when he was alone.

He came home. Yet the past night had left a powerful impression on him. The world had seemed bright to him, and within himself he felt a stirring and crawling toward an abyss to which an inexorable power was drawing him. Now he burrowed within himself. He ate little; half the night in prayer and feverish dreams. A powerful urge, then beaten back in exhaustion; he lay bathed in the hottest tears, and then suddenly strength returned, and he arose cold and indifferent, his tears were like ice then, he had to laugh. The higher he raised himself up, the deeper he fell. Everything streamed together again. Visions of his former state flashed through his mind and threw searchlights into the wild chaos of his spirit. During the day he usually sat in the room downstairs, Madame Oberlin went back and forth, he drew, painted, read, clutched at every diversion, always hastily from one thing to another. Now he attached himself to Madame Oberlin, especially when she sat there, her black hymnal before her, next to a plant grown in the room, her youngest child between her knees; he also spent much time with the child. Once when he was sitting there he grew anxious, jumped up, paced back and forth. The door ajar, he heard the maid singing, first unintelligibly, then the words came:

> In all this world no joy for me,
> I have a love, far off is he.

This crushed him, he almost dissolved from the sound. Madame Oberlin looked at him. He steeled himself, he could no longer remain silent, he had to talk about it. Dearest Madame Oberlin, can't you tell me how the lady[10] is, whose fate lies like a hundredweight on my heart? "But Mr. Lenz, I know nothing about it."

He fell silent again and paced hastily back and forth in the room; then he began again: you see, I want to leave; God, these are the only people whom I can bear, and yet—yet I must go, to *her*—but I can't, I mustn't.—He was highly agitated and went out. Toward evening Lenz returned, the room was in twilight; he sat down beside Madame Oberlin. You see, he began again, when she used to walk through the room like that, and singing half to herself, and each step was music, there was such happiness in her, and it overflowed into me. I was always at peace when I looked at her or when she leaned her head against me like this, and—God! God—I haven't been at peace for a long time [. . .][11] Completely like a child; it was as if the world were too vast for her, she withdrew into herself so, she looked for the smallest place in the whole house, and there she sat as if all her happiness were focused on one little spot, and

10. Friederike Brion, beloved of Goethe and Lenz.

11. Gap in text.

then I felt the same; then I could have played like a child. Now I feel so confined, so confined, you see, sometimes it's as if my hands were hitting the sky; oh, I'm suffocating! Sometimes I feel as if I'm in physical pain, here on the left side, in the arm that used to embrace her. But I can't visualize her anymore, the image escapes me, and that torments me, only sometimes when my mind is completely clear do I feel much better. —He often spoke about this afterwards with Madame Oberlin, but mostly only in fragmented sentences; she could say only little in response, but it did him good.

Meanwhile his religious torments continued. The emptier, the colder, the deader he felt inwardly, the more he felt urged to ignite a blaze within himself, he remembered the times when everything seethed within him, when he panted under the weight of all his sensations; and now so dead. He despaired of himself, then he threw himself down, he wrung his hands, he stirred up everything inside him; but dead! Dead! Then he begged God for a sign, then he burrowed within himself, fasted, lay dreaming on the floor. On the third of February he heard that a child had died in Fouday,[12] he took this up like an obsession. He retired to his room and fasted for a day. On the fourth he suddenly entered the room where Madame Oberlin was, he had smeared his face with ashes and demanded an old sack; she was alarmed, he was given what he wanted. He wrapped the sack around himself like a penitent and set out for Fouday. The people in the valley were already used to him; they told all sorts of strange stories about him. He came into the house where the child lay. The people went about their business indifferently; they showed him to a room, the child lay in a nightgown on straw, on a wooden table. Lenz shuddered as he touched the cold limbs and saw the half-opened, glassy eyes. The child seemed so abandoned, and he so alone and lonely; he threw himself over the corpse; death frightened him, violent pain seized him, these features, this quiet face must decay, he dropped to his knees, he prayed in all the misery of despair that God should grant him a sign and revive the child, how weak and unhappy he was; then he sank into himself completely and focussed all of his willpower on one point, he sat rigidly like this for a long time. Then he rose and grasped the child's hands and said loudly and firmly: arise and walk! But the echo from the sober walls seemed to mock him, and

12. Oberlin mentions in his diary that the child was named Friederike.

the corpse remained cold. He collapsed, half insane, then he was driven up, out into the mountains. Clouds moved swiftly across the moon; at times all was dark, at times in the moonlight the landscape was revealed, shrouded in fog. He ran up and down. Hell's song of triumph was in his breast. The wind sounded like a song of titans, he felt as if he could thrust a gigantic fist up into Heaven and tear God down and drag Him through His clouds; as if he could grind up the world in his teeth and spit it into the Creator's face; he swore, he blasphemed. So he came to the crest of the mountain ridge, and the uncertain light spread down to the white masses of stone, and the sky was a stupid blue eye and the moon hung in it most ludicrously, foolishly. Lenz had to laugh out loud, and in that laughter atheism seized and held him quite securely and calmly and firmly. He no longer knew what had disturbed him so before, he was freezing, he thought he would go to bed now, and he went coldly and stolidly through the uncanny darkness—all seemed empty and hollow to him, he had to run and went to bed.

The following day great horror overcame him because of his state the day before, he was now standing at the abyss, where a mad desire urged him to look down into it again and again and to relive this torment. Then his fear increased, the sin against the Holy Ghost loomed before him.

A few days later Oberlin returned from Switzerland, much earlier than expected. This disturbed Lenz. But he cheered up when Oberlin told him about his friends in Alsace. Oberlin went back and forth in the room meanwhile, unpacked, put things away. He talked about Pfeffel[13] praising the happy life of a country pastor. He admonished him to comply with his father's wishes, to live in keeping with his profession, to return home. He told him: "Honor your father and mother" and more of the same. During the conversation Lenz grew highly agitated; he sighed deeply, tears welled from his eyes, he spoke disjointedly. Yes, but I won't be able to bear it; do you want to turn me out? In you alone is the way to God. But it's all over with me! I have sinned, I'm damned for eternity, I'm the Wandering Jew. Oberlin told him Christ had died for that, he should turn to Him with all his heart and he would partake of His grace.

Lenz raised his head, wrung his hands and said: ah! Ah! Divine

13. Gottlieb Konrad Pfeffel (1736–1809), blind poet and author of fables, active in educational and religious enterprises.

consolation. Then suddenly he asked affably how the lady was. Oberlin said he knew nothing about this, yet he would help and advise him in all things, but he must tell him the place, circumstances, and the name. He answered only in broken words: ah, she's dead! Is she still alive? You angel, she loved me—I loved her, she was worthy of it, oh, you angel. Damned jealousy, I sacrificed her—she still loved another—I loved her, she was worthy of it—oh, good mother, she loved me too. I'm a murderer. Oberlin answered: perhaps all these people were still alive, perhaps content; be that as it may, if he would turn to God, then God could and would do them so much good that the benefit they would gain through Lenz's prayers and tears would perhaps far outweigh the injury he had inflicted upon them. He gradually grew quieter and went back to his painting.

He returned in the afternoon with a piece of fur on his left shoulder and a bundle of rods in his hand, which had been given to Oberlin along with a letter for Lenz. He handed Oberlin the rods with the request that he should beat him with them. Oberlin took the rods from his hand, pressed several kisses on his mouth and said: these are the blows he would give him, he should be calm, settle his affairs alone with God, no amount of blows would erase a single sin; Jesus had seen to that, to Him should he turn. He went away.

At supper he was somewhat pensive as usual. Yet he talked about all sorts of things, but in anxious haste. At midnight Oberlin was awakened by a noise. Lenz was running through the yard, calling out the name Friederike in a hollow, harsh voice with extreme rapidity, confusion, and despair, then he threw himself into the basin of the fountain, splashed around, out again and up to his room, down again into the basin, and so on several times, finally he grew quiet. The maids who slept in the nursery below him said they had often, but especially that night, heard a droning sound that they could compare only to the sound of a shepherd's pipe. Perhaps it was his whining in a hollow, ghastly, despairing voice.

Next morning Lenz did not appear for a long time. Finally Oberlin went up to his room, he was lying quietly and motionless in bed. Oberlin questioned him repeatedly before he received an answer; at last he said: yes, Pastor, you see, boredom! Boredom! Oh! So boring. I no longer know what to say, I've already drawn all sorts of figures on the wall. Oberlin told him to turn to God; he laughed at that and said: yes, if I were as happy as you to have found such a comforting pastime, yes, one could indeed spend one's time that way. Everything out of boredom. For most people pray out of boredom; others fall in love out of boredom, a third group is virtuous, a fourth corrupt, and I'm nothing, nothing at all. I don't even want to kill myself: it's too boring![14]

O God, Thy waves of radiant light,
Thy glowing midday shining bright,
Have made my watchful eyes so sore,
Will not the night come evermore?

Oberlin looked at him angrily and started to go. Lenz rushed after him and, looking at him with haunted eyes: you see, now I've finally thought of something, if I could only determine whether I'm dreaming or awake: you see, that's very true, we must look into it; then he rushed back to bed. That afternoon Oberlin wanted to pay a visit nearby; his wife had already left; he was just about to leave when there was a knock at his door and Lenz entered, his body bent forward, his head hanging down, ashes all over his face and here and there on his clothes, holding his left arm with his right hand. He asked Oberlin to pull on his arm, he had sprained it, he had thrown himself from the window, but since no one had seen it, he did not want to tell anyone. Oberlin was seriously alarmed, but he said nothing, he did what Lenz asked, at the same time he wrote to the schoolmaster at Bellefosse, asking him to come down and giving him instructions. Then he rode off. The man came. Lenz had already seen him often and had grown attached to him. He pretended he had wanted to discuss something with Oberlin, then started to leave again. Lenz asked him to stay, and so they remained together. Lenz suggested a walk to Fouday. He visited the grave of the child he had tried to resurrect, knelt down several times, kissed the earth on the grave, seemed to be praying, though in great confusion, tore off part of the bouquet of flowers on the grave as a souvenir, returned to Waldbach, turned back again and Sebastian[15]

14. See *Leonce and Lena,* Act I, Scene 1.

15. Sebastian Scheidecker, the schoolmaster.

with him. At times he walked slowly and complained about great weakness in his limbs, then he walked in desperate haste, the landscape frightened him, it was so confining that he was afraid of bumping into everything. An indescribable feeling of discomfort came over him, his companion finally got on his nerves, he probably guessed his purpose and looked for a way to be rid of him. Sebastian appeared to give in to him but secretly found a way to inform his brothers of the danger, and now Lenz had two guardians instead of one. He continued to lead them around, finally he returned to Waldbach, and as they neared the village he turned like a flash and ran like a deer back toward Fouday. The men chased after him. While they were looking for him in Fouday, two shopkeepers came and told them that a stranger who called himself a murderer had been tied up in a house, but he could not possibly be a murderer. They ran into the house and found it was so. A young man had been frightened into tying him up at his vehement insistence. They untied him and brought him safely to Waldbach, where Oberlin had since returned with his wife. He looked confused, but when he noticed he was received with kindness and friendship, he took courage, his expression changed for the better, he thanked his two companions affably and tenderly and the evening passed quietly. Oberlin implored him not to take any more baths, to spend the night quietly in bed, and if he could not sleep, to converse with God. He promised and did so that night, the maids heard him praying almost all night long.—Next morning he came to Oberlin's room looking cheerful. After they had discussed various things, he said with exceptional friendliness: dear Pastor, the lady I was telling you about has died, yes, died, the angel. "How do you know that?"—Hieroglyphics, hieroglyphics—and then looking up to heaven, and again: yes, died—hieroglyphics. Then nothing else could be gotten out of him. He sat down and wrote several letters and gave them to Oberlin, asking him to add a few lines.

Meanwhile his condition had become ever bleaker, all the peace he had derived from Oberlin's nearness and the valley's stillness was gone; the world he had wished to serve had a gigantic crack, he felt no hate, no love, no hope, a terrible void and yet a tormenting anxiety to fill it. He had *nothing*. Whatever he did, he did consciously and yet an inner instinct drove him on. Whenever he was alone, he was so horribly lonely that he constantly talked out loud to himself, called out, and then he was startled again, and it seemed as if a strange voice had been speaking with him. He often stammered in conversation, an indescribable fear came over him, he had lost the end of his sentence; then he thought he ought to hold on to the last word spoken and keep repeating it, only with great effort did he suppress these desires. The good people were deeply concerned when at times in quiet moments he was sitting with them and speaking freely, and then he stammered and an unspeakable fear came over his features, he convulsively seized the arms of those sitting closest to him and only gradually came to his senses. When he was alone, or reading, it was even worse, at times all his mental activity would hang on one thought; if he thought about or visualized another person vividly, it seemed as if he were becoming that person, he became utterly confused, and at the same time he had a boundless urge to internalize everything around him arbitrarily; nature, people, Oberlin alone excepted, everything dreamlike, cold; he amused himself by standing houses on their roofs, dressing and undressing people, concocting the maddest pranks imaginable. At times he felt an irresistible urge to do something, and then he made horrible faces. Once he was sitting next to Oberlin, the cat was lying on a chair opposite, suddenly his eyes became fixed, he held them riveted on the animal, then he slipped slowly off the chair, so did the cat, as if transfixed by his gaze, it grew terribly frightened, it bristled with fear, Lenz making the same sounds, with a horribly distorted face, they threw themselves at each other as though in desperation, then finally Madame Oberlin rose to separate them. Once again he was deeply ashamed. The attacks during the night increased dreadfully. He fell asleep only with the greatest effort after he had attempted to fill the dreadful void. Then, between sleep and waking, he entered into a horrifying state; he bumped against something hideous, horrible, insanity seized him, he started up with terrible screams, drenched in sweat, and only gradually he found himself again. He then had to begin with the simplest things in order to come to his senses again. It was actually not he who did this but a powerful instinct of self-preservation, it seemed as if he were double and one part were trying to save the other, and called out to itself; he told stories, he recited poems in the most acute fear until he came to his senses again. These attacks occurred also during the day, then they were even more appalling; previously daylight had protected him from them. Then he seemed to be existing alone, as if the world were merely in his imagination, as if there were nothing besides him, he was the eternally damned, he was Satan; alone with his tormenting fantasies. He rushed with blinding speed through his past life and then he said: consistent, consistent; when someone said something: inconsistent, inconsistent; it was the abyss of incurable insanity, an insanity throughout eternity. The instinct of preserving his mind aroused him; he flung himself into Oberlin's arms, he clung to him as if he wanted to force himself into him, he was the only being who was alive for him and through whom life was revealed to him. Gradually Oberlin's words brought him to his senses, he knelt before Oberlin, his hands in Oberlin's hands, his face drenched in cold sweat in his lap, his whole body trembling and shivering. Oberlin felt boundless compassion, the family knelt and prayed for the unfortunate one, the maids fled and thought he was possessed. And when he calmed down it was like a child's misery, he sobbed, he felt deep, deep pity for himself; these were also his happiest moments. Oberlin talked to him about God. Lenz quietly drew away and looked at him with an expression of endless suffering and finally said: but I, if I were almighty, you see, if I were, and I couldn't bear this suffering, I would save, save, I just want nothing but peace, peace, just a little peace and to be able to sleep. Oberlin said this was blasphemy. Lenz shook his head dejectedly. His half-hearted suicide attempts that he undertook regularly were not wholly serious, it was less a wish to die, for him there was after all no peace nor hope in death; it was more an attempt to bring himself to his senses through physical pain in moments of most terrifying fear or of apathetic inactivity bordering on nonexistence. Those moments when his mind seemed to be riding on some sort of insane idea were still the happiest ones. That provided at least some peace, and his wild look was not as terrible as that fear thirsting for salvation, the eternal torment of anxiety! He often beat his head against the wall or inflicted violent physical pain on himself in other ways.

On the morning of the 8th he remained in bed, Oberlin went up; he was lying in bed nearly naked and was violently agitated. Oberlin wanted to cover him, but he complained much about how heavy everything was, so heavy, he doubted greatly he could walk, now at last he felt the immense weight of the air. Oberlin urged him to take courage. But he remained in this condition for most of the day, and he ate nothing. Toward evening Oberlin was called to visit a sick person in Bellefosse. The weather was mild and there was moonlight. On the way back Lenz met him. He seemed quite rational and spoke calmly and affably with Oberlin. Oberlin begged him not to go too far, he promised; walking away, he suddenly turned and came up very close to Oberlin again and said quickly: you see, Pastor, if only I didn't have to hear that anymore, that would do me good. "Hear what, my dear friend?" Don't you hear anything, don't you hear the terrible voice, usually called silence, screaming around the entire horizon, ever since I've been in this silent valley I always hear it, it won't let me sleep, yes, Pastor, if only I could sleep once again. Then he went away shaking his head. Oberlin went back to Waldbach and was about to send someone after him when he heard him going upstairs to his room. A moment later something crashed in the yard with such a loud noise that Oberlin thought it could not possibly have been caused by a falling human body. The nursemaid came, deathly pale and trembling all over. [. . .]

In cold resignation he sat in the coach as they rode out of the valley toward the west. He did not care where they were taking him; several times when the coach was endangered by the bad road he remained sitting quite calmly; he was totally indifferent. In this state he traveled through the mountains. Toward evening they were in the Rhine valley. Gradually they left the mountains behind, which now rose up like a deep blue crystal wave into the sunset, and on its warm flood the red rays of evening played; above the plain at the foot of the mountains lay a shimmering, bluish web. It grew darker as they approached Strassburg; a high full moon, all distant objects in the dark, only the mountain nearby formed a sharp line, the earth was like a golden bowl from which the foaming golden waves of the moon overflowed. Lenz stared out quietly, no perception, no impulse; only a dull fear grew in him the more things became lost in darkness. They had to stop for the night; again he made several attempts on his life but he was too closely watched. Next morning he arrived in Strassburg in dreary, rainy weather. He seemed quite rational, spoke with people; he acted like everyone else, yet there was a terrible void within him, he no longer felt any fear, any desire; his existence was a necessary burden.—So he lived on.

Notes

Büchner began his investigation into the life of the Storm and Stress poet Jacob Michael Reinhold Lenz in the spring of 1835. In October he wrote to his family from Strassburg: "I've obtained many interesting notes about a friend of Goethe, an ill-starred poet named Lenz, who resided here with Goethe and who went half-insane. I'm thinking of publishing an essay on this in the *Deutsche Revue.*" The editor of the *German Review*, Karl Gutzkow, had already been informed about "a story about [the shipwrecked poet] Lenz" and suggested to Büchner a "better publisher" than Sauerländer. On September 28, 1835, Gutzkow mentions "Memories of Lenz," which Büchner was due to publish soon in the *German Review*; obviously, the project underwent many changes before its actual appearance in print. On February 6, 1836, Gutzkow was still interested: "I appreciate hearing of your activities. At one time you planned a novella about Lenz. Didn't you write to me how Lenz assumed Goethe's place vis-a-vis Friederike? The way Goethe tells what Lenz did in Strassburg—the way he tried to protect the loved one with whose welfare he was charged—that's really quite appropriate stuff." Presumably, Büchner wrote the prose fragment "Lenz" between spring and fall of 1836 and Gutzkow finally published it in January 1839 in the *Telegraph for Germany* under the title: "Lenz. A Relic of Georg Büchner." In the *Telegraph* he briefly sketched its content as follows:

> The story is that of the well-known Storm and Stress poet, Lenz, during his stay in Strassburg and it is based on authentic research which Büchner did while residing in the city. Unfortunately, the novella was never finished. We would hesitate to publish it in this form were it not for the fact that it contains material concerning Lenz which will surprise a number of our readers. Is it possible that Lenz, a member of that literary movement which has been accused of being frivolous and philosophical, could ever have had any sort of relationship with the famous Pietist Pastor Oberlin of Steintal, who is so aptly described by Steffens in his otherwise worthless novel, *Revolution*? Büchner took everything concerning this relationship from credible family papers.

At the end of the story, Gutzkow summarizes his personal reaction to it:

> What a description of nature! What a portrait of the soul! How well does the one poet understand the refined nervous condition of the other, whose disposition is so like his own! [Büchner] empathizes with everything: we are in awe of this anatomy of a disturbed life and mind. G. Büchner demonstrates in this relic a reproductive imagination that was not so clearly and so truly evident even in Jean Paul.

Ludwig Büchner was the first to note the elective affinity between his brother Georg and the Latvian writer. It was no coincidence that Büchner suggestively arranged portions of Lenz's poem *Love in the Country* into a complex play of associations in a letter to his fiancée. Büchner probably took some of his material from Tieck's edition of Lenz's *Collected Works* (Berlin, 1828), but otherwise he relied on the Stöber brothers, his friends in Alsace, for the "authentic research done in Strassburg." These sources included Oberlin's diary-like account; some previously unknown and unpublished letters written by Lenz, particularly his letters to Salzmann, which August Stöber published in the Stuttgart *Morning Paper for the Educated Classes (Morgenblatt für gebildete Stände)* from October through December 1831; presumably, Lenz's *Study on the First Principle of Morality*, subsequently published by August Stöber in 1874; and possibly Lenz's sermon *On the Nature of Our Spirit.*

Büchner's story of Lenz, Goethe's unhappy and talented "poetic twin," is limited to his stay in Waldbach in the Steintal with Johann Friedrich Oberlin (1740–1826), in his day a well-known Pietist and philanthropist. Jakob Michael Reinhold Lenz (1751–92) was the author of *The Tutor* (1774), *The Soldiers* (1776), and *Notes on the Theater* (1774). To this day it is not known what he did to cause his dismissal, despite Herder's and Knebel's intercession on his behalf, from the "court of muses" at Weimar. Upon leaving Weimar, he first went to Goethe's sister Cornelia (1750–77) and her husband, Johann Georg Schlosser (1739–99) in Emmendingen. He subsequently traveled to Basel, Zurich, and Schaffhausen until, towards the end of 1777, he suffered a physical and mental collapse during a visit with "God's bloodhound" and "apostle of the genius movement," Christoph Kaufmann (1753–95). In January of 1778,

Lenz traveled alone across the Vosges to Oberlin who watched the sick man closely and tried to help him. Finally, in February 1778, he had no alternative but to have Lenz returned to Emmendingen near Strassburg. There, Schlosser selflessly cared for him (Cornelia had died on June 8, 1777), until Lenz's brother arrived and took him back to his family in Riga in 1779.

Sources

Daniel Ehrenfried Stöber, *Vie de Fredéric Oberlin*, Strasbourg, 1831.

August Stöber, "The Poet Lenz" in *Morgenblatt für gebildete Stände*, Stuttgart, 1831 (October 19–December 15).

Johann Friedrich Oberlin's account of Lenz, "The Poet Lenz, in the Steintal." Ed. by Dedert, Gersch, Oswald, Spiess. In: *Revue des Langues Vivantes* 42 (1976), 357–85 (O).

August Stöber, *The Poet Lenz and Friederike von Sesenheim*, Basel, 1842.

August Stöber, Johann Gottfried Roderer of Strassburg and his friends: Bibliographical accounts and letters to him from Goethe, Kayser, Schlosser, etc. Appendix includes letters to Röderer and Lenz, Colmar, 1874.

Johann Wolfgang von Goethe, *The Sorrows of Young Werther*, Leipzig, 1774.

Johann Wolfgang von Goethe, *Aus meinen Leben. Dichtung und Wahrheit*, Tübingen, 1812–22.

First Printings

a) "Lenz. A Relic of Georg Büchner." (Ed. with Foreword and Afterword by Karl Gutzkow.) In: *Telegraph for Germany*, January 1839, No. 5, 7–11, 13, 14 (J).

"Lenz. Leonce and Lena." In Karl Gutzkow, ed., *Mosaic. Novellas and Sketches*. Leipzig: Lorck, 1842.

"Lenz." In *Posthumous Writings of Georg Büchner*, ed. by Ludwig Büchner, Frankfurt/Main: J. D. Sauerländer, 1850 (N).

Versions

Gutzkow's first printing (J) is based on a "clean copy" by Minna Jaeglé (h). Ludwig Büchner may have been able to refer to the lost manuscript (H) or (h) for his edition (N). Besides J and N, only pastor Oberlin's account of Lenz in Waldbach from January 20–February 8, 1778, exists (O).

Leonce and Lena

A Comedy

PROLOGUE

Alfieri: "E la fama?"
Gozzi: "E la fame?"

CHARACTERS

KING PETER *of the Kingdom of Popo*
PRINCE LEONCE, *his son, engaged to*
PRINCESS LENA *of the Kingdom of Peepee*
VALERIO
THE GOVERNESS
THE TUTOR
THE MASTER OF CEREMONIES
THE PRESIDENT OF THE STATE COUNCIL
THE COURT CHAPLAIN
THE DISTRICT MAGISTRATE
THE SCHOOLMASTER
ROSETTA
SERVANTS, COUNCILLORS, PEASANTS, *etc.*

Act One

O that I were a fool!
I am ambitious for a motley coat.
—*As You Like It*

1

A garden.

LEONCE *reclining on a bench. The* TUTOR.

LEONCE. Sir, what do you want from me? To prepare me for my profession? I have my hands full, I'm so busy I don't know which way to turn. Look, first I have to spit on this stone here three hundred sixty-five times in a row. Haven't you tried it yet? Do it, it's uniquely entertaining. Then—you see this handful of sand?—(*He picks up some sand, throws it in the air and catches it on the back of his hand.*)—Now I'll throw it in the air. Shall we bet? How many grains do I now have on the back of my hand? Odd or even?—What? You don't want to bet? Are you a heathen? Do you believe in God? I usually bet with myself and can keep it up for days. If you could find me someone who would like to bet with me, I'd be much obliged. Then—I must figure out how I could manage to see the top of my head for once.—Oh, if only a person could see the top of his head for once! That's one of my ideals. That would do me good. And then—and then more of the same, endlessly.—Am I an idler? Don't I have anything to do?—Yes, it's sad . . .

TUTOR. Very sad, Your Highness.

LEONCE. That the clouds have been moving from west to east for three weeks now. It's making me quite melancholy.

TUTOR. A very well-founded melancholy.

LEONCE. Why don't you contradict me, man? You have urgent business, don't you? I'm sorry I've detained you so long. (*The* TUTOR *exits with a deep bow.*) Sir, I congratulate you on the beautiful parentheses your legs make when you bow. (*Alone,* LEONCE *stretches out on the bench.*) The bees sit so slothfully on the flowers, and the sunshine lies so lazily on the ground. A horrible idleness prevails.—Idleness is the root of all evil.—What people won't do out of boredom! They study out of boredom, they pray out of boredom, they fall in love, marry, and reproduce out of boredom and finally die out of boredom, and—and that's the humor of it—they do everything with the most serious faces, without realizing why and God knows what they mean by it. All these heroes, these geniuses, these idiots, these saints, these sinners, these fathers of families are basically nothing but refined idlers.—Why must *I* be the one to know this? Why can't I take myself seriously and dress this poor puppet in tails and put an umbrella in its hand so that it will become very proper and very useful and very moral?—That man who just left me—I envied him, I could have beaten him out of envy. Oh, to be someone else for once! Just for one minute.—(VALERIO, *half drunk, comes running in.*) How that man runs! If only I knew of one thing under the sun that could still make me run.

VALERIO. (*Stands close to* LEONCE, *puts a finger next to his nose and stares at him.*) Yes!

LEONCE. (*Does the same.*) Correct!

VALERIO. You understand?

LEONCE. Perfectly.

VALERIO. Well, then let's change the subject. (*He lies down in the grass.*) Meanwhile I'll lie in the grass and let my nose bloom through the blades and inhale romantic sensations when the bees and butterflies sway on it as on a rose.

LEONCE. But don't sniff so hard, my dear fellow, or the bees and butterflies will starve because you're inhaling immense pinches of pollen from the flowers.

VALERIO. Ah, my Lord, what a feeling I have for nature! The grass looks so beautiful that I wish I were an ox so I could eat it, and then a human being again to eat the ox that has eaten such grass.

LEONCE. Unhappy man, you too seem to be suffering from ideals.

VALERIO. What a pity. You can't jump off a church steeple without breaking your neck. You can't eat four pounds of cherries with the pits without getting a bellyache. Look, my Lord, I could sit in a corner and sing from morning to night: "Hey, there's a fly on the wall! Fly on the wall! Fly on the wall!" and so on for the rest of my life.

LEONCE. Shut up with your song, it could turn a man into a fool.

VALERIO. Then at least he'd be something. A fool! A fool! Who will trade his folly for my reason? Ha, I'm Alexander the Great! Look how the sun shines a golden crown in my hair, how my uniform glitters! Generalissimo Grasshopper, let the troops advance! Finance Minister Spider, I need money! Dear Lady Dragonfly, how is my beloved wife, Beanstalk? Ah, dear Royal Physician Spanish Fly, I need an heir to the throne. And on top of these delicious fantasies you get a good soup, good meat, good bread, a good bed, and a free haircut—in the madhouse, that is—while I with my sound mind could at best hire myself out to a cherry tree as a promoter of ripening in order to—well?—in order to?

LEONCE. In order to make the cherries red with shame at the holes in your pants. But, noblest sir, your trade, your profession, your occupation, your rank, your art?

VALERIO. (*With dignity.*) My Lord, I have the great occupation of being idle, I am incredibly skilled in doing nothing, I have an enormous capacity for laziness. No callus desecrates my hands, the earth has not drunk a drop of sweat from my brow; as for work, I'm a virgin, and if it weren't too much trouble, I would take the trouble to expound on these merits in greater detail.

LEONCE. (*With comic enthusiasm.*) Come to my bosom! Are you one of those godlike beings who wander effortlessly with a clear brow through sweat and dust on the highway of life and who enter Olympus with gleaming feet and glowing bodies like the blessed gods? Come! Come!

VALERIO. (*Sings as he leaves.*) Hey! There's a fly on the wall! Fly on the wall! Fly on the wall! (*They go off arm in arm.*)

2

A room.

KING PETER *is being dressed by two valets.*

KING PETER. (*While being dressed.*) Man must think, and I must think for my subjects, for they do not think, they do not think.—The substance is the "thing-in-itself," that is I. (*He runs around the room almost naked.*) Understood? In-itself is in-itself, you understand? Now for my attributes, modifications, affections, and accessories: where is my shirt, my pants?—Stop! Ugh! Free will is wide open here in front. Where is morality, where are my cuffs? The categories are in the most scandalous disorder, two buttons too many are buttoned, the snuffbox is in the right-hand pocket. My whole system is ruined.—Ha, what is the meaning of this knot in my handkerchief? Varlet, what does the knot mean, what did I want to remind myself of?

FIRST VALET. When Your Majesty deigned to tie this knot in your handkerchief, you wished . . .

KING PETER. Well?

FIRST VALET. To remind yourself of something.

KING PETER. A complicated answer!—My! Well, what do *you* think?

SECOND VALET. Your Majesty wished to remind yourself of something when you deigned to tie this knot in your handkerchief.

KING PETER. (*Runs up and down.*) What? What? These people mix me up, I am utterly confused. I am at my wit's end. (*A servant enters.*)

SERVANT. Your Majesty, the State Council is assembled.

KING PETER. (*Happily.*) Yes, that's it, that's it—I wanted to remind myself of my people! Come, gentlemen! Walk symmetrically. Isn't it very hot? Take your handkerchiefs and wipe your faces. I am always so embarrassed when I have to speak in public. (*All go off.*)

KING PETER. *The State Council.*

KING PETER. My dear and faithful subjects, I wish you to know by these presents, to know by these presents—because either my son marries or not (*Puts a finger next to his nose.*)—either, or—

you understand, of course? There is no third possibility. Man must think. (*Stands musing for a while.*) When I speak out loud like that, I don't know who it really is—I or someone else: that frightens me. (*After long reflection.*) I am I.—What do you think of that, President?

PRESIDENT. (*Slowly, with gravity.*) Your Majesty, perhaps it is so, but perhaps it is also not so.

THE STATE COUNCIL. (*In chorus.*) Yes, perhaps it is so, but perhaps it is also not so.

KING PETER. (*Emotionally.*) Oh, my wise men!—Now what were we talking about? What did I want to say? President, how can you have such a short memory on such a solemn occasion? The meeting is adjourned. (*He leaves solemnly, the State Council follows him.*)

3

A richly decorated hall with burning candles.

LEONCE *with several servants.*

LEONCE. Are all the shutters closed? Light the candles! Away with day! I want night, deep, ambrosial night. Put the lamps under crystal globes among the oleanders, so that they peer out dreamily like girls' eyes under leafy lashes. Bring the roses nearer, so that the wine may sparkle on their petals like dewdrops. Music! Where are the violins? Where is Rosetta? Away! Everybody out! (*The servants go off.* LEONCE *stretches out on a couch.* ROSETTA *enters, prettily dressed. Music in the distance.*)

ROSETTA. (*Approaches coquettishly.*) Leonce!

LEONCE. Rosetta!

ROSETTA. Leonce!

LEONCE. Rosetta!

ROSETTA. Your lips are lazy. From kissing?

LEONCE. From yawning!

ROSETTA. Oh!

LEONCE. Ah, Rosetta, I have the terrible chore . . .

ROSETTA. Well?

LEONCE. Of doing nothing . . .

ROSETTA. Besides loving?

LEONCE. That's certainly a chore!

ROSETTA. (*Insulted.*) Leonce!

LEONCE. Or an occupation.

ROSETTA. Or idleness.

LEONCE. You're right as usual. You're a clever girl, and I admire your keenness.

ROSETTA. So you love me out of boredom?

LEONCE. No, I'm bored because I love you. But I love my boredom as I love you. You are one and the same. O *dolce far niente,*[1] I dream about your eyes as magical springs, deep and hidden; your caressing lips lull me to sleep like murmuring waves. (*He embraces her.*) Come, dear boredom, your kisses are voluptuous yawns and your steps a delicate hiatus.

ROSETTA. You love me, Leonce?

LEONCE. Why not?

ROSETTA. And forever?

LEONCE. That's a long word: forever! Now if I love you for five thousand years and seven months, is that enough? It's far less than forever, of course, but it's still a considerable length of time, and we can take time to love each other.

ROSETTA. Or time can take love from us.

LEONCE. Or love can take time from us. Dance, Rosetta, dance, let time pass to the beat of your dainty feet!

ROSETTA. My feet would rather pass out of time. (*She dances and sings.*)

O tired feet, why must you dance
In shoes so bright?
You'd rather lie, so deep, so deep
In earth's dark night.

O fiery cheeks, why must you burn
In wild delight?
You'd rather bloom, not roses red,
But roses white.

O poor dear eyes, why must you gleam
In candle's glow?

1. "Oh, delightful idleness!"

You'd rather sleep, until is gone
All pain and woe.

LEONCE. (*Dreamily to himself meanwhile.*) Oh, a dying love is more beautiful than a growing one. I'm a Roman; for dessert at our lavish banquet, golden fish play in their death's colors. How her red cheeks fade, how softly her eyes dim, how gently her swaying limbs rise and fall! *Addio, addio,* my love, I shall love your dead body. (ROSETTA *approaches him again.*) Tears, Rosetta? A fine Epicureanism—to be able to cry. Go stand in the sun and let the precious drops crystallize, they'll be magnificent diamonds. You can have a necklace made of them.

ROSETTA. Yes, diamonds. They're cutting my eyes. Oh, Leonce! (*Tries to embrace him.*)

LEONCE. Careful! My head! I've buried our love in it. Look into the windows of my eyes. Do you see how nice and dead the poor thing is? Do you see the two white roses on its cheeks and the two red roses on its breast? Don't nudge me, or a little arm might break off, that would be a pity. I must carry my head straight on my shoulders, like a mourning woman with a child's coffin.

ROSETTA. (*Jokingly.*) Fool!

LEONCE. Rosetta! (ROSETTA *makes a face.*) Thank God! (*Covers his eyes.*)

ROSETTA. (*Frightened.*) Leonce, look at me.

LEONCE. Not for the world.

ROSETTA. Just one look!

LEONCE. Not one! Are you crying? The slightest thing would bring my beloved love to life again. I'm happy to have buried it. I'll retain the impression.

ROSETTA. (*Goes off sadly and slowly, singing.*)

I'm a poor orphan girl,
Afraid and all alone.
Ah, sorrow, dear,
Will you not see me home?

LEONCE. (*Alone.*) Love is a peculiar thing. You lie half-asleep in bed for a year, then one fine morning you wake up, drink a glass of water, get dressed, and run your hand across your forehead and come to your senses—and come to your senses.—My God, how many women does one need to sing up and down the scale of love? One woman is scarcely enough for a single note. Why is the mist above the earth a prism that breaks the white-hot ray of love into a rainbow?—(*He drinks.*) Which bottle contains the wine that will make me drunk today? Can't I even get that far anymore? It's as if I were sitting under a vacuum pump. The air so sharp and thin that I'm freezing, as if I were going ice skating in cotton pants.—Gentlemen, gentlemen, do you know what Caligula and Nero were? I know.—Come, Leonce, let's have a soliloquy, I'll listen. My life yawns at me like a large white sheet of paper that I have to fill, but I can't write a single letter. My head is an empty dance hall, a few withered roses and crumpled ribbons on the floor, broken violins in the corner, the last dancers have taken off their masks and look at each other with dead-tired eyes. I turn myself inside out twenty-four times a day, like a glove. Oh, I know myself, I know what I'll be thinking and dreaming in a quarter of an hour, in a week, in a year. God, what have I done that you make me recite my lesson so often like a schoolboy?—

Bravo, Leonce! Bravo! (*He applauds.*) It does me good to cheer for myself like this. Hey! Leonce! Leonce!

VALERIO. (*From under a table.*) Your Highness really seems to be well on the way to becoming a genuine fool.

LEONCE. Yes, seen in that light it looks the same to me.

VALERIO. Wait, we'll discuss this in detail in a minute. I just have to finish a piece of roast beef I stole from the kitchen, and some wine I stole from your table. I'm almost through.

LEONCE. How he smacks his lips. That fellow brings on the most idyllic feelings; I could begin again with the simplest things, I could eat cheese, drink beer, smoke tobacco. Hurry up, don't grunt like that with your snout and don't rattle your tusks.

VALERIO. Most worthy Adonis, do you fear for your thighs? Don't worry. I'm neither a broommaker nor a schoolmaster. I need no twigs for my rods.

LEONCE. You're never at a loss.

VALERIO. I wish it were the same with you, my Lord.

LEONCE. So that you'll get a thrashing, you mean? Are you so concerned about your education?

VALERIO. Oh heavens, procreation is easier to come by than education. It's a pity that propagation can cause such a sorry situation! What labor have I known since my mother was in labor! What good have I received from being conceived?

LEONCE. Concerning your conception, its enunciation deserves repression. Improve your expression, or you'll experience a most unpleasant impression of my negative reception.

VALERIO. When my mother sailed around the Cape of Good Hope . . .

LEONCE. And your father was shipwrecked on Cape Horn . . .

VALERIO. Right, for he was a nightwatchman. But he didn't put the horn to his lips as often as to the foreheads of fathers of well-born sons.

LEONCE. Man, your impertinence is sublime. I feel a certain desire to become more closely acquainted with it. I have a passion to thrash you.

VALERIO. That is a striking response and an impressive proof.

LEONCE. (*Goes after him.*) Or you are a stricken response. Because you'll be struck for your response.

VALERIO. (*Runs away,* LEONCE *trips and falls.*) And you are a proof that remains to be proven, because it trips over its own legs, which are fundamentally unproven as yet. These are highly improbable calves and very problematic thighs. (*The State Council enters.* LEONCE *remains seated on the floor.*)

PRESIDENT. Pardon me, Your Highness . . .

LEONCE. And myself! And myself! I pardon myself for being kind enough to listen to you. Won't you take a seat, gentlemen?—What faces people make when they hear the word "seat"! Just sit on the ground and make yourselves at home. After all, that's the last seat you'll ever have, but it's of no value to anyone besides the gravedigger.

PRESIDENT. (*Snapping his fingers in embarrassment.*) May it please Your Highness . . .

LEONCE. But don't snap your fingers like that, unless you want to make a murderer of me.

PRESIDENT. (*Snapping ever more violently.*) If Your Highness would most graciously consider . . .

LEONCE. My God, put your hands in your pockets or sit on them. He's ready to burst. Pull yourself together.

VALERIO. Children must not be interrupted while they are pissing, or they'll become repressed.

LEONCE. Control yourself, man. Think of your family and the state. You'll risk a stroke if you hold back your speech.

PRESIDENT. (*Pulls a piece of paper from his pocket.*) May it please Your Highness . . .

LEONCE. What, you can read? Well now . . .

PRESIDENT. His Royal Majesty desires to inform Your Highness that the awaited arrival of Your Highness's betrothed, Her Most Serene Highness, Princess Lena of Peepee, is to take place tomorrow.

LEONCE. If my betrothed awaits me, then I'll do as she wishes and let her wait. I saw her last night in a dream, her eyes were so large that my Rosetta's dancing shoes could have fit as eyebrows, and instead of dimples her cheeks had drainage ditches for her laughter. I believe in dreams. Do you ever dream, President? Do you have premonitions?

VALERIO. Of course. Every night before a roast for His Majesty's table burns, a capon drops dead, or His Royal Majesty gets a bellyache.

LEONCE. Apropos, didn't you have something else on the tip of your tongue? Go ahead, relieve yourself of everything.

PRESIDENT. On the wedding day it is the intention of the Highest Will to transmit the exalted disposition of His Will to Your Highness's hands.

LEONCE. Tell the Highest Will that I shall do anything except that which I forbear to do, which, however, shall in any case not be as much as if it were twice as much.—Gentlemen, you will excuse me if I do not see you out, right now I have a passion for sitting, but my goodwill is so great that I can't possibly measure it with my legs. (*He spreads his legs.*) President, measure this so you can remind me of it later. Valerio, bring the gentlemen out.

VALERIO. Ring them out? Shall I hang a bell on the President? Shall I direct them as if they could not walk erect?

LEONCE. Man, you are nothing more than a bad pun. You have neither father nor mother—the five vowels gave birth to you.

VALERIO. And you, Prince, are a book without letters, with nothing but dashes.—Now come, gentlemen! It's a pity about the word "come": if you want an income, you must steal; you won't come up in the world except when you're hanged; your only accommodation is a comedown to the grave; and a shortcoming is the lack of an accomplished comeback, when one is completely at a loss for words, as I am now, and as you are *before* you commence to speak. Discomfited by such a comeuppance, you are commanded to come away. (*The State Council and* VALERIO *go off.*)

LEONCE. (*Alone.*) How vilely I played the cavalier to those poor devils! And yet there's a kind of pleasure in a certain kind of vileness.—Hm! To marry! In other words, to drink a well dry. Oh, Shandy, old Shandy, if only I had your clock![2]—(VALERIO *returns.*) Ah, Valerio, did you hear that?

VALERIO. Well, you're to be king—that's a lot of fun. You can ride around all day and make people wear out their hats because they have to take them off all the time; you can carve decent soldiers out of decent people, so that will become the natural order of things; you can turn black frock coats and white ties into state officials, and when you die every shiny button will tarnish and the bell-ropes will tear like threads from all that tolling. Isn't that entertaining?

LEONCE. Valerio! Valerio! We've got to find something else to do. Think!

VALERIO. Ah, science, science! Let's be scholars! *A priori?* Or *a posteriori?*[3]

LEONCE. *A priori* you can learn from my father, and *a posteriori* always begins like an old fairy tale: once upon a time!

VALERIO. Then let's be heroes. (*He marches up and down trumpeting and drumming.*) Trara-ta-ta!

LEONCE. But heroism stinks terribly of liquor and gets hospital fever and can't exist without lieutenants and recruits. Get away with your Alexander and Napoleon romanticism!

VALERIO. Then let's be geniuses.

LEONCE. The nightingale of poetry warbles over our heads all day long, but the best of it goes to the devil until we tear out its feathers and dip them into ink or paint.

VALERIO. Then let's be useful members of human society.

LEONCE. I'd rather resign from the human race.

VALERIO. Then let's go to the devil.

LEONCE. Oh, the devil exists only for the sake of contrast, so that we'll believe there's something to the idea of Heaven. (*Jumping up.*) Ah, Valerio, now I've got it! Don't you feel the breeze from the south? Don't you feel the surging, deep blue, glowing ether, the light flashing from the golden, sunny earth, from the holy

2. In Laurence Sterne's *Tristram Shandy*, Shandy's father performed his marital obligations once a month after winding the clock.

3. Deductive versus inductive reasoning.

salt sea and the marble columns and statues? Great Pan sleeps, and in the shade above the deep, rushing waves, bronze figures dream of the old magician Virgil, of tarantellas and tambourines and dark, wild nights, full of masks, torches, and guitars. A *lazzarone!*[4] Valerio! A *lazzarone!* We're going to Italy.

4

A garden.

PRINCESS LENA *in bridal clothes. The* GOVERNESS.

LENA. Yes, now! Here it is. Up to now I didn't think about anything. Time passed, and suddenly *that* day looms before me. The bridal wreath is in my hair—and the bells, the bells! (*She leans back and shuts her eyes.*) Look, I wish the grass would grow over me and the bees would hum above me. Look, now I'm all dressed and have rosemary in my hair. Isn't there an old song:

In the earth I'd lay my head
Like a child in its bed . . .

GOVERNESS. Poor child, how pale you are under your glittering jewels.

LENA. Oh God, I could love, why not? We walk all alone and reach out for a hand to hold until the undertaker separates the hands and folds them over our breasts. But why drive a nail through two hands that weren't searching for each other? What has my poor hand done? (*She draws a ring from her finger.*) This ring stings me like a viper.

GOVERNESS. And yet—they say he's a real Don Carlos.

LENA. But—a man—

GOVERNESS. Well?

LENA. Whom I don't love. (*She rises.*) Bah! You see, I'm ashamed.—Tomorrow I'll be stripped of all fragrance and luster. Am I like a poor, helpless stream whose quiet depths must reflect every image that bends over it? Flowers open and shut to the morning

4. A Neapolitan beggar.

sun and evening breeze as they please. Is a king's daughter less than a flower?

GOVERNESS. (*Weeping.*) Dear angel, you're really a sacrificial lamb.

LENA. Yes—and the priest is already raising his knife.—My God, my God, is it true that we must redeem ourselves through pain? Is it true that the world is a crucified Savior, the sun its crown of thorns, and the stars the nails and spears in its feet and sides?

GOVERNESS. My child, my child! I can't bear to see you like this. This can't go on, it will kill you. Perhaps, who knows! I've got an idea. We'll see. Come! (*She leads the* PRINCESS *away.*)

Act Two

Did not once a voice resound
    Deep within me,
And instantly within me drowned
    All my memory.
        —Adelbert von Chamisso[5]

1

Open field. An inn in the background.

Enter LEONCE *and* VALERIO, *carrying a pack.*

VALERIO. (*Panting.*) On my honor, Prince, the world is an incredibly spacious building.

LEONCE. Not at all! Not at all! I hardly dare stretch out my hands, as if I were in a narrow room of mirrors, afraid of bumping against everything—then the beautiful figures would lie in fragments on the floor and I'd be standing before the bare, naked wall.

VALERIO. I'm lost.

5. A Romantic poet (1781–1838); altered stanza from his "*Die Blinde*" ("The Blind Girl"), published in 1834.

LEONCE. That's a loss only to whoever finds you.

VALERIO. Soon I'll go stand in the shadow of my shadow.

LEONCE. You're evaporating in the sun. Do you see that beautiful cloud up there? At least a quarter of it is from you. It's looking down quite contentedly at your grosser material substance.

VALERIO. That cloud would do your head no harm if your head were shaved and the cloud were to drip on it, drop by drop.—A delightful thought. We've walked through a dozen principalities, half a dozen duchies, and several kingdoms with the greatest haste in half a day, and why? Because you're to become king and marry a beautiful princess. And in such a situation you're still alive? I can't understand your resignation. I can't understand why you haven't taken arsenic, climbed on a parapet of a church steeple, and put a bullet through your head, just to be on the safe side.

LEONCE. But Valerio, my ideals! I have the ideal woman in my mind, and I must search for her. She's infinitely beautiful and infinitely stupid. Her beauty is so helpless, so touching, like a newborn child. The contrast is exquisite. Those gloriously stupid eyes, that divinely simple mouth, that mutton-headed Greek profile, that spiritual death in that spiritual body.

VALERIO. Damn! Here we're at a border again; this country is like an onion, nothing but skins—or like boxes, one inside another: in the largest there's nothing but boxes and in the smallest, nothing at all. (*He throws down his pack.*) Shall this pack be my tombstone? Look, Prince, I'm getting philosophical—an image of human existence: I haul this pack with sore feet through frost and broiling sun because I want to put on a clean shirt in the evening, and when the evening finally comes, my brow is wrinkled, my cheeks are hollow, my eye is dim, and I just have enough time to put on my shirt as a shroud. Now wouldn't it have been smarter to take my bundle off its stick and sell it in the nearest bar, and get drunk and sleep in the shade till evening—without sweating and getting corns on my feet? And now, Prince, the practical application: out of sheer modesty we shall now clothe the inner man and put on a coat and pants internally. (*Both go toward the inn.*) Hey, you dear pack, what a delicious aroma, what scents of wine and roast beef! Hey, you dear pants, how you root in the earth and turn green and bloom, and the long, heavy grapes hang into my mouth, and the new wine ferments in the winepress. (*They go off.*)

(PRINCESS LENA *and the* GOVERNESS *enter.*)

GOVERNESS. The day must be bewitched; the sun won't set, and it's been an eternity since we ran off.

LENA. Not at all, my dear; the flowers I picked as we left the garden have hardly wilted.

GOVERNESS. And where will we rest? We haven't come across a thing. I see no convent, no hermit, no shepherd.

LENA. I guess we dreamed things differently behind our garden wall with our books, among the myrtles and oleanders.

GOVERNESS. Oh, the world is horrible! We can't begin to think about a stray prince.

LENA. Oh, the world is beautiful and so vast, so infinitely vast. I'd like to go on like this day and night.

Nothing is stirring. Look how the red glow from the orchids plays over the meadow and the distant mountains lie on the earth like resting clouds.

GOVERNESS. Jesus, what will people say? And yet, it's all so delicate and feminine! It's a renunciation. It's like the flight of Saint Odilia.[6] But we must look for shelter. Night is coming!

LENA. Yes, the plants are closing their leaves in sleep and the sunbeams are swaying on blades of grass like weary dragonflies.

2

The inn on a hill beside a river, wide view.
The garden in front of the inn.

VALERIO. LEONCE.

VALERIO. Well, Prince, don't your pants provide a delicious drink? Don't your boots slide down your throat with the greatest of ease?

6. Patron saint of Alsace. Having dedicated her life to Christ, she fled from her father, who wished her to marry a man he had selected.

LEONCE. Look at those old trees, the hedges, the flowers. They all have their legends, their dear, secret legends. Look at the old, friendly faces under the vines at the front door. How they sit holding hands, afraid because they're so old and the world is still so young. Oh, Valerio, and I'm so young, and the world is so old. Sometimes I'm afraid for myself and could sit in a corner and weep hot tears in self-pity.

VALERIO. (*Gives him a glass.*) Take this bell, this diving-bell, and immerse yourself in the sea of wine till bubbles foam over you. Look how the elves float over the flowers of the wine-bouquet, in golden shoes, clashing their cymbals.

LEONCE. (*Jumping up.*) Come, Valerio, we've got to do something, do something. Let's busy ourselves with profound thoughts: let's investigate why a stool stands on three legs but not on two, why we blow our noses with our hands and not with our feet as flies do. Come, let's dissect ants, count flower filaments; I'll manage to find some kind of princely hobby yet. I'll find a child's rattle that will fall from my hand only when I'm woolgathering and plucking at the blanket on my deathbed. I still have a certain dose of enthusiasm to use up, but when I've warmed everything up, it takes me an eternity to find a spoon for the meal, and it goes stale.

VALERIO. *Ergo bibamus.*[7] This bottle is not a mistress, not an idea, it causes no labor pains, it won't be boring nor unfaithful—it stays the same from the first to the last drop. You break the seal and all the dreams slumbering inside bubble out at you.

LEONCE. Oh God! I'll spend half my life in prayer if I could only have a blade of straw on which to ride as on a splendid steed, until I lie on the straw myself.—What an uncanny evening! Down there everything is quiet, and up there the clouds change and drift and the sunshine comes and goes. Look what strange shapes chase each other up there, look at the long white shadows with horribly skinny legs and bats' wings—and all so swift, so chaotic, and down there not a leaf, not a blade of grass is stirring. The earth has curled up like a frightened child, and ghosts stalk over its cradle.

VALERIO. I don't know what you're after—I feel quite comfortable.

7. "Therefore let's drink!"

The sun looks like the sign of an inn and the fiery clouds over it like the inscription: "Inn of the Golden Sun." The earth and the water down there are like wine spilled on a table, and we lie on it like playing cards, with which God and the Devil are playing a game out of boredom, and you're the king and I'm the jack, and all we need is a queen, a beautiful queen with a large gingerbread heart on her breast and with a giant tulip, into which her long nose sentimentally sinks. . . . (*The* GOVERNESS *and the* PRINCESS *enter.*) . . . and—by God, there she is! But it's not really a tulip but a pinch of snuff, and it's not really a nose but a trunk. (*To the* GOVERNESS.) Why do you walk so fast, gracious lady, that one can see your former calves up to your respectable garters?

GOVERNESS. (*Very angry, stops.*) Why do you, most honorable sir, open your mouth so wide that you tear a hole in the landscape?

VALERIO. So that you, honorable madam, won't bloody your nose on the horizon. Thy nose is as the tower of Lebanon which looketh toward Damascus.[8]

LENA. (*To the* GOVERNESS.) My dear, is the way so long?

LEONCE. (*Musing to himself.*) Oh, every way is long! The ticking of the death-watch beetle in our breast is slow, and each drop of blood measures its time, and our life is a lingering fever. For tired feet every way is too long . . .

LENA. (*Listening to him anxiously, pensively.*) And for tired eyes every light is too bright and for tired lips every breath too heavy, (*Smiling.*) and for tired ears every word too much. (*She enters the inn with the* GOVERNESS.)

LEONCE. Oh, dear Valerio! Couldn't I, too, say: "Would not this and a forest of feathers with two Provincial roses on my razed shoes—"?[9] I believe I said it quite melancholically. Thank God I'm beginning to come down with a case of melancholy. The air isn't so clear and cold anymore, the glowing sky is sinking down closely around me, and heavy drops are falling.—Oh, that voice:

8. Song of Solomon 7:5.

9. *Hamlet*, Act III, Scene 2: "Would not this, sir, and a forest of feathers—if the rest of my fortunes turn Turk with me—with two Provincial roses on my razed shoes, get me a fellowship in a cry of players, sir?" The feathers, roses, and shoes were traditionally part of an actor's costume.

"Is the way so long?" Many voices talk about the world, and you'd think they're speaking of other things, but I understood it. It rests upon me like the Spirit moving upon the face of the waters before there was light. What ferment in the depths, what growth in me, how the voice pours through space!—"Is the way so long?" (*Exit.*)

VALERIO. No. The way to the madhouse is not so long, it's easy to find; I know every footpath, every highway and byway leading to it. I can see him now: going there down a broad avenue on an icy winter day, his hat under his arm, standing in the long shadows under the bare trees, fanning himself with his handkerchief.—He's a fool! (*Follows him.*)

3

A room.

LENA. *The* GOVERNESS.

GOVERNESS. Don't think about him.

LENA. He was so old under his blond curls. Spring on his cheeks and winter in his heart. That's sad. A tired body finds a pillow everywhere, but when the spirit is tired, where shall it rest? I've just had a horrible thought: I think there are people who are unhappy, incurable, just because they *exist*. (*She rises.*)

GOVERNESS. Where are you off to, my child?

LENA. I want to go down to the garden.

GOVERNESS. But . . .

LENA. But, dear mother—I should have been placed in a flowerpot, you know. I need dew and night air, like flowers. Do you hear the evening harmonies? How the crickets sing the day to sleep and the violets lull it with their fragrance! I can't stay in this room. The walls are falling in on me.

4

The garden. Night and moonlight.

LENA *is sitting on the grass.*

VALERIO. (*At a certain distance.*) Nature is a pleasant thing, but it would be even more pleasant if there weren't any gnats, if the beds in the inn were a little cleaner, and the death-watch beetles wouldn't tick so in the walls. Inside, people are snoring and outside, frogs are croaking; inside, house crickets are chirping and outside, it's the field crickets. Dear ground, this is a well-grounded decision. (*He lies down on the grass.*)

LEONCE. (*Enters.*) O night, balmy as the first that descended on Paradise. (*He notices the* PRINCESS *and approaches her quietly.*)

LENA. (*To herself.*) The warbler chirped in its dreams, the night sleeps more deeply, its cheeks grow paler and its breath calmer. The moon is like a sleeping child, its golden curls have fallen over its dear face.—Oh, its sleep is death. Look how the dead angel rests on its dark pillow and the stars burn around it like candles. Poor child, will the bogeymen come to get you soon? Where is your mother? Doesn't she want to kiss you once more? Ah, it's sad, dead and so alone.

LEONCE. Arise in your white dress and follow the corpse through the night and sing its requiem.

LENA. Who said that?

LEONCE. A dream.

LENA. Dreams are blessed.

LEONCE. Then dream yourself blessed and let me be your blessed dream.

LENA. Death is the most blessed dream.

LEONCE. Then let me be your angel of death. Let my lips sink like its wings onto your eyes. (*He kisses her.*) Dear corpse, you rest so beautifully on the black pall of night that nature begins to hate life and falls in love with death.

LENA. No, let me be. (*She jumps up and rushes off.*)

LEONCE. Too much! Too much! My whole being is in this one moment. Now die. More is impossible. How Creation struggles out of Chaos toward me, breathing freshly, glowing beautifully!

The earth is a bowl of dark gold—how the light foams in it and overflows and the stars bubble out brightly. My lips suck their fill; this one drop of bliss turns me into a priceless vessel. Down with you, holy chalice! (*He tries to throw himself into the river.*)

VALERIO. (*Jumps up and grabs him.*) Stop, my Serene Highness!

LEONCE. Let me be!

VALERIO. I'll let you be as soon as you let yourself be calm and promise to let the water be.

LEONCE. Idiot!

VALERIO. Hasn't Your Highness outgrown that lieutenants' romanticism yet—throwing the glass out of the window after you've drunk to your sweetheart's health?

LEONCE. I almost think you're right.

VALERIO. Console yourself. Even if you won't sleep *under* the grass tonight, at least you'll sleep *on* it. It would be an equally suicidal venture to sleep on one of those beds. You lie on the straw like a dead man and the fleas bite you like a living one.

LEONCE. All right. (*He lies down in the grass.*) Man, you ruined a most beautiful suicide. I'll never find such a marvelous moment for it again in my whole life, and the weather is so perfect. Now I'm not in the mood anymore. That fellow with his yellow vest and his sky-blue pants[10] spoiled everything for me.—Heaven grant me a good and healthy, solid sleep.

VALERIO. Amen.—And I've saved a human life, and I'll keep myself warm tonight with my good conscience. To your health, Valerio!

Act Three

1

LEONCE. VALERIO.

VALERIO. Marriage? Since when has Your Highness decided to be bound by a perpetual calendar?

10. The costume of Goethe's Werther (*The Sorrows of Young Werther,* 1774), who committed suicide out of rejected love.

LEONCE. Do you know, Valerio, that even the most insignificant human being is so great that life is far too short to love him? And yet I can say to those people who imagine that nothing is so beautiful and holy that they can't make it even more beautiful and holier: go ahead and enjoy yourselves. There's a certain pleasure in this dear arrogance. Why shouldn't I indulge them?

VALERIO. Very humane and philobestial. But does she know who you are?

LEONCE. She knows only that she loves me.

VALERIO. And does Your Highness know who she is?

LEONCE. Idiot! Try asking a carnation and a dewdrop what their names are.

VALERIO. That is, assuming she's anything at all, if that isn't already too indelicate and smacks of personal description.—But what then? Hm!—Prince, will I be your Minister of State when you are joined today before your father in holy matrimony with the unspeakable, nameless one? Your word on that?

LEONCE. I give you my word.

VALERIO. The poor devil Valerio takes his leave of His Excellency the Minister of State, Valerio of Valerianshire.—"What does the fellow want? I do not know him. Off with you, rascal!" (*He runs off,* LEONCE *follows.*)

2

Open square before KING PETER*'s palace.*

The DISTRICT MAGISTRATE. *The* SCHOOLMASTER. *Peasants in Sunday clothes, holding pine branches.*

MAGISTRATE. How are your people holding up, schoolmaster?

SCHOOLMASTER. They're holding up so well in their suffering that for quite a while they've been holding on to each other. They're downing a lot of liquor, otherwise they couldn't possibly hold out in this heat. Courage, people! Hold your branches out straight, so they'll think you're a pine forest and your noses the strawberries and your three-cornered hats the antlers and your leather pants the moonlight in it, and remember: the last one always walks ahead of the first, so that it looks as if your number had been squared.

MAGISTRATE. And, you, schoolmaster, stand for sobriety.

SCHOOLMASTER. That's understood, since I'm so sober I can hardly stand.

MAGISTRATE. Pay attention, people. The program states: "All subjects shall voluntarily assemble along the highway, neatly dressed, well fed, and with contented faces." Don't give us a bad name!

SCHOOLMASTER. Stand firm! Don't scratch behind your ears and don't blow your noses with your fingers while the royal couple rides past, and show proper emotion, or we'll use emotive means on you. Look what we're doing for you: we've placed you so the breeze from the kitchen passes over you, and for once in your life you'll smell a roast. Do you still know your lesson? Hey? Vi!

PEASANTS. Vi!

SCHOOLMASTER. Vat!

PEASANTS. Vat!

SCHOOLMASTER. Vivat!

PEASANTS. Vivat!

SCHOOLMASTER. There, Mr. Magistrate. You see how intelligence is on the upswing. Just think, it's *Latin*. Besides, tonight we'll hold a transparent ball thanks to the holes in our jackets and pants, and we'll beat rosettes onto our heads with our fists.

3

Large hall.

Well-dressed gentlemen and ladies, carefully arranged in groups. The MASTER OF CEREMONIES *with several servants in the foreground.*

MASTER OF CEREMONIES. What a shame! Everything's going to pot. The roasts are drying up. Congratulations are going stale. Stand-up collars are all bending over like melancholy pigs' ears. The peasants' nails and beards are growing again. The soldiers' curls are drooping. Among the twelve bridesmaids there is none who wouldn't prefer a horizontal position to a vertical one. In their white dresses they look like exhausted Angora rabbits, and the Court Poet grunts around them like a distressed guinea pig. The officers are going limp. (*To a servant.*) Go tell our curate to let his boys make water.—The poor Court Chaplain! His frock coat is hanging its tails most dejectedly. I think he has ideals and is changing all the chamberlains into chamber stools. He's tired of standing.

FIRST SERVANT. All meat spoils from standing. The Court Chaplain is at a stale standstill too, after standing up this morning.

MASTER OF CEREMONIES. The ladies-in-waiting stand there like saltworks, the salt is crystallizing on their necklaces.

SECOND SERVANT. At least they're making themselves comfortable. You can't accuse them of bearing a weight on their shoulders. If they aren't exactly openhearted, at least they're open down to the heart.

MASTER OF CEREMONIES. Yes, they're good maps of the Turkish Empire—you can see the Dardanelles and the Sea of Marmara. Out, you rascals! To the windows! Here comes His Majesty! (KING PETER *and the State Council enter.*)

KING PETER. So the Princess has disappeared as well? Has no trace been found of our beloved Crown Prince? Have my orders been carried out? Are the borders being watched?

MASTER OF CEREMONIES. Yes, Your Majesty. The view from this hall allows us the strictest surveillance. (*To the* FIRST SERVANT.) What have you seen?

FIRST SERVANT. A dog ran through the kingdom looking for its master.

MASTER OF CEREMONIES. (*To another.*) And you?

SECOND SERVANT. Someone is taking a walk on the northern border, but it's not the prince, I'd recognize him.

MASTER OF CEREMONIES. And you?

THIRD SERVANT. Begging your pardon, nothing.

MASTER OF CEREMONIES. That's very little. And you?

FOURTH SERVANT. Nothing either.

MASTER OF CEREMONIES. That's even less.

KING PETER. But Council, have I not resolved that My Royal Majesty shall rejoice today and that the wedding shall be celebrated? Was this not our most solemn resolution?

PRESIDENT. Yes, Your Majesty, it is so registered and recorded.

KING PETER. And would I not compromise myself, if I did not carry out my resolution?

PRESIDENT. If it were at all possible for Your Majesty to compromise yourself, this would be an instance in which Your Majesty could compromise yourself.

KING PETER. Have I not given my Royal Word? Yes, I shall carry out my resolution immediately: I shall rejoice. (*He rubs his hands.*) Oh, I am exceptionally happy!

PRESIDENT. We join in sharing Your Majesty's emotion, insofar as it is possible and proper for subjects to do so.

KING PETER. Oh, I am beside myself with joy. I shall have red coats made for my chamberlains, I shall promote some cadets to lieutenants, I shall permit my subjects to—but, but, the wedding? Does not the other half of the resolution state that the wedding shall be celebrated?

PRESIDENT. Yes, Your Majesty.

KING PETER. Yes, but if the Prince does not come and neither does the Princess?

PRESIDENT. Yes, if the Prince does not come and neither does the Princess—then—then—

KING PETER. Then, then?

PRESIDENT. Then indeed they cannot get married.

KING PETER. Wait, is the conclusion logical? If—then.—Correct! But my Word, my Royal Word!

PRESIDENT. Take comfort, Your Majesty, with other majesties. A Royal Word is a thing—a thing—a thing—of nothing.

KING PETER. (*To the servants.*) Do you see anything yet?

SERVANTS. Nothing, Your Majesty, nothing at all.

KING PETER. And I had resolved to be so happy. I wanted to begin at the stroke of twelve and wanted to rejoice a full twelve hours.—I am becoming quite melancholy.

PRESIDENT. All subjects are commanded to share the feelings of His Majesty.

MASTER OF CEREMONIES. For the sake of decorum, those who carry no handkerchiefs are nonetheless forbidden to cry.

FIRST SERVANT. Wait! I see something! It's something like a protuberance, like a nose—the rest isn't over the border yet—and now I see another man and two people of the opposite sex.

MASTER OF CEREMONIES. In which direction?

FIRST SERVANT. They're coming closer. They're approaching the palace. Here they are. (VALERIO, LEONCE, *the* GOVERNESS, *and the* PRINCESS *enter, masked.*)

KING PETER. Who are you?

VALERIO. Do I know? (*He slowly takes off several masks, one after another.*) Am I this? Or this? Or this? I'm truly afraid I could peel myself away completely like this.

KING PETER. (*Confused.*) But—but you must be something, after all?

VALERIO. If Your Majesty commands it. But gentlemen, then turn the mirrors around and hide your shiny buttons somewhat and don't look at me so that I'm mirrored in your eyes, or I'll really no longer know who I actually am.

KING PETER. This man makes me confused, desperate. I am thoroughly mixed up.

VALERIO. But actually I wanted to announce to this exalted and honored company that the two world-famous automatons have arrived, and that I'm perhaps the third and most peculiar of them all, if only I really knew who I am, which by the way shouldn't surprise you, since I myself don't know what I'm talking about—in fact, I don't even know that I don't know it, so that it's highly probable that I'm merely being *made* to speak, and it's actually nothing but cylinders and air hoses that are saying all this. (*In a strident voice.*) Ladies and gentlemen, here you see two persons of opposite sexes, a male and a female, a gentleman and a lady. Nothing but art and machinery, nothing but cardboard and watchsprings. Each one has a tiny, tiny ruby spring under the nail of the little toe of the right foot—press on it gently and the mechanism runs a full fifty years. These persons are so perfectly constructed that one couldn't distinguish them from other people if one didn't know that they're simply cardboard; you could actually make them members of human society. They are very noble, for they speak the Queen's English. They are very moral, for they get up punctually, eat lunch punctually, and go to bed punctually; they also have a good digestion, which proves they have a good conscience. They have a fine sense of propriety, for the lady has no word for the concept "pants," and it is absolutely impossible for the gentleman to follow a lady going upstairs or to precede her downstairs. They are highly educated, for the lady sings all the new operas and the gentleman wears cuffs. Take note, ladies and gentlemen: they are now in an interesting state. The mechanism of love is beginning to function: the gentleman has already carried the lady's shawl several times, the lady has turned her eyes up to heaven. Both have whispered more than once: "Faith, hope, charity!" Both already appear to be completely in accord; all that is lacking is the tiny word "amen."

KING PETER. (*Puts a finger next to his nose.*) In effigy? In effigy? President, if you hang a man in effigy, isn't that just as good as hanging him properly?

PRESIDENT. Begging Your Majesty's pardon, it's very much better, because no harm comes to him, yet he is hanged nevertheless.

KING PETER. Now I've got it. We shall celebrate the wedding in effigy. (*Pointing to* LEONCE *and* LENA.) This is the Prince, this is the Princess. I shall carry out my resolution—I shall rejoice. Let the bells ring, prepare your congratulations! Quickly, Court Chaplain! (*The* COURT CHAPLAIN *steps forward, clears his throat, looks toward heaven several times.*)

VALERIO. Begin! Leave thy damnable faces, and begin![11] Come on!

COURT CHAPLAIN. (*In the greatest confusion.*) When we—or—but—

VALERIO. Whereas and because—

COURT CHAPLAIN. For—

VALERIO. It was before the creation of the world—

COURT CHAPLAIN. That—

VALERIO. God was bored—

KING PETER. Just make it short, my good man.

COURT CHAPLAIN. (*Composing himself.*) May it please Your Highness Prince Leonce from the Kingdom of Popo and may it please Your Highness Princess Lena from the Kingdom of Peepee, and may it please Your Highnesses mutually to want each other respectively, then say a loud and audible "I do."

LENA AND LEONCE. I do.

COURT CHAPLAIN. Then I say amen.

VALERIO. Well done, short and sweet—thus man and woman are created and all the animals of paradise surround them. (LEONCE *takes off his mask.*)

11. *Hamlet*, Act III, Scene 2.

ALL. The Prince!

KING PETER. The Prince! My son! I'm lost, I've been deceived! (*He rushes over to the* PRINCESS.) Who is this person? I shall declare everything invalid.

GOVERNESS. (*Takes off the* PRINCESS's *mask, triumphantly.*) The Princess!

LEONCE. Lena?

LENA. Leonce?

LEONCE. Why Lena, I think that was an escape into paradise. I've been deceived.

LENA. I've been deceived.

LEONCE. Oh, Fortune!

LENA. Oh, Providence!

VALERIO. I can't help laughing. I can't help laughing. Fate has certainly been fortuitous for the two of you. I hope Your Highnesses will be so fortunate as to find favor with each other forthwith.

GOVERNESS. That my old eyes could see this! A wandering prince! Now I can die in peace.

KING PETER. My children, I am deeply moved, I am almost beside myself with emotion. I am the happiest of all men! I shall now, however, most solemnly place the kingdom in your hands, my son, and shall immediately begin to do nothing but think without interruption. My son, you will leave me these wise men (*He points to the State Council.*), so they can support me in my efforts. Come, gentlemen, we must think, think without interruption. (*He leaves with the State Council.*) That person confused me before—I must find my way out again.

LEONCE. (*To those present.*) Gentlemen, my spouse and I are terribly sorry that you have had to attend us for so long today. Your deportment is so tenuous that we do not intend to test your tenacity any longer. Go home now, but don't forget your speeches, sermons, and verses, because tomorrow, in peace and comfort, we'll begin the game all over again. Good-bye! (*All leave except* LEONCE, LENA, VALERIO, *and the* GOVERNESS.)

LEONCE. Well, Lena, now do you see how our pockets are full of dolls and toys? What shall we do with them? Shall we give them beards and hang swords on them? Or shall we dress them up in tails and let them play at protozoan politics and diplomacy and watch them through a microscope? Or would you prefer a barrel organ on which milk-white aesthetic shrews are scurrying about? Shall we build a theater? (LENA *leans against him and shakes her head.*) But I know what you really want: we'll have all the clocks smashed, all calendars prohibited, and we'll count hours and months only by flower-clocks, only by blossoms and fruit. And then we'll surround the little country with heat reflectors so there'll be no more winter, and in the summer we'll make it as warm as Ischia and Capri, and we'll spend the whole year among roses and violets, among oranges and laurels.

VALERIO. And I'll be Minister of State, and it shall be decreed that whoever gets calluses on his hands shall be placed in custody, that whoever works himself sick shall be criminally prosecuted, that anyone who boasts of eating his bread in the sweat of his brow shall be declared insane and dangerous to human society, and then we'll lie in the shade and ask God for macaroni, melons, and figs, for musical voices, classical bodies, and a comfortable religion!

Variant to Act One, Scene 1

1

. . . [*The beginning of the variant is almost identical to the later version on page 166*].

VALERIO. Ah, my Lord, what a feeling I have for nature! The grass looks so beautiful that I wish I were an ox so I could eat it, and then a human being again to eat the ox that has eaten such grass.

LEONCE. Unhappy man, you too seem to be suffering from ideals.

VALERIO. Oh God! For a week I've been running after an ideal roast beef without finding it anywhere in reality. (*He sings.*)

Our hostess has a pretty maid,
She's in her garden night and day,
She sits inside her garden,
Until the bells have all struck twelve
And stares at all the soo-ooldiers.[1]

(*He sits on the ground.*) Look at these ants, dear children, it's amazing what instinct is in these little creatures—order, diligence—My Lord, there are only four ways a man can earn money: find it, win it in a lottery, inherit it, or steal it in God's name, if you're clever enough not to suffer any conscience pangs.

LEONCE. You've grown rather old on these principles without dying of hunger or on the gallows.

VALERIO. (*Always staring at him.*) Yes, my Lord, and I maintain that whoever earns money in any other way is a scoundrel.

LEONCE. Because one who works is subtly committing suicide, and a suicide is a criminal, and a criminal is a scoundrel: therefore whoever works is a scoundrel.

VALERIO. Yes.—All the same, ants are most useful pests, but they'd be even more useful if they didn't do any damage. Nevertheless, most honored vermin, I can't deny myself the pleasure of kicking a few of you in the ass with my heel, blowing your noses and cutting your nails. (*Two policemen enter.*)[2]

1. Eventually incorporated into *Woyzeck*, Scene 4,10.

2. If the following episode is to be used in a production of the play, it would seem more appropriate to place it into Act II, after Leonce and Valerio have fled, perhaps before the entrance of Lena and the Governess in Scene 1.

FIRST POLICEMAN. Halt—where's the rascal?

SECOND POLICEMAN. There are two over there.

FIRST POLICEMAN. Check if either of them is running away.

SECOND POLICEMAN. I don't think anyone is running away.

FIRST POLICEMAN. Then we'll have to interrogate them both.—Gentlemen, we're looking for someone—a subject, an individual, a person, a delinquent, a suspect, a rascal. (*To the other policeman.*) Check if either of them is blushing.

SECOND POLICEMAN. Nobody blushed.

FIRST POLICEMAN. Then we'll have to try something else. —Where's the warrant, the description, the certificate? (*The* SECOND POLICEMAN *takes a paper out of his pocket and hands it over.*) Inspect the subjects as I read: a human being—

SECOND POLICEMAN. Doesn't match, there are two of them.

FIRST POLICEMAN. Idiot!—walks on two feet, has two arms; in addition, a mouth, a nose, two eyes, two ears. Distinguishing characteristics: is a highly dangerous individual.

SECOND POLICEMAN. That fits both. Shall I arrest them both?

FIRST POLICEMAN. Two—that's dangerous—there are only two of us. But I'll make a report. It's a case of highly criminal complexity or highly complex criminality. For if I get drunk and lie down in bed, that's my affair and doesn't concern anyone, but if I squander my bed on drink, whose affair is that, you rogue?

SECOND POLICEMAN. Well, I don't know.

FIRST POLICEMAN. Well, I don't know either, but that's the point. (*They go off.*)

VALERIO. Just try to deny destiny. Look what one can accomplish with a flea. If it hadn't crawled over me last night, I wouldn't have carried my bed into the sun this morning, and if I hadn't carried it into the sun, I wouldn't have ended up with it next to the Inn of the Moon, and if sun and moon hadn't shone on it, I couldn't have pressed any wine out of my straw mattress and gotten drunk from it—and if all that hadn't happened I wouldn't be in your company now, most honored ants, letting you strip me to a skeleton and being dried up by the sun, but I'd be carving up a piece of meat and drying up a bottle of wine—in the hospital, namely.

LEONCE. A pleasant way of life.

VALERIO. I have a racy way of life. Because only my racing in the course of the war saved me from receiving a round of rifle bullets in my ribs. As a result of this rescue, I got a rasping cough, and the doctor resolved that my racing had become a galloping and that I had galloping consumption. But since I realized I had nothing to consume, I fell into or rather upon a consuming fever, during which I was required to eat good soup, good beef, good bread and drink good wine every day in order to sustain myself as a defender of the Fatherland.

LEONCE. But, noblest sir, your trade, your métier, your profession, your occupation, your rank, your art?

VALERIO. My Lord, I have the great occupation of being idle, I am incredibly skilled in doing nothing, I have an enormous capacity for laziness.

Notes

Like Clemens Brentano's *Ponce de Leon* (1801) and E. T. A. Hoffmann's *The Prize* (1803), Büchner's comedy was written in response to a public competition. On February 3, 1836, the publishing firm of Cotta had printed an announcement in the so-called "Intelligence Sheet" ("*Intelligenzblatt*"), a special section of the *Morning Paper for the Educated Classes* (*Morgenblatt für gebildete Stände*), offering a prize for the "best one- or two-act comedy in prose or verse" and inviting readers to submit their entries. Büchner apparently missed the deadline for the receipt of entries, July 1, since one presumes that the "white sheets of paper" which he was supposed to fill, mentioned in his letter to Eugen Boeckel on June 1, were a reference to the comedy project. If this were the case, Büchner could not have begun the play before that date. In a letter to his brother Wilhelm written on September 2, 1836, he indicated that he was in the process of "letting several people kill each other or get married on paper," and in the same month he also mentioned to his family that he had not yet "released [his] two dramas." But these statements were doubtless strategic in nature and can hardly be considered sufficient evidence for a terminus ad quem: Büchner had probably begun the play before June 1 of that year.

The comedy *Leonce and Lena* is Büchner's only work not based on historical sources. Nevertheless, its structure is still based on a montage of quotations. Büchner works into the text numerous ideas, references, and quotes from the works of Shakespeare, Sterne, Musset, Goethe, Holberg, Tieck, Brentano, Jean Paul, Friedrich Schlegel, Bonaventura's *Nightwatches,* and the tradition of the *commedia dell'arte.* But it would be quite wrong and indeed ridiculous to presume, as did Gutzkow, that the extensive use of quotation was an indication of a lack of talent on the part of the author. On the contrary, literary quotation in *Leonce and Lena* is the decisive aesthetic principle upon which the play is built and is a part of its communicative strategy.

Foreword: Wolfgang Pross recently identified the quotation "E la fama?" ("And fame?"), "E la fame?" ("And hunger?") in Carlo Goldoni's comedy *Il poeta fanatico.* The quotation might point to the difference between an idealistic and a more realistic aesthetic concept in Büchner's program (cf. Introduction, pp. 13–17). However, it is also possible to interpret the quotations in the Foreword on the basis of Büchner's comment about his literary activity: "I want fame from it, not bread."

Characters: The character constellation of Princess Lena and the Governess is similar to that of Isidora and Juanna in Brentano's *Ponce de Leon* and Princess Elsbeth and the Governess in Musset's *Fantasio* and of Isabelle and Hameline in Scott's *Quentin Durward.* The characters in Büchner's *Leonce and Lena,* however, are so simplified as to permit many parallels to be drawn between them and other plays. For example, one could find a connection between the King, Leonce, Valerio, and Rosetta—and Pantalon, Tartaglia, Truffaldin, and Smeraldina in Gozzi's comedies. But such writers as Holberg and E.T.A. Hoffmann (*Princess Brambilla,* chapter 2), Goethe (*Faust, Fair at Plundersweilern*), and, as ever, Shakespeare (*As You Like It, Twelfth Night, Hamlet, Love's Labors Lost, Henry IV,* and others) also provide numerous parallel characters. The kingdom of Peepee, for example, is first mentioned in Goethe's poem *The New Amadis,* in which a Prince Peepee chivalrously frees a Princess Fish. A nearer source, however, would be E. T. A. Hoffmann's "a letter by Milo, an educated ape, to his friend Peepee in North America" (from: *Fantastic Pieces in the Manner of Callot. Kreisleriana, News of an Educated Man*). In this work by Hoffmann a baron also appears and skillfully spits on a stone.

First Editions

a) "Leonce and Lena" in *Telegraph for Germany* 1 (*Telegraph für Deutschland*) (1838), May numbers (edition by Karl Gutzkow of a major portion of the comedy, but abridged and fragmented) (J).

b) "Lenz. Leonce and Lena" in Karl Gutzkow, ed., *Mosaic. Novellas and Sketches,* Leipzig: Lorck 1842 (version of *Leonce and Lena* is identical to J).

c) "Leonce and Lena" in *Posthumous Works,* ed. by Ludwig Büchner, Frankfurt/Main: J. D. Sauerländer, 1850 (first complete version of *Leonce and Lena*) (N).

Versions

Although in the case of *Leonce and Lena* Karl Gutzkow speaks of a clean copy "in the handwriting of his fiancée," neither the "clean copy" (h) nor the original manuscript (H) is extant, with the exception of two outlines in Büchner's hand which include fragments of Act I (with a complete Scene 1) and fragments of Act II.

An authoritative text of *Leonce and Lena* cannot be established beyond the shadow of a doubt for every detail because of the questionable nature of the various versions. As Karl Gutzkow put it, one must be satisfied with the "ruin of a devastation."

WOYZECK

A RECONSTRUCTION

[consisting of Büchner's incomplete revision (Fourth Draft), scenes from the First Draft, and two optional scenes]

CHARACTERS

FRANZ WOYZECK
MARIE
CAPTAIN
DOCTOR
DRUM MAJOR
SERGEANT
ANDRES
MARGRET
BARKER
ANNOUNCER
OLD MAN
CHILD
JEW
INNKEEPER
FIRST APPRENTICE
SECOND APPRENTICE
KARL, *an idiot*
KATEY
GRANDMOTHER
FIRST CHILD
SECOND CHILD
FIRST PERSON
SECOND PERSON
COURT CLERK
JUDGE
SOLDIERS, STUDENTS, YOUNG MEN, GIRLS, CHILDREN

4,1.

Open field. The town in the distance.

WOYZECK *and* ANDRES *are cutting branches in the bushes.*

WOYZECK. Yes, Andres—that stripe there across the grass, that's where heads roll at night; once somebody picked one up, he thought it was a hedgehog. Three days and three nights, and he was lying in a coffin. *(Softly.)* Andres, it was the Freemasons, that's it, the Freemasons—shh!

ANDRES. (*Sings.*)

I saw two big rabbits
Chewing up the green, green grass . . .

WOYZECK. Shh! Something's moving!

ANDRES. Chewing up the green, green grass
Till it was all gone.

WOYZECK. Something's moving behind me, under me. (*Stamps on the ground.*) Hollow—you hear that? It's all hollow down there. The Freemasons!

ANDRES. I'm scared.

WOYZECK. It's so strangely quiet. You feel like holding your breath. Andres!

ANDRES. What?

WOYZECK. Say something! (*Stares off into the distance.*) Andres! Look how bright it is! There's fire raging around the sky, and a noise is coming down like trumpets. It's coming closer! Let's go! Don't look back! (*Drags him into the bushes.*)

ANDRES. (*After a pause.*) Woyzeck! Do you still hear it?

WOYZECK. Quiet, it's all quiet, like the world was dead.

ANDRES. Listen! They're drumming. We've got to get back.

4,2.

[*The town.*][1]

MARIE *with her* CHILD *at the window.* MARGRET. *A military patrol goes by, the* DRUM MAJOR *leading.*

MARIE. *(Rocking the* CHILD *in her arms.)* Hey, boy! Ta-ra-ra-ra! You hear it? They're coming.

MARGRET. What a man, like a tree!

MARIE. He stands on his feet like a lion. (*The* DRUM MAJOR *greets them.*)

MARGRET. Say, what a friendly look you gave him, neighbor—we're not used to that from you.

MARIE. (*Sings.*)

A soldier is a handsome fellow . . .

MARGRET. Your eyes are still shining.

MARIE. So what? Why don't you take *your* eyes to the Jew and have them polished—maybe they'll shine enough to sell as two buttons.

MARGRET. What? Why, Mrs. Virgin, I'm a decent woman, but you—you can stare through seven pairs of leather pants!

MARIE. Bitch! *(Slams the window shut.)* Come, my boy. What do they want from us, anyway? You're only the poor child of a whore, and you make your mother happy with your bastard face. Ta-ta! *(Sings.)*

Maiden, now what's to be done?
You've got no ring, you've a son.
Oh, why worry my head,
I'll sing here at your bed:
Rockabye baby, my baby are you,
Nobody cares what I do.

Johnny, hitch up your six horses fleet,
Go bring them something to eat.
From oats they will turn,
From water they'll turn,

1. Brackets indicate additions to the text (as in this case) or doubtful readings.

Only cool wine will be fine, hooray!
Only cool wine will be fine.

(*A knock at the window.*)

MARIE. Who's that? Is that you, Franz? Come on in!

WOYZECK. I can't. Have to go to roll call.

MARIE. What's the matter with you, Franz?

WOYZECK. (*Mysteriously.*) Marie, there was something out there again—a lot. Isn't it written: "And lo, the smoke of the country went up as the smoke of a furnace"?

MARIE. Man alive!

WOYZECK. It followed me until I reached town. What's going to happen?

MARIE. Franz!

WOYZECK. I've got to go. (*He leaves.*)

MARIE. That man! He's so upset. He didn't look at his own child. He'll go crazy with those thoughts of his. Why are you so quiet, son? Are you scared? It's getting so dark, you'd think you were blind. Usually there's a light shining in. I can't stand it. I'm frightened. (*Goes off.*)

4,3.

Carnival booths. Lights. People.[2]

OLD MAN. DANCING CHILD.

How long we live, just time will tell,
We all have got to die,
We know that very well!

[WOYZECK.] Hey! Whee! Poor man, old man! Poor child! Young child! Hey, Marie, shall I carry you? . . . Beautiful world!

CARNIVAL BARKER. (*In front of a booth.*) Gentlemen! Gentlemen! [(*Points to a monkey.*)] Look at this creature, as God made it: he's nothing, nothing at all. Now see the effect of art: he walks upright, wears coat and pants, carries a sword! Ho! Take a bow!

2. In his revision, Büchner wrote only this title and left one and a half pages blank. The scene has been reconstructed from earlier drafts.

Good boy. Give me a kiss! ([*Monkey*] *trumpets.*) The little dummy is musical!

Ladies and gentlemen, here is to be seen the astronomical horse and the little cannery-birds[3]—they're favorites of all potentates of Europe and members of all learned societies. They'll tell you everything: how old you are, how many children you have, what kind of illnesses. [(*Points to the monkey.*)] He shoots a pistol, stands on one leg. It's all a matter of upbringing; he has merely a beastly reason, or rather a very reasonable beastliness—he's no brutish individual like a lot of people, present company excepted. Enter! The presentation will begin. The commencement of the beginning will start immediately.

Observe the progress of civilization. Everything progresses—a horse, a monkey, a cannery-bird. The monkey is already a soldier—that's not much, it's the lowest level of the human race!

[WOYZECK.] Want to?

MARIE. All right. It ought to be good. Look at his tassels, and the woman's got pants on!

(SERGEANT. DRUM MAJOR. [MARIE. WOYZECK.])

SERGEANT. Hold it! Over there. Look at her! What a piece!

DRUM MAJOR. Damn! Good enough for the propagation of cavalry regiments and the breeding of drum majors.

SERGEANT. Look how she holds her head—you'd think that black hair would pull her down like a weight. And those eyes, black . . .

DRUM MAJOR. It's like looking down a well or a chimney. Come on, after her!

MARIE. Those lights!

WOYZECK. Yeah, like a big black cat with fiery eyes. Hey, what a night!

(*Inside the booth.*)

CARNIVAL ANNOUNCER. [*Presenting a horse.*] Show your talent! Show your beastly wisdom! Put human society to shame! Gentlemen, this animal that you see here, with a tail on his body, with his four hooves, is a member of all learned societies, is a professor

3. The Barker says *Canaillevogel* instead of *Kanarienvögel,* which means "canaries." *Canaille* means "scoundrel."

at our university, with whom the students learn to ride and fight duels. That was simple comprehension! Now think with double *raison.* What do you do when you think with double *raison?* Is there in the learned *société* an ass? (*The horse shakes its head.*) Now you understand double *raison!* That is beastiognomy.[4] Yes, that's no brutish individual, that's a person! A human being, a beastly human being, but still an animal, a *bête.* (*The horse behaves improperly.*) That's right, put *société* to shame! You see, the beast is still nature, unspoiled nature! Take a lesson from him. Go ask the doctor, it's very unhealthy![5] It is written: man, be natural; you were created from dust, sand, dirt. Do you want to be more than dust, sand, dirt? Observe his power of reason! He can add, but he can't count on his fingers—why is that? He simply can't express himself, explain himself—he's a transformed person! Tell the gentlemen what time it is. Who among the ladies and gentlemen has a watch—a watch?

DRUM MAJOR. A watch! (*Slowly and grandly he pulls a watch out of his pocket.*) There you are, sir.

MARIE. This I've got to see. (*She climbs into the first row. The* DRUM MAJOR *helps her.*)

4,4.

[*Room.*]

MARIE *sits with her* CHILD *on her lap, a piece of mirror in her hand.*

MARIE. (*Looks at herself in the mirror.*) These stones really sparkle! What kind are they? What did he say?—Go to sleep, son! Shut your eyes tight. (*The* CHILD *covers his eyes with his hands.*) Tighter—stay quiet or he'll come get you. (*Sings.*)

Close up your shop, fair maid,
A gypsy boy's in the glade.
He'll lead you by the hand
Off into gypsyland.

4. *Viehsionomik:* a pun on "beast" and "physiognomy."

5. Meaning "to hold it in."

(Looks in the mirror again.) It must be gold. The likes of us only have a little corner in the world and a little piece of mirror, but I have just as red a mouth as the great ladies with their mirrors from top to toe and their handsome lords who kiss their hands. I'm just a poor woman. (*The* CHILD *sits up.*) Shh, son, eyes shut—look, the sandman! He's running along the wall. (*She flashes with the mirror.*) Eyes shut, or he'll look into them, and you'll go blind.

(WOYZECK *enters behind her. She jumps up with her hands over her ears.*)

WOYZECK. What's that you got there?

MARIE. Nothing.

WOYZECK. Something's shining under your fingers.

MARIE. An earring—I found it.

WOYZECK. I've never found anything like that. Two at once.

MARIE. What am I—a whore?

WOYZECK. It's all right, Marie.—Look, the boy's asleep. Lift him up under his arms, the chair's hurting him. There are shiny drops on his forehead; everything under the sun is work—sweat, even in our sleep. Us poor people! Here's some more money, Marie, my pay and some from my captain.

MARIE. Bless you, Franz.

WOYZECK. I have to go. See you tonight, Marie. Bye.

MARIE. (*Alone, after a pause.*) What a bitch I am. I could stab myself.—Oh, what a world! Everything goes to hell anyhow, man and woman alike.

4,5.

The CAPTAIN. WOYZECK.

The CAPTAIN *in a chair,* WOYZECK *shaves him.*

CAPTAIN. Take it easy, Woyzeck, take it easy. One thing at a time; you're making me quite dizzy. You're going to finish early today—what am I supposed to do with the extra ten minutes? Woyzeck, just think, you've still got a good thirty years to live, thirty years!

That's 360 months, and days, hours, minutes! What are you going to do with that ungodly amount of time? Get organized, Woyzeck.

WOYZECK. Yes, Cap'n.

CAPTAIN. I fear for the world when I think about eternity. Activity, Woyzeck, activity! Eternal, that's eternal, that's eternal—you realize that, of course. But then again it's not eternal, it's only a moment, yes, a moment.—Woyzeck, it frightens me to think that the earth rotates in one day—what a waste of time, what will come of that? Woyzeck, I can't look at a mill wheel anymore or I get melancholy.

WOYZECK. Yes, Cap'n.

CAPTAIN. Woyzeck, you always look so upset. A good man doesn't act like that, a good man with a good conscience. Say something, Woyzeck. What's the weather like today?

WOYZECK. It's bad, Cap'n, bad—wind.

CAPTAIN. I can feel it, there's something rapid out there. A wind like that reminds me of a mouse. (*Cunningly.*) I believe it's coming from the south-north.

WOYZECK. Yes, Cap'n.

CAPTAIN. Ha! Ha! Ha! South-north! Ha! Ha! Ha! Oh, are you stupid, terribly stupid. (*Sentimentally.*) Woyzeck, you're a good man, a good man—(*With dignity.*) but Woyzeck, you've got no morality. Morality—that's when you are moral, you understand. It's a good word. You have a child without the blessing of the church, as our Reverend Chaplain says, without the blessing of the church—*I* didn't say it.

WOYZECK. Cap'n, the good Lord isn't going to look at a poor little kid only because amen was said over it before it was created. The Lord said: "Suffer little children to come unto me."

CAPTAIN. What's that you're saying? What kind of a crazy answer is that? You're getting me all confused with your answer. When I say *you,* I mean you—you!

WOYZECK. Us poor people. You see, Cap'n—money, money. If you don't have money. Just try to raise your own kind on morality in this world. After all, we're flesh and blood. The likes of us are wretched in this world and in the next; I guess if we ever got to Heaven, we'd have to help with the thunder.

CAPTAIN. Woyzeck, you have no virtue, you're not a virtuous person. Flesh and blood? When I'm lying at the window after it has rained, and I watch the white stockings as they go tripping down the street—damn it, Woyzeck, then love comes all over me. I've got flesh and blood, too. But Woyzeck, virtue, virtue! How else could I make time go by? I always say to myself: you're a virtuous man, (*Sentimentally.*) a good man, a good man.

WOYZECK. Yes, Cap'n, virtue! I haven't figured it out yet. You see, us common people, we don't have virtue, we act like nature tells us—but if I was a gentleman, and had a hat and a watch and an overcoat and could talk refined, then I'd be virtuous, too. Virtue must be nice, Cap'n. But I'm just a poor guy.

CAPTAIN. That's fine, Woyzeck. You're a good man, a good man. But you think too much, that's unhealthy—you always look so upset. This discussion has really worn me out. You can go now—and don't run like that! Slow, nice and slow down the street.

4,6.

MARIE. DRUM MAJOR.

DRUM MAJOR. Marie!

MARIE. (*Looking at him expressively.*) Go march up and down for me.—A chest like a bull and a beard like a lion. Nobody else is like that.—No woman is prouder than me.

DRUM MAJOR. Sundays when I have my plumed helmet and my white gloves—goddamn, Marie! The prince always says: man, you're quite a guy!

MARIE. (*Mockingly.*) Aw, go on! (*Goes up to him.*) What a man!

DRUM MAJOR. What a woman! Hell, let's breed a race of drum majors, hey? (*He embraces her.*)

MARIE. (*Moody.*) Leave me alone!

DRUM MAJOR. You wildcat!

MARIE. (*Violently.*) Just try to touch me!

DRUM MAJOR. Is the devil in your eyes?

MARIE. For all I care. What does it matter?

4,7.

MARIE. WOYZECK.

WOYZECK. (*Stares at her, shakes his head.*) Hm! I don't see anything, I don't see anything. Oh, I should be able to see it; I should be able to grab it with my fists.
MARIE. (*Intimidated.*) What's the matter, Franz? You're out of your mind, Franz.
WOYZECK. A sin so fat and so wide—it stinks enough to smoke the angels out of Heaven. You've got a red mouth, Marie. No blister on it? Good-bye, Marie, you're as beautiful as sin.—Can mortal sin be so beautiful?
MARIE. Franz, you're delirious.
WOYZECK. Damn it!—Was he standing here like this, like this?
MARIE. As the day is long and the world is old, lots of people can stand on one spot, one after another.
WOYZECK. I saw him.
MARIE. You can see all sorts of things if you've got two eyes and aren't blind, and the sun is shining.
WOYZECK. [With my own eyes!]
MARIE. (*Fresh.*) So what!

4,8.

WOYZECK. *The* DOCTOR.

DOCTOR. What's this I saw, Woyzeck? A man of his word!
WOYZECK. What is it, Doctor?
DOCTOR. I saw it, Woyzeck—you pissed on the street, you pissed on the wall like a dog. And even though you get two cents a day. Woyzeck, that's bad. The world's getting bad, very bad.
WOYZECK. But Doctor, the call of nature . . .
DOCTOR. The call of nature, the call of nature! Nature! Haven't I proved that the *musculus constrictor vesicae* is subject to the will? Nature! Woyzeck, man is free; in man alone is individuality exalted to freedom. Couldn't hold it in! (*Shakes his head, puts his hands behind his back, and paces back and forth.*) Did you

eat your peas already, Woyzeck?—I'm revolutionizing science, I'll blow it sky-high. Urea ten per cent, ammonium chloride, hyperoxidic. Woyzeck, don't you have to piss again? Go in there and try.

WOYZECK. I can't, Doctor.

DOCTOR. (*With emotion.*) But pissing on the wall! I have it in writing, here's the contract. I saw it all, saw it with my own eyes—I was just holding my nose out the window, letting the sun's rays hit it, so as to examine the process of sneezing. (*Starts kicking him.*) No, Woyzeck, I'm not getting angry; anger is unhealthy, unscientific. I am calm, perfectly calm—my pulse is beating at its usual sixty, and I'm telling you this in all cold-bloodedness! Who on earth would get excited about a human being, a human being! Now if it were a Proteus lizard that were dying! But you shouldn't have pissed on the wall . . .

WOYZECK. You see, Doctor, sometimes you've got a certain character, a certain structure.—But with nature, that's something else, you see, with nature—(*He cracks his knuckles.*) that's like—how should I put it—for example . . .

DOCTOR. Woyzeck, you're philosophizing again.

WOYZECK. (*Confidingly.*) Doctor, have you ever seen anything of double nature? When the sun's standing high at noon and the world seems to be going up in flames, I've heard a terrible voice talking to me!

DOCTOR. Woyzeck, you've got an *aberratio!*

WOYZECK. (*Puts his finger to his nose.*) The toadstools, Doctor. There—that's where it is. Have you seen how they grow in patterns? If only someone could read that.

DOCTOR. Woyzeck, you've got a marvelous *aberratio mentalis partialis,* second species, beautifully developed. Woyzeck, you're getting a raise. Second species: obsession with a generally rational condition. You're doing everything as usual—shaving your captain?

WOYZECK. Yes, sir.

DOCTOR. Eating your peas?

WOYZECK. Same as ever, Doctor. My wife gets the money for the household.

DOCTOR. Going on duty?

WOYZECK. Yes, sir.

DOCTOR. You're an interesting case. Subject Woyzeck, you're getting a raise. Now behave yourself. Show me your pulse! Yes.

4,9.

CAPTAIN. DOCTOR.

CAPTAIN. Doctor, I'm afraid for the horses when I think that the poor beasts have to go everywhere on foot. Don't run like that! Don't wave your cane around in the air like that! You'll run yourself to death that way. A good man with a good conscience doesn't go so fast. A good man. (*He catches the* DOCTOR *by the coat.*) Doctor, allow me to save a human life. You're racing . . .

Doctor, I'm so melancholy, I get so emotional, I always start crying when I see my coat hanging on the wall—there it is.

DOCTOR. Hm! Bloated, fat, thick neck, apoplectic constitution. Yes, Captain, you might be stricken by an *apoplexia cerebralis*. But you might get it just on one side and be half paralyzed, or—best of all—you might become mentally affected and just vegetate from then on: those are approximately your prospects for the next four weeks. Moreover, I can assure you that you will be a most interesting case, and if, God willing, your tongue is partially paralyzed, we'll make immortal experiments.

CAPTAIN. Doctor, don't frighten me! People have been known to die of fright, of pure, sheer fright.—I can see them now, with their hats in their hands—but they'll say, he was a good man, a good man.—You damn coffin nail!

DOCTOR. [(*Holds out his hat.*)] What's this, Captain? That's brainless!

CAPTAIN. (*Makes a crease.*) What's this, Doctor? That's in-crease!

DOCTOR. I take my leave, most honorable Mr. Drillprick.

CAPTAIN. Likewise, dearest Mr. Coffin Nail.

4,10.

The guardroom.

WOYZECK. ANDRES.

ANDRES. *(Sings.)*

Our hostess has a pretty maid,
She's in her garden night and day,
She sits inside her garden . . .

WOYZECK. Andres!

ANDRES. Huh?

WOYZECK. Nice weather.

ANDRES. Sunday weather. There's music outside town. All the broads are out there already, everybody's sweating—it's really moving along.

WOYZECK. (*Restlessly.*) A dance, Andres, they're dancing.

ANDRES. Yeah, at the Horse and at the Star.

WOYZECK. Dancing, dancing.

ANDRES. Big deal. (*Sings.*)

She sits inside her garden,
Until the bells have all struck twelve,
And stares at all the soo-ooldiers.

WOYZECK. Andres, I can't keep still.

ANDRES. Fool!

WOYZECK. I've got to get out of here. Everything's spinning before my eyes. How hot their hands are. Damn it, Andres!

ANDRES. What do you want?

WOYZECK. I've got to go.

ANDRES. With that whore.

WOYZECK. I've got to get out. It's so hot in here.

4,11.

Inn.

The windows are open, a dance. Benches in front of the house. APPRENTICES.

FIRST APPRENTICE.

This shirt I've got, I don't know whose,
My soul it stinks like booze . . .

SECOND APPRENTICE. Brother, shall I in friendship bore a hole in your nature? Dammit, I want to bore a hole in your nature. I'm quite a guy, too, you know—I'm going to kill all the fleas on his body.

FIRST APPRENTICE. My soul, my soul it stinks like booze.—Even money eventually decays. Forget-me-not! Oh, how beautiful this world is. Brother, I could cry a rain barrel full of tears. I wish our noses were two bottles and we could pour them down each other's throats.

OTHERS. (*In chorus.*)

A hunter from the west
Once went riding through the woods.
Hip-hip, hooray! A hunter has a merry life,
O'er meadow and o'er stream,
Oh, hunting is my dream!

(WOYZECK *stands at the window.* MARIE *and the* DRUM MAJOR *dance past without seeing him.*)

MARIE. (*Dancing by.*) On! and on, on and on!

WOYZECK. (*Chokes.*) On and on—on and on! (*Jumps up violently and sinks back on the bench.*) On and on, on and on. (*Beats his hands together.*) Spin around, roll around. Why doesn't God blow out the sun so that everything can roll around in lust, man and woman, man and beast. Do it in broad daylight, do it on our hands, like flies.—Woman!—That woman is hot, hot! On and on, on and on. (*Jumps up.*) The bastard! Look how he's grabbing her, grabbing her body! He—he's got her now, [like I used to have her.][6]

6. Or: "like it always is at the beginning!"

FIRST APPRENTICE. *(Preaches on the table.)* Yet when a wanderer stands leaning against the stream of time or gives answer for the wisdom of God, asking himself: Why does man exist? Why does man exist?—But verily I say unto you: how could the farmer, the cooper, the shoemaker, the doctor exist if God hadn't created man? How could the tailor exist if God hadn't given man a feeling of shame? How could the soldier exist, if men didn't feel the necessity of killing one another? Therefore, do not ye despair, yes, yes, it is good and pleasant, yet all that is earthly is passing, even money eventually decays.—In conclusion, my dear friends, let us piss crosswise so that a Jew will die.

4,12.

Open field.

WOYZECK. On and on! On and on! Shh—music. (*Stretches out on the ground)*) Ha—what, what are you saying? Louder, louder—stab, stab the bitch to death? Stab, stab the bitch to death. Should I? Must I? Do I hear it over there too, is the wind saying it too? Do I hear it on and on—stab her to death, to death.

4,13.

Night.

ANDRES *and* WOYZECK *in a bed.*

WOYZECK. (*Shakes* ANDRES.) Andres! Andres! I can't sleep—when I close my eyes, everything starts spinning, and I hear the fiddles, on and on, on and on. And then there's a voice from the wall—don't you hear anything?

ANDRES. Oh, yeah—let them dance! God bless us, amen. (*Falls asleep again.*)

WOYZECK. And it floats between my eyes like a knife.

ANDRES. Drink some brandy with a painkiller in it. That'll bring your fever down.

4,14.

Inn.

DRUM MAJOR. WOYZECK. PEOPLE.

DRUM MAJOR. I'm a man! (*Pounds his chest.*) A man, I say. Who wants to start something? If you're not drunk as a lord, stay away from me. I'll shove your nose up your ass. I'll . . . (*To* WOYZECK.) Man, have a drink. A man gotta drink. I wish the world was booze, booze.

WOYZECK. (*Whistles.*)

DRUM MAJOR. You bastard, you want me to pull your tongue out of your throat and wrap it around you? (*They wrestle,* WOYZECK *loses.*) Shall I leave you as much breath as an old woman's fart? Shall I?

(WOYZECK *sits on the bench, exhausted and trembling.*)

DRUM MAJOR. He can whistle till he's blue in the face. Ha!

Oh, brandy, that's my life,
Oh, brandy gives me courage!

A PERSON. He sure got what was coming to him.

ANOTHER. He's bleeding.

WOYZECK. One thing after another.

4,15.

WOYZECK. *The* JEW.

WOYZECK. The pistol costs too much.

JEW. Well, do you want it or don't you?

WOYZECK. How much is the knife?

JEW. It's good and straight. You want to cut your throat with it? Well, how about it? I'll give it to you as cheap as anybody else; your death'll be cheap, but not for nothing. How about it? You'll have an economical death.

WOYZECK. That can cut more than just bread.

JEW. Two cents.

WOYZECK. There! (*Goes off.*)
JEW. There! Like it was nothing. But it's money! The dog.

4,16.

[MARIE. KARL, *the idiot*. CHILD.]

MARIE. (*Leafs through the Bible.*) "And no guile is found in his mouth" . . . My God, my God! Don't look at me. (*Pages further.*) "And the scribes and Pharisees brought unto him a woman taken in adultery, and set her in the midst . . . And Jesus said unto her, 'Neither do I condemn thee: go, and sin no more.' " *(Clasps her hands together.)* My God! My God! I can't. God, just give me enough strength to pray. (*The* CHILD *snuggles up to her.*) The boy is like a knife in my heart. [Karl! He's sunning himself!]

KARL. (*Lies on the ground and tells himself fairy tales on his fingers.*) This one has a golden crown—he's a king. Tomorrow I'll go get the queen's child. Blood sausage says, come, liver sausage! *(He takes the* CHILD *and is quiet.)*

[MARIE.] Franz hasn't come, not yesterday, not today. It's getting hot in here. (*She opens the window.*) "And stood at his feet weeping, and began to wash his feet with tears, and did wipe them with the hairs of her head, and kissed his feet, and anointed them with ointment." (*Beats her breast.*) It's all dead! Savior, Savior, I wish I could anoint your feet.

4,17.

The barracks.

ANDRES. WOYZECK *rummages through his things.*

WOYZECK. This jacket isn't part of the uniform, Andres; you can use it, Andres. The crucifix is my sister's, and the little ring. I've got an icon, too—two hearts and nice gold. It was in my mother's Bible, and it says:

May pain be my reward,
Through pain I love my Lord.

Lord, like Thy body, red and sore,
So be my heart forevermore.

My mother can only feel the sun shining on her hands now. That doesn't matter.

ANDRES. (*Blankly, answers to everything.*) Yeah.

WOYZECK. (*Pulls out a piece of paper.*) Friedrich Johann Franz Woyzeck, enlisted infantryman in the second regiment, second battalion, fourth company, born . . . Today[7] I'm thirty years, seven months, and twelve days old.

ANDRES. Franz, you better go to the infirmary. You poor guy—drink brandy with a painkiller in it. That'll kill the fever.

WOYZECK. You know, Andres, when the carpenter nails those boards together, nobody knows who'll be laying his head on them.

[End of Büchner's revision.]

[Scenes from the First Draft:]

1,14.

[*Street.*]

MARIE *with girls in front of the house door.* [GRANDMOTHER. *Then* WOYZECK.]

GIRLS. How bright the sun on Candlemas Day,
On fields of golden grain.
As two by two they marched along
Down the country lane.
The pipers up in front,
The fiddlers in a chain.
Their red socks . . .

FIRST CHILD. That's not nice.

SECOND CHILD. What do you want, anyway?

[OTHERS.] Why'd you start it?

Yeah, why?

7. Büchner inserted here: "on the Feast of the Annunciation, the 20th of July" (actually March 25).

I can't.

Because!

Who's going to sing?

Why because?

Marie, you sing to us.

MARIE. Come, you little shrimps.

([*Children's games:*] *"Ring-around-a-rosy" and "King Herod."*)

Grandmother, tell a story.

GRANDMOTHER. Once upon a time there was a poor child with no father and no mother, everything was dead, and no one was left in the whole world. Everything was dead, and it went and searched day and night. And since nobody was left on the earth, it wanted to go up to the heavens, and the moon was looking at it so friendly, and when it finally got to the moon, the moon was a piece of rotten wood and then it went to the sun and when it got there, the sun was a wilted sunflower and when it got to the stars, they were little golden flies stuck up there like the shrike sticks 'em on the blackthorn and when it wanted to go back down to the earth, the earth was an overturned pot and was all alone and it sat down and cried and there it sits to this day, all alone.

WOYZECK.[8] Marie!

MARIE. (*Startled.*) What is it?

WOYZECK. Marie, we have to go. It's time.

MARIE. Where to?

WOYZECK. How do I know?

1,15.

MARIE *and* WOYZECK.

MARIE. So the town is over there—it's dark.

WOYZECK. Stay here. Come on, sit down.

MARIE. But I have to get back.

WOYZECK. You won't get sore feet.

MARIE. What's gotten into you!

8. Actually, Woyzeck is named "Louis" and Marie is "Margret" in this draft.

WOYZECK. Do you know how long it's been, Marie?
MARIE. Two years since Pentecost.
WOYZECK. And do you know how long it's going to be?
MARIE. I've got to go, the evening dew is falling.
WOYZECK. Are you freezing, Marie? But you're warm. How hot your lips are!—Hot, the hot breath of a whore—and yet I'd give heaven and earth to kiss them once more. And when you're cold, you don't freeze anymore. The morning dew won't make you freeze.
MARIE. What are you talking about?
WOYZECK. Nothing. (*Silence.*)
MARIE. Look how red the moon is.
WOYZECK. Like a bloody blade.
MARIE. What are you up to? Franz, you're so pale. (*He pulls out the knife.*) Franz—wait! For God's sake—help!
WOYZECK. Take that and that! Can't you die? There! There! Ah—she's still twitching—not yet? Not yet? Still alive? (*Stabs once again.*) Are you dead? Dead! Dead! (*People approach, he runs off.*)

1,16.

Two people.

FIRST PERSON. Wait!
SECOND PERSON. You hear it? Shh! Over there.
FIRST PERSON. Ooh! There! What a sound.
SECOND PERSON. That's the water, it's calling. Nobody has drowned for a long time. Let's go—it's bad to hear things like that.
FIRST PERSON. Ooh! There it is again. Like someone dying.
SECOND PERSON. It's weird. It's so fragrant—some gray fog, and the beetles humming like broken bells. Let's get out of here!
FIRST PERSON. No—it's too clear, too loud. Up this way. Come on.

1,17.

The inn.

[WOYZECK. KATEY. KARL. INNKEEPER. *People.*]

WOYZECK. Dance, all of you, on and on, sweat and stink—he'll get you all in the end. (*Sings.*)

Our hostess has a pretty maid,
She's in her garden night and day,
She sits inside her garden,
Until the bells have all struck twelve,
And stares at all the soldiers.

(*He dances.*) Come on, Katey! Sit down! I'm hot! Hot. (*He takes off his jacket.*) That's the way it is: the devil takes one and lets the other go. Katey, you're hot! Why? Katey, you'll be cold someday, too. Be reasonable. Can't you sing something?

[KATEY.] For Swabian hills I do not yearn,
And flowing gowns I always spurn,
For flowing gowns and pointed shoes
A servant girl should never choose.

[WOYZECK.] No, no shoes—you can go to hell without shoes, too.

[KATEY.] For shame, my love, I'm not your own,
Just keep your money and sleep alone.

[WOYZECK.] Yes, that's right, I don't want to make myself bloody.

KATEY. But what's that on your hand?

WOYZECK. Who? Me?

KATEY. Red! Blood! (*People gather around.*)

WOYZECK. Blood? Blood?

INNKEEPER. Ooh, blood.

WOYZECK. I guess I must have cut myself, there on my right hand.

INNKEEPER. But how'd it get on your elbow?

WOYZECK. I wiped it off.

INNKEEPER. What, with your right hand on your right elbow? You're talented.

KARL. And then the giant said: I smell, I smell, I smell human flesh. Phew! That stinks already.

WOYZECK. Damn it, what do you want? What's it got to do with you? Get away, or the first one who—damn it! You think I killed someone? Am I a murderer? What are you staring at? Look at yourselves! Out of my way! (*He runs out.*)

1,18.

Children.

FIRST CHILD. Come on! Marie!

SECOND CHILD. What is it?

FIRST CHILD. Don't you know? Everybody's gone out there already. Someone's lying there!

SECOND CHILD. Where?

FIRST CHILD. To the left through the trench, near the red cross.

SECOND CHILD. Let's go, so we can still see something. Otherwise they'll carry her away.

1,19.

WOYZECK *alone.*

WOYZECK. The knife? Where's the knife? Here's where I left it. It'll give me away! Closer, still closer! What kind of a place is this? What's that I hear? Something's moving. Shh! Over there. Marie? Ah—Marie! Quiet. Everything's quiet! Why are you so pale, Marie? Why is that red thread around your neck? Who helped you earn that necklace, with your sins? They made you black, black! Now I've made you white. Why does your black hair hang so wild? Didn't you do your braids today? Something's lying over there! Cold, wet, still. Got to get away from here. The knife, the knife—is that it? There! People—over there. (*He runs off.*)

1,20.

WOYZECK *at a pond.*

WOYZECK. Down it goes! (*He throws the knife in.*) It sinks into the dark water like a stone! The moon is like a bloody blade! Is the whole world going to give me away? No, it's too far in front—when people go swimming—(*He goes into the pond and throws it far out.*) All right, now—but in the summer, when they go diving for shells—bah, it'll rust. Who'll recognize it? I wish I'd smashed it! Am I still bloody? I've got to wash myself. There's a spot—and there's another.

1,21.

COURT CLERK. BARBER. DOCTOR. JUDGE.

[CLERK.] A good murder, a real murder, a beautiful murder—as good a murder as you'd ever want to see. We haven't had one like this for a long time.

[Optional Scenes:]

3,1.

The PROFESSOR*'s courtyard.*

STUDENTS *below, the* PROFESSOR *at the attic window.*

[PROFESSOR.] Gentlemen, I am on the roof like David when he saw Bathsheba, but all I see is underwear on a clothesline in the garden of the girls' boarding house. Gentlemen, we are dealing with the important question of the relationship of subject to object. If we take only one of the things in which the organic self-affirmation of the Divine manifests itself to a high degree, and examine its relationship to space, to the earth, to the planetary system—gentlemen, if I throw this cat out of the window, how will this organism relate to the *centrum gravitationis* and to its own instinct? Hey, Woyzeck. (*Shouts.*) Woyzeck!

WOYZECK. Professor, it bites!

PROFESSOR. The fellow holds the beast so tenderly, like it was his grandmother!

WOYZECK. Doctor [*sic*], I've got the shivers.

DOCTOR. (*Elated.*) Say, that's wonderful, Woyzeck! (*Rubs his hands. He takes the cat.*) What's this I see, gentlemen—a new species of rabbit louse, a beautiful species, quite different, deep in the fur. (*He pulls out a magnifying glass.*) Ricinus, gentlemen! (*The cat runs off.*) Gentlemen, that animal has no scientific instinct. Ricinus—the best examples—bring your fur collars. Gentlemen, instead of that you can see something else: take note of this man—for a quarter of a year he hasn't eaten anything but peas. Notice the result—feel how uneven his pulse is. There—and the eyes.

WOYZECK. Doctor, everything's getting black. (*He sits down.*)

DOCTOR. Courage, Woyzeck—just a few more days, and then it'll be all over. Feel him, gentlemen, feel him. (STUDENTS *feel his temples, pulse, and chest.*) Apropos, Woyzeck, wiggle your ears for the gentlemen; I meant to show it to you before. He uses two muscles. Come on, hop to it!

WOYZECK. Oh, Doctor!

DOCTOR. You dog, shall I wiggle them for you, are you going to act like the cat? So, gentlemen, this represents a transition to the donkey, frequently resulting from being brought up by women and from the use of the mother tongue. How much hair has your mother pulled out for a tender memory? It's gotten very thin in the last few days. Yes, the peas, gentlemen.

3,2.

[KARL,] *the idiot. The* CHILD. WOYZECK.

KARL. (*Holds the* CHILD *on his lap.*) He fell in the water, he fell in the water, he fell in the water.

WOYZECK. Son—Christian!

KARL. (*Stares at him.*) He fell in the water.

WOYZECK. (*Wants to caress the* CHILD, *who turns away and screams.*) My God!

KARL. He fell in the water.

WOYZECK. Christian, you'll get a hobbyhorse. Da-da! (*The* CHILD *resists. To* KARL.) Here, go buy the boy a hobbyhorse.

KARL. (*Stares at him.*)

WOYZECK. Hop! Hop! Horsey!

KARL. (*Cheers.*) Hop! Hop! Horsey! Horsey! (*Runs off with the* CHILD.)

Synopsis:

CORRESPONDENCES AMONG DRAFTS

PRELIMINARY DRAFTS	REVISION
Scene(s): 2,1.	Scene: 4,1. *Open field.*
2,2.	4,2. *The town.*
1,1; 1,2; 2,3; (2,5).	(4,3. *Carnival booths. Lights. People.)*
	4,4. *Room.*
	4,5. *The* CAPTAIN. WOYZECK.
	4,6. MARIE. DRUM MAJOR.
2,8.	4,7. MARIE. WOYZECK.
2,6.	4,8. WOYZECK. *The* DOCTOR.
2,7.	4,9. CAPTAIN. DOCTOR.
1,4.	4,10. *The guardroom.*
1,5; 2,4.	4,11. *Inn.*
1,6.	4,12. *Open field.*
1,7; 1,8; 1,13.	4,13. *Night.*
(1,10).	4,14. *Inn.*
	4,15. WOYZECK. *The* JEW.
(2,9).	4,16. MARIE. KARL, *the idiot.* CHILD.
	4,17. *The barracks.*

1,14. *Street.*
1,15. MARIE *and* WOYZECK.
1,16. *Two people.*
1,17. *The inn.*
1,18. *Children.*
1,19. WOYZECK *alone.*
1,20. WOYZECK *at a pond.*
1,21. COURT CLERK. BARBER. DOCTOR. JUDGE.
3,1. *The* PROFESSOR'*s courtyard.*
3,2. KARL, *the idiot. The* CHILD. WOYZECK.

Woyzeck

The Drafts

First Draft

1,1. *Booths. People.*

CARNIVAL BARKER. (*In front of a booth.*) Gentlemen! Gentlemen! Look at this creature as God made it: he's nothing, nothing at all. Now see the effect of art: he walks upright, wears coat and pants, carries a sword! Ho! Take a bow! Good boy. Give me a kiss! (*He trumpets.*) The little dummy is musical! Ladies and gentlemen, here is to be seen the astronomical horse and the little cannery-birds—they're favorites of all crowned heads. The presentation will begin! The beginning of the beginning! The commencement of the commencement will start immediately!

SOLDIER. Want to?

MARGRET.[1] All right. It ought to be good. Look at his tassels, and the woman's got pants on!

1,2. *Inside the booth.*

CARNIVAL ANNOUNCER. Show your talent! Show your beastly wisdom! Put human society to shame! Gentlemen, this animal that you see here, with a tail on his body, with his four hooves, is a member of all learned societies, is a professor at our university, with whom the students learn to ride and fight duels. That was

1. I.e., Marie.

simple comprehension! Now think with double *raison*. What do you do when you think with double *raison?* Is there in the learned *société* an ass? (*The horse shakes its head.*) Now you understand double *raison!* That is beastiognomy. Yes, that's no brutish individual, that's a person! A human being, a beastly human being, but still an animal, a *bête*. (*The horse behaves improperly.*) That's right, put *société* to shame. You see, the beast is still nature, unspoiled nature! Take a lesson from him. Go ask the doctor, it's very unhealthy! It is written: man, be natural; you were created from dust, sand, dirt. Do you want to be more than dust, sand, dirt? Observe his power of reason! He can add, but he can't count on his fingers—why is that? He simply can't express himself, explain himself—he's a transformed person! Tell the gentlemen what time it is. Who among the ladies and gentlemen has a watch—a watch?

SERGEANT. A watch! (*Slowly and grandly he pulls a watch out of his pocket.*) There you are, sir. (What a piece! She can stare through seven layers of leather pants!)

MARGRET. This I've got to see. (*She climbs into the first row. The* SERGEANT *helps her.*)

SERGEANT. —

1,3. MARGRET *alone.**[2]

MARGRET. The other one gave him an order and he had to go. Ha! What a man!

1,4. *Barracks courtyard.**

ANDRES. LOUIS.[3]

ANDRES. (*Sings.*)

Our hostess has a pretty maid,
She's in her garden night and day,

2. An asterisk indicates that Büchner crossed out the scene while he was revising the play.

3. I.e., Woyzeck.

She sits inside her garden,
Until the bells have all struck twelve,
And stares at all the soldiers.

LOUIS. Hey, Andres, I can't keep still.
ANDRES. Fool!
LOUIS. What do you know about it? So tell me!
ANDRES. Well?
LOUIS. Why do you think I'm here?
ANDRES. 'Cause it's nice weather and they're dancing today.
LOUIS. I've got to get out there, got to see it!
ANDRES. What do you want?
LOUIS. To get out there!
ANDRES. You spoilsport, because of that whore?
LOUIS. I've got to get out.

1,5. *Inn.**

The windows are open. People are dancing. On the bench in front of the house LOUIS *looks through the window.*

LOUIS. It's him—with her! Hell! (*He sits down, shivering. He goes to the window again.*) They're really moving! Yeah, roll around on each other! Look at her—on! and on, on and on.

IDIOT. Phew! That stinks!

LOUIS. Yeah, that stinks! She's got red, red cheeks, but why does she stink already? Karl, what's on your mind?

IDIOT. I smell, I smell blood.

LOUIS. Blood? Why is everything turning red in front of my eyes? It's like they were rolling around in a sea of blood, all of them together! Ha! a red sea!

1,6. *Open field.**

LOUIS. On! and on!—On and on! Shssh, shssh, that's how the fiddles and flutes go. On and on! On and on! What's that talking down there? There—out of the earth, very softly, something. What? (*He stoops down.*) Stab! Stab! Stab the Woyzeck woman to death. Stab, stab the Woyzeck woman to death. It's hissing and moaning and thundering.

1,7. *A room.**

LOUIS *and* ANDRES.

ANDRES. Hey!
LOUIS. Andres!
ANDRES. (*Mumbles in his sleep.*)
LOUIS. Hey, Andres!
ANDRES. Well, what is it?
LOUIS. I can't keep still, I keep hearing it, the fiddling and the jumping, on and on! On and on! And then when I shut my eyes, I see flashes, and there's a big broad knife lying on a table by the window—it's in a dark alley and an old man is sitting behind the table. And the knife's always between my eyes.
ANDRES. Go to sleep, fool!

1,8. *Barracks courtyard.*

LOUIS. Didn't you hear anything?
ANDRES. He went past with a friend.
LOUIS. He said something.
ANDRES. How do you know? How shall I say it? Well, he laughed, and then he said: "What a piece! She's got thighs, and it's all so firm!"
LOUIS. (*Very coldly.*) So that's what he said? What was I dreaming about last night? Wasn't it about a knife? What foolish dreams we get.
ANDRES. Where're you going, friend?
LOUIS. To get wine for my officer.—But Andres, she was one in a million.
ANDRES. Who was?
LOUIS. Never mind. Bye.

1,9. *The* OFFICER. LOUIS.*

LOUIS. (*Alone.*) What did he say? Well, don't count your chickens.

1,10. *An inn.**

BARBER. SERGEANT.

BARBER. Oh daughter, dear daughter,
What's got into you?
You took up with coachmen
And stablemen too!

What is it that God can't do, huh? Undo what's been done, that's what. Heh heh heh!—But that's the way it is, and that's good. But just to be on the safe side. (*Sings.*)

Booze, that's my life,
Booze gives me courage.

And a decent person loves life, and a person who loves life has no courage, a virtuous person has no courage. Whoever's got courage is a dog.

SERGEANT. (*With dignity.*) You're forgetting yourself in the presence of a brave man.

BARBER. I'm not speaking politely, like the French do, and it was nice of you.—But whoever's got courage is a dog!

SERGEANT. Damn you! You broken shaving basin, you stale soapsuds! I'll make you drink your piss and swallow your razor!

BARBER. Sir, you're wronging yourself! Was I talking about you, did I say that you had courage? Sir, leave me alone! I am science. Every week I get half a florin for my scientific self—don't break me apart or I'll go hungry. I am a *spinosa pericyclyda;* I have a Latin backbone. I'm a living skeleton, all mankind studies me.—What is man? Bones! Dust, sand, dirt. What is nature? Dust, sand, dirt. But those stupid people, those stupid people. Let's be friends. If I had no courage, there wouldn't be any science. Only nature, no amputation. What is an arm, flesh, bones, veins? What is dirt? Where will it be sticking in the dirt? So should I cut my arm off? No, man is egoistic, but he hits, shoots, stabs. There, now. We must. Friends, I'm touched. Look, I wish our noses were two bottles and we could pour them down each other's throats. Oh, how beautiful the world is! Friend! My friend! The world! (*Moved.*) Look how the sun's coming out of the clouds, like a bedpan being emptied out. (*He cries.*)

1,11. *The inn.*

LOUIS *sits in front of the inn. People go out.* ANDRES.

ANDRES. What are you doing there?

LOUIS. What time is it?

ANDRES. —

LOUIS. Isn't it later than that? I thought it would go faster, and I wish it was the day after tomorrow.

ANDRES. Why?

LOUIS. Then it'd be over.

ANDRES. What?

LOUIS. Scram.

[ANDRES.] Why're you sitting there in front of the door?

LOUIS. I'm all right sitting here, and I know it, but lots of people sit in front of a door and they *don't* know it; a lot get carried out the door feet first.

[ANDRES.] Come on, let's go!

[LOUIS.] I'm all right sitting here, and I'd be even better lying here. If everybody knew what time it is, they'd get undressed and put on a clean shirt and have their coffin measured.

[ANDRES.] He's drunk.

LOUIS. What's that lying over there? It's flashing. It's always floating between my eyes. Look how it's shining. I got to have it.

1,12. *Open field.*

LOUIS. (*Lays the knife in a hole.*) Thou shalt not kill. Stay there! Got to get out of here! (*He runs off quickly.*)

1,13. *Night. Moonlight.*

ANDRES *and* LOUIS *in a bed.*

LOUIS. (*Softly.*) Andres!
ANDRES. (*Dreams.*) There! Wait!—Yes.
LOUIS. Hey, Andres!
ANDRES. Well?
LOUIS. I can't keep still! Andres.
ANDRES. You had a nightmare?
LOUIS. Something's lying out there. In the earth. They're always pointing to it. You hear that—and that? How they're knocking inside the walls? One of them just looked in at the window. Don't you hear it? I hear it all day long. On and on. Stab, stab the Woyzeck woman.
ANDRES. Lie down, Louis. You better go to the infirmary. Drink some brandy with a painkiller in it; that'll bring the fever down.

[For 1,14 to 1,21[4]: see Reconstruction, pp. 217–22.]

4. Note to Scene, 1,21: after the Clerk's words, this fragment contains the following: "*Barber. Tall, haggard, cowardly.*"

Second Draft

2,1. *Open field. The town in the distance.**

WOYZECK. ANDRES. *They are cutting branches in the bushes.*

ANDRES. (*Whistles and sings.*)

A hunter's life for me,
A hunter's always free;
Where I can hunt
That's where I'll go.

One day a rabbit I did see,
"Are you a hunter?" he asked me.
A hunter I used to be,
But shooting I can't do.

WOYZECK. Yeah, Andres, it really is—this place is haunted. Do you see that shining stripe there across the grass, where the toadstools are growing? That's where heads roll at night; once somebody picked one up, thought it was a hedgehog. Three days and two nights, and he was dead. (*Softly.*) It was the Freemasons, I figured it out.

ANDRES. It's getting dark. You're almost making me scared. (*He sings.*)

WOYZECK. (*Grabs him.*) You hear it, Andres? Do you hear it, it's moving! Next to us, under us. Let's go—the ground's swaying under our feet. The Freemasons! How they're burrowing underground! (*He drags him away.*)

ANDRES. Leave me alone! Are you crazy? Damn it!

WOYZECK. Are you a mole, are your ears full of sand? Don't you hear that terrible noise in the sky? Over the town it's all in flames! Don't look back. Look how it's shooting up, and everything's thundering.

ANDRES. You're scaring me.

WOYZECK. Don't look back. (*They hide in the bushes.*)

ANDRES. Woyzeck, I can't hear anything anymore.

WOYZECK. Quiet, all quiet, like death.

ANDRES. They're drumming. We've got to get back.

2,2. *The town.**

LOUISE.[1] MARGRET *at the window. A military patrol goes by, the* DRUM MAJOR *leading.*

LOUISE. Hey, boy! Tra-ra-ra-ra!

MARGRET. A handsome man!

LOUISE. Like a tree. (*The* DRUM MAJOR *greets them.*)

MARGRET. Say, what a friendly look you gave him, neighbor—we're not used to that from you.

LOUISE. A soldier is a handsome fellow . . .

MARGRET. Your eyes are still shining!

LOUISE. What's it to you? Why don't you take your eyes to the Jew and have them polished—maybe they'll shine enough to sell as two buttons.

MARGRET. Why, Mrs. Virgin! I'm a decent woman, but you—everybody knows you can stare through seven pairs of leather pants!

LOUISE. Bitch! (*Slams the window shut.*) Come, my boy, shall I sing you something? What do they want from us, anyway? You're only the child of a whore, and you make your mother happy with your bastard face.

> Johnny, hitch up your six horses fleet,
> Go bring them something to eat.
> From oats they will turn,
> From water they'll turn,
> Only cool wine will be fine, hooray!
> Only cool wine will be fine.
>
> Maiden, now what's to be done?
> You've got no ring, you've a son.
> Oh, why worry my head,
> I'll sing here at your bed:
> Rockabye baby, my baby are you,
> Nobody cares what I do.

1. I.e., Marie.

(*A knock at the window.*)

Is that you, Franz? Come on in.

WOYZECK. I can't. Have to go to roll call.

LOUISE. Did you cut wood for the major?

WOYZECK. Yes, Louise.

LOUISE. What's the matter with you, Franz? You look so upset.

WOYZECK. Shh! Quiet! I figured it out. The Freemasons! There was a terrible noise in the sky and everything was in flames! I'm on the track of something! Something big!

LOUISE. Fool!

WOYZECK. Don't you think so? Look around! Everything's rigid, hard, dark—something's moving behind it all. Something that we don't understand, that drives us insane, but I figured it out. I've got to go!

LOUISE. And your child?

WOYZECK. Oh, the boy! Tonight—at the carnival. I saved something up again. (*Goes off.*)

LOUISE. That man'll go crazy. He frightened me. It's eerie—I don't like to stay around when it gets dark, I think I'm going blind, I catch it from him. Usually there's a light shining in. Oh, us poor people. (*She sings.*)

Rockabye baby, on the treetop,
When the wind blows, your cradle will rock.

(*She goes off.*)

2,3. *Open square. Booths. Lights.*

OLD MAN. DANCING CHILD.

How long we live, just time will tell,
We all have got to die,
We know that very well!

———. Hey! Whee! Poor man, old man! Poor child! Young child! Cares and fairs! Hey, Louise, shall I carry you? . . . Beautiful world!

CARNIVAL BARKER. (*In front of a booth.*) Ladies and gentlemen, here is to be seen the astronomical horse and the little cannery-birds—they're favorites of all potentates of Europe and members of all learned societies. They'll tell you everything: how old you are, how many children you have, what kind of illnesses. He shoots a pistol, stands on one leg. It's all a matter of upbringing; he has merely a beastly reason, or rather a very reasonable beastliness—he's no brutish individual like a lot of people, present company excepted. Enter! The presentation will begin. The commencement of the beginning will start immediately.

Observe the progress of civilization. Everything progresses—a horse, a monkey, a cannery-bird! The monkey is already a soldier—that's not much, it's the lowest level of the human race!

———. Are you an atheist, too? I'm a dogmatic atheist.

———. Is it grotesque? I'm a friend of the grotesque. You see that? What a grotesque effect.

———. I'm a dogmatic atheist. Grotesque!

2,4. APPRENTICES.*

[AN APPRENTICE.] Brother! Forget-me-not! Friendship! I could cry a rain barrel full. Sadness! If I only had another one! I think it stinks, it smells. Why is this world so beautiful? If I close one eye and look out over my nose, then everything's red as a rose. Brandy, that's my life.

ANOTHER. He'll see everything red as a rose when a cross is looking over his nose.

[AN APPRENTICE.] It's all out of order! Why did the street-lamp cleaner forget to sweep out my eyes—it's all dark. May God go to the devil! I'm lying in my own way and have to jump over myself. What happened to my shadow? There's no safety in this stable anymore. Somebody shine the moon between my legs to see if I've still got my shadow.

Chewing up the green, green grass,
Chewing up the green, green grass
Till all the grass was go-o-ne.

Shooting star, I have to blow the noses of all the stars.

[ANOTHER.] Don't make a hole in nature.

[AN APPRENTICE.] Why did God create man? That has its reasons: what would the farmer, the shoemaker, the tailor do, if he couldn't make shoes or pants for people? Why did God give man a feeling of shame? So that the tailor can exist. Yes! Yes! So there! That's why! For that reason! Therefore! Or, on the other hand, if He hadn't done it—but in that we see His wisdom, that the animals He created would be respected by man, because mankind would otherwise have eaten up the animals. This infant, this weak, helpless creature, this infant.—Now let's piss crosswise so that a Jew will die.

Brandy, that's my life,
Brandy gives me courage.

2,5. SERGEANT. DRUM MAJOR.

SERGEANT. Hold it! Over there. Look at her! What a piece!

DRUM MAJOR. Damn! Good enough for the propagation of cavalry regiments and the breeding of drum majors!

SERGEANT. Look how she holds her head—you'd think that black hair would pull her down like a weight. And those eyes, black . . .

DRUM MAJOR. It's like looking down a well or a chimney. Come on, after her!

LOUISE. Those lights!

FRANZ. Yeah, like a big black cat with fiery eyes. Hey, what a night!

2,6. WOYZECK. DOCTOR.*

DOCTOR. What's this I saw, Woyzeck? A man of his word? You! You! You?

WOYZECK. What is it, Doctor?

DOCTOR. I saw it, Woyzeck! You pissed on the street like a dog. For that I give you three cents and board every day? The world's getting bad, very bad, bad, I say. Oh! Woyzeck, that's bad.

WOYZECK. But Doctor, if you can't help it?

DOCTOR. Can't help it, can't help it. Superstition, horrible superstition! Haven't I proved that the *musculus constrictor vesicae* is subject to the will? Woyzeck, man is free, in man individuality is exalted to freedom.—Couldn't hold it in! That's cheating, Woyzeck. Did you eat your peas already? Nothing but peas, nothing but legumes, *cruciferae*—remember that. Then next week we'll start on mutton. Don't you have to go to the toilet? Go ahead. I'm telling you to. I'm revolutionizing science. A revolution! According to yesterday's report: ten per cent urea, and ammonium chloride . . . But I saw how you pissed on the wall! I was just holding my head outside . . . Did you catch some frogs for me? Got any fish eggs? No fresh-water polyps? No hydra, *vestillae, cristatellae?* Don't bump into my microscope. I've just got the left molar of a protozoon under it. I'll blow them sky-high, all of them together. Woyzeck, no spiders' eggs, no toads? But pissing on the wall! I saw it. (*Starts kicking him.*) No, Woyzeck, I'm not getting angry; anger is unhealthy, unscientific. I am calm, perfectly calm, and I'm telling you this in all cold-bloodedness. Who on earth would get excited about a human being! A human being! Now if it were a Proteus lizard that were dying! But you shouldn't have pissed on the wall.

WOYZECK. Yes, nature, Doctor, when nature has run out.

DOCTOR. What's that when nature has run out?

WOYZECK. When nature has run out, that's when nature has run out! When the world gets so dark that you have to feel your way around it with your hands, and you think it'll dissolve like spiderwebs! That's when something is and yet isn't. When everything is dark and there's only a red glow in the west, like from a furnace. When . . . (*Paces up and down in the room.*)

DOCTOR. Man, you're tapping around with your feet like a spider.

WOYZECK. (*Stands rigidly.*) Have you seen the rings of toadstools on the ground yet? Long lines, crooked circles, figures—that's where it is! There! If only someone could read that. When the sun's standing high and bright at noon and the world seems to be going up in flames. Don't you hear anything? When the world speaks, you see, the long lines, it's like someone's talking with a terrible voice.

DOCTOR. Woyzeck! You're going to the insane asylum. You've got a beautiful obsession, a marvelous *alienatio mentis*. Look at me—now what are you supposed to do? Eat your peas, then eat your mutton, polish your rifle; you know all that. And then the obsessions. That's good, Woyzeck! You'll get a raise of one cent a week. My theory, my new theory—brave, eternally youthful. Woyzeck, I'll be immortal. Show me your pulse! I have to feel your pulse mornings and evenings.

2,7. *Street.*

CAPTAIN. DOCTOR. *The* CAPTAIN *comes panting down the street, stops, pants, looks around.*

CAPTAIN. Where to so fast, most honorable Mr. Coffin Nail?
DOCTOR. Where to so slowly, most honorable Mr. Drillprick?
CAPTAIN. Take your time, honorable tombstone.
DOCTOR. I don't waste my time like you, honorable . . .
CAPTAIN. Don't run like that, Doctor—a good man doesn't go so fast, sir, a good man. (*Pants.*) A good man. You'll run yourself to death that way. You're really frightening me.
DOCTOR. I'm in a hurry, Captain, I'm in a hurry.
CAPTAIN. Mr. Coffin Nail, you're wearing out your little legs on the pavement. Don't ride off in the air on your cane.
DOCTOR. She'll be dead in four weeks. She's in her seventh month—I've had twenty patients like that already. In four weeks—you can count on that.
CAPTAIN. Doctor, don't frighten me—people have been known to die of fright, of pure, sheer fright!
DOCTOR. In four weeks, the stupid beast. She'll be an interesting specimen. I'm telling you . . .
CAPTAIN. May you get struck by lightning! I'll hold you by the wing, I won't let you go. Dammit, four weeks? Doctor, coffin nail, shroud, I'll [live] as long as I exist—four weeks—and the people with their hats in their hands, but they'll say, he was a good man, a good man.
DOCTOR. Say, good morning, Captain. (*Swinging his hat and cane.*) Cock-a-doodle-doo! My pleasure! My pleasure! (*Holds out his hat.*) What's this, Captain? That's brain-less. Ha?
CAPTAIN. (*Makes a crease.*) What's this, Doctor? That's an in-crease! Ha-ha-ha! No harm meant. I'm a good man—but I can when I want to, Doctor, ha-ha-ha, when I want to. [WOYZECK *comes running down the street.*] Hey, Woyzeck, why are you running past me like that? Stay here, Woyzeck. You're running around like an open razor blade—you might cut someone! You're running like you had to shave a regiment of Cossacks and would be hanged by the last hair. But about those long beards—what was I going to say? Woyzeck—those long beards . . .

DOCTOR. A long beard on the chin—Pliny already speaks of it. Soldiers should be made to give them up.

CAPTAIN. (*Continues.*) Hey? What about those long beards? Say, Woyzeck, haven't you found a hair from a beard in your soup bowl yet? Hey? You understand of course, a human hair, from the beard of an engineer, a sergeant, a—a drum major? Hey, Woyzeck? But you've got a decent wife. Not like others.

WOYZECK. Yes, sir! What are you trying to say, Cap'n?

CAPTAIN. Look at the face he's making! Now, it doesn't necessarily have to be in the soup, but if you hurry around the corner, you might find one on a pair of lips—a pair of lips, Woyzeck. I know what love is, too, Woyzeck. Say! You're as white as chalk!

WOYZECK. Cap'n, I'm just a poor devil—and that's all I have in the world. Cap'n, if you're joking . . .

CAPTAIN. Joking? Me? Who do you think you are?

DOCTOR. Your pulse, Woyzeck, your pulse—short, hard, skipping, irregular.

WOYZECK. Cap'n, the earth is hot as hell—for me it's ice cold, ice cold—hell is cold, I'll bet. It can't be! God! God! It can't be!

CAPTAIN. Listen, fellow, how'd you like to be shot, how'd you like to have a couple of bullets in your head? You're looking daggers at me, but I only mean well, because you're a good man, Woyzeck, a good man.

DOCTOR. Facial muscles rigid, tense, occasionally twitching. Posture tense.

WOYZECK. I'm going. A lot is possible. A human being! A lot is possible. The weather's nice, Cap'n. Look: such a beautiful, hard, gray sky—you'd almost feel like pounding a block of wood into it and hanging yourself on it, only because of the hyphen between yes and no—yes and no. Cap'n, yes and no? Is no to blame for yes, or yes for no? I'll have to think about that. (*Goes off with long strides, first slowly, then ever faster.*)

DOCTOR. (*Races after him.*) A phenomenon, Woyzeck! A raise!

CAPTAIN. These people make me dizzy. Look at them go—that tall rascal takes off like the shadow before a spider, and the short one—he's trotting along. The tall one is lightning and the short one is thunder. Ha-ha! After them. I don't like that! A good man loves life, a good man has no courage! A scoundrel has courage! I just went to war to strengthen my love for life . . . Grotesque! Grotesque!

2,8. WOYZECK. LOUISE.*

LOUISE. Hello, Franz.

FRANZ. (*Looking at her.*) Oh, it's you! Well, well! No, I don't see anything, I should be able to see it! Louise, you're beautiful!

LOUISE. Why are you looking so strange, Franz? I'm scared.

FRANZ. What a nice street—you can get corns walking on it. But it's good to stand on the street, and good to be in society.

LOUISE. Society?

FRANZ. Lots of people go through the streets, don't they? And you can talk to anyone you want; that's none of my business! Was he standing here like this? Like this? Close to you like this? I wish I'd been him.

LOUISE. What "he"? I can't tell anybody to stay off the streets or leave their mouths at home when they go past.

FRANZ. Or their lips at home. That'd be a shame—they're so beautiful. But wasps like to sit on them.

LOUISE. And what kind of wasp stung you? You look as crazy as a cow chased by hornets.

FRANZ. Whore! (*Goes after her.*)

LOUISE. Don't you touch me, Franz! I'd rather have a knife in my body than your hand on mine. When I was ten years old, my father didn't dare touch me when I looked at him.

FRANZ. Woman!—No, it should show on you! Everyone's an abyss—you get dizzy when you look down into it. It could be! She looks like Innocence herself. Now, Innocence, you have a mark on you. Do I know it? Do I know it? Who can tell?

2,9. LOUISE *alone. Prayer.*

LOUISE. And no guile is found in his mouth. My God!

Third Draft

[See "Optional Scenes" 3,1 and 3,2 on pp. 223–24.]

Fourth Draft

[See Scenes 4,1–17 of the Reconstruction.]

Notes

Like *Danton's Death* and *Lenz, Woyzeck* is not a piece of freely invented fiction. It is assumed to be based on three case histories of impoverished former soldiers who murdered their lovers. One of the three was named Johann Christian Woyzeck, born in Leipzig in 1780, an itinerant wigmaker, barber, and engraver, who served for several years in various military regiments but who today would be classified as chronically unemployed. After returning to Leipzig in 1818, often unable to pay his rent, he began an affair with a Mrs. Woost, the widow of a surgeon. Jealous of her relationships with other men, he abused her physically and in June 1821 stabbed her to death. After his arrest, a controversy arose over his soundness of mind and his legal accountability for his act, a debate that centered on the reports published by J. C. A. Clarus, Woyzeck's medical examiner. Ultimately the crime was judged to be premeditated, appeals for clemency were denied, and on August 27, 1824, Woyzeck was beheaded in a public square filled with onlookers.

Büchner's extant letters contain no direct reference to the play. In letters written in 1836 to his brother Wilhelm and to his parents, he referred to two unfinished dramas, and just before the onset of his fatal illness he announced that *Leonce and Lena* and two other dramas would be ready for publication "in a week at most." He evidently considered *Woyzeck* to be on the verge of completion. Whereas *Leonce and Lena* and *Lenz* were published by Gutzkow soon after Büchner's death and reappeared in Ludwig Büchner's 1850 edition of his brother's works, *Woyzeck* was to remain unpublished until the 1870s. Ludwig Büchner had pronounced himself unable to decipher adequately his brother's handwriting, and he had found the content of the work to be "trivial" and "cynical." For a generation the *Woyzeck* manuscripts lay in an attic, exposed to rain, dust, and rodents, until they came into the hands of Karl Emil Franzos, a prolific Jewish novelist. His transcription was first published in the Viennese newspaper *New Free Press* in 1875, and the play was then incorporated into Franzos's complete edition of Büchner's works (1879).

Franzos rescued *Woyzeck* from almost certain oblivion, yet he was responsible for inaugurating a long tradition of *Woyzeck* falsifications. The ink on the forty-year-old manuscripts had faded considerably by the time they were rediscovered; to make them more legible, he treated them with chemicals that hastened their further deterioration. Being an author himself, he allowed his inventiveness to prevail over editorial accuracy, liberally altering and adding to the text, clarifying where he thought the play needed clarification. Büchner had not indicated a title, so, misreading the protagonist's name, Franzos provided one: "*Wozzeck:* A Fragment of a Tragedy." Although the misspelling was corrected in 1920, it survives in the title of Alban Berg's opera, which was based on Franzos's edition of the play.

The *Woyzeck* manuscripts consist of five double-pages in folio format (First and Second Drafts), one page in quarto format (Third Draft), and six double-pages in quarto format (Fourth Draft), containing groups of scenes and scene fragments, some apparently written in such haste that numerous passages are nearly illegible. The Fourth Draft is clearly a revision of earlier attempts, and it therefore must take precedence over them when one attempts to reconstruct the play without seriously violating the author's intentions. Büchner's revision begins with "Open field. The town in the distance" (4,1) and breaks off after "The barracks" (4,17). Traditionally the scenes from the First Draft beginning with "Marie with girls in front of the house door" (1,14) through "Court Clerk. Barber. Doctor. Judge" (1,21)—the "murder-complex"—are added at this point. The ending nevertheless remains inconclusive: is Woyzeck eventually arrested and brought to trial? The "Court Clerk" fragment might seem to imply this, but it is doubtful that Woyzeck and the Barber are the same person. The only certainty is that Woyzeck disappears from view after Scene 1,20, experiencing neither divine retribution, perpetual isolation, nor punishment at the hands of society.

There is general agreement about the order in which the drafts were written and the arrangement of pages within them. Using as a guide the incomplete revision and the assumption that Büchner planned to include the murder of Marie in the drama, we can roughly determine the work's genesis: Büchner first sketched out the infidelity-jealousy-murder action (First Draft), interspersed with scenes of generalized, often ironic commentary (the Carnival Barker, the Barber, the Grandmother). In retrospect, these scenes function as the middle and end of the plot. Then he added a beginning (Second Draft), in which the name "Woyzeck" is introduced for the first time, and where the protagonist is placed in confrontation with figures that constitute his social environment. The Fourth Draft is a revision of the beginning and the middle, in which some scenes were incorporated with only minor changes (e.g., 4,1 and 4,2); some were considerably altered or expanded (e.g., 4,14 and 4,16); and five were completely new (4,4–6; 4,15; 4,17). As noted in the text, Scene 4,3 consists only of the title, "Carnival booths. Lights. People," followed by one and a half blank pages. While revising, Büchner crossed out many but by no means all scenes in his earlier drafts, leaving the question unresolved as to what material might eventually have been included, had Büchner lived to complete the work. The "Synopsis" on p. 225 gives an approximate idea of the correspondences among the drafts. When examining the relationship between Scenes 2,7 and 4,9, one may wonder why Büchner omitted Woyzeck's dramatic confrontation with the Captain and the Doctor in his revision. Two reasons suggest themselves: Woyzeck seems to be somewhat out of character at the end of the scene when he speculates about the "hyphen between yes and no." More important, the Captain's taunts about Marie's infidelity appear to take Woyzeck entirely by surprise. In the Fourth Draft this would be illogical, because Woyzeck has already accused Marie of infidelity two scenes earlier. In the Second Draft, however, the equivalent scene with Marie takes place immediately *after* the Captain/Doctor/Woyzeck dialogue.

The Third Draft consists of only two scenes, and we do not know where Büchner intended to place them in his final version. Instead of incorporating them arbitrarily into the reconstruction, as numerous editors have done, we present them here as "Optional Scenes," which readers ought not overlook and which might well be performed in theatrical productions. A portion of "The Professor's courtyard" (3,1) derives from an experience of Büchner's in Giessen: one of his professors habitually brought his son to class to demonstrate that the ear muscles have become obsolete in human beings, but not in apes. His son was then obliged to stand and wiggle his ears. The second scene, "The idiot. The child. Woyzeck," would seem to take place after Woyzeck returns from the pond ("He fell in the water . . ."). But one might also argue that Karl's line, which is also a children's counting rhyme, might *anticipate* Woyzeck's search for the knife, and we are left once again without conclusive evidence of his ultimate fate.

Letters

Strassburg
1831–1833

To his parents

Strassburg, [after December 4] 1831

[. . .]* When the rumor spread that Ramorino would pass through Strassburg, the students immediately organized a march in his direction with a black flag. Finally we heard the news that Ramorino would arrive during the afternoon with Generals Schneider and Langermann. We immediately gathered in the academy, but as we attempted to march through the gate, the officer whom the government had ordered not to let us pass with our flag stationed the armed watch across our path. But we forced our way through, and three to four hundred of us assembled at the great bridge over the Rhine. The National Guard joined us. Finally Ramorino appeared, accompanied by a number of cavalry; a student makes a speech, which he answers, so does a soldier of the National Guard. The Guard surrounds his coach and pulls it, we join the head of the parade with our flag, a large musical choir precedes us. We march into town like this, accompanied by a huge crowd singing the Marseillaise and the Carmagnole; everywhere the cry resounds: "Vive la liberté! Vive Ramorino! A bas les ministres! A bas le juste milieu!" The city is illuminated, women wave their kerchiefs at their windows, and Ramorino is borne in triumph to the inn, where our

*Deletions date from Ludwig Büchner's original edition of his brother's letters (see Notes).

dows, and Ramorino is borne in triumph to the inn, where our flagbearer presents him the flag with the wish that this flag of mourning would soon be transformed into Poland's flag of freedom. Then Ramorino appears on the balcony, thanks the crowd, it cries "Vivat!"—and the comedy is complete. [. . .]

To his parents

Strassburg, December 1831

[. . .] War is very much in the air; if it comes, then there will be Babylonian confusion in Germany, and heaven knows how the song will end. *Everything* can be won or lost, but if the Russians cross the Oder, then I'll take up arms, even if I have to do so in France. May God be merciful to our Most Serene and Anointed Muttonheads; on the earth, I hope, they will no longer be granted mercy. [. . .]

To his parents

Strassburg, [before May 16] 1832

[. . .] The only matter of political interest is that the local republican coxcombs run around in red hats, and that Herr Périer got cholera, but cholera unfortunately didn't get him. [. . .]

To Edouard Reuss

Darmstadt, August 20, 1832

Dear Edouard,

I ought to begin with several dozen excuses, right? But heavens, I already did that in the enclosed letter, and I don't like to repeat such things. I therefore beg your pardon most humbly as an irresponsible delinquent. I expect that you will accept this paper olive branch and flag of peace without further preliminaries and won't quarrel with me any longer and won't keep me waiting for three full weeks just because I kept you waiting that long. I'm really happy that this scrap of paper will go to a place that has become my second hometown, and if I die as a princely biped, longimanus and omnivore, I'd bequeath it a chamber of my heart along with the rest of my Most Serene Corpse, whereas I would probably bequeath the other chamber to the house of my fathers, but only to that, for alas! I poor crossbearer am sitting *first* in the dear Holy German Empire, *second* in the Grandduchy of Hesse, *third* in the capital city of Darmstadt, and finally I'm still sitting in the midst of my family, but unfortunately I have not become patriarchal enough to forget in this bosom of Abraham the other three classifications.

The first includes the Sect of the Navel-Contemplators, which is of course to be distinguished from the old sect only in that it no longer thinks of God when contemplating the navel but of the navel when contemplating God. The second, a subcategory, includes a section of the part where navel-and-stomach-worship is performed as constitutionally enlightened liberalism. The third includes the ordained clerics and its monastic garb is courtly livery and its coat of arms is the Civilian Order of Merit of the House of Hesse, etc.

You can imagine how comfortable that makes me feel, but I adapt to the situation and have become such a decent, upright, civilized young man that I could have tea with a minister, sit on the sofa with his wife and dance a gavotte with his daughter. We're in the nineteenth century—think of what that means!

Oh, dear Edouard, write to me soon so that I receive at least something from Strassburg. I do have parents and siblings here, but all my friends are gone and I'm almost totally isolated. I was happy at first, but I can't stand the air here—it's as repulsive to me as when I left. I'm complaining to you while you probably want to hear something sensible from me, but it's impossible to write anything like that either about or in Darmstadt—nor has it ever been. Only this: your requests have been met, Zimmermann's son is still the editor of the church newspaper, but it's said he'll share the duties with Bretschneider, and a cleric from Mainz, whose name I've forgotten, will take Zimmermann's place here. This may interest you, but me damned little. Farewell, write soon, best regards to your aunt, to Pauline, and Madame Bauer.

from your G. Büchner

To August Stöber

Darmstadt, August 24, 1832

Dear brothers,

Although this is addressed only to one of you, it's for both; but look first at the enclosure, for my letter is only the shell and acts as wrapping paper. When you've read the other paper you'll know that it's a matter of no less than the Muse of German Poetry. Only the future will show whether you will act as midwives or grave-diggers. You are requested to help revive the corpse with your poetic house-and-field dispensary. Best of all, one should try to warm the corpse in an oven, because that's the only work of art the dear German folk knows how to build and enjoy! But jokes aside, I urge you to consider this seriously; if those who have promised to help keep their word, something worthwhile will be accomplished. Without trying to flatter you, I know that you have much to offer. I know the editors personally—Künzel is a theology student, Metz runs a bookstore, both very well-educated young people. The Zimmermanns are twins and are studying in Heidelberg, they're among my best and oldest friends. One of them has exceptional poetic talent. Please address your answer to me; I hope it will include some friendly words for me. I left you only three weeks ago, but I could already write you some epistolas ex ponto! Oh, if only I were sitting with you again in the Drescher! Best regards to the noble "Eugenides," namely Boeckel and Baum.

Farewell!

Your G. Büchner

To Adolph Stöber

Strassburg, November 3, 1832

Dear Adolph,

My greetings come to you this time only in a few short lines. I've just come from the deathly miasma and the Golgotha where I now cross myself again daily for several hours, and after all the cold breasts and dead hearts I encountered there, I was refreshed again by your live, warm one, against which you pressed me over the few miles that separate our cadavers. The dragon you mentioned is certainly not so dangerous—we would be poor wretches indeed if our arms could not reach across those thirty hours. I hope to see you when spring comes. I've been back here for a week; I despise the damp, cold German-Dutch climate, I prefer the sultry French air before the thunderstorm.

Farewell,

Your G. Büchner

To his parents

Strassburg, December 1832

[. . .] I almost forgot to say that the place is under a state of siege (because of the unrest in Holland). Cannons constantly rattle by under my window, troops drill on the open squares, and artillery is being mounted on the city walls. I have no more time for a political treatise, it wouldn't be worth the effort, the whole thing is only a comedy. The king and the legislatures rule, and the people applaud and pay. [. . .]

To his parents

Strassburg, January 1833

[. . .] At Christmas I went to the cathedral at four in the morning for the early mass. The gloomy vaults with their columns, the rose window, the stained glass, and the kneeling masses were only partly lit by the lamps. The singing of the invisible choir seemed to be floating over the chancel and the altar, answering the full tones of the powerful organ. I'm not Catholic and I care little about the ringing and kneeling of the multicolored priests, but the singing alone impressed me more than the stale, repetitious cliches of most of our clerics, who year after year on Christmas day can hardly say anything more sensible than: the Lord God was truly a clever man to allow Christ to be born just at this time.

To his parents

Strassburg, April 5, 1833

Today I received your letter with the news from Frankfurt. My opinion is this: if anything can help in these times, it is *violence.* We know what to expect from our princes. All they have granted us has been forced from them by necessity. And even their concessions were thrown at our feet like a favor we had begged for, like a wretched child's toy, to make that eternal monkey, the German folk, forget its too tightly wrapped swaddling clothes. Only a German could indulge in the absurdity of playing soldier with a tin rifle and a wooden sword. Our legislatures are a satire against good sense; we could continue like this for another century, and the people would still end up paying more for their representatives' beautiful speeches than did the Roman emperor who gave his court poet twenty thousand florins for two broken verses. Young people are accused of using violence. But aren't we in an eternal state of violence? Because we were born and raised in a prison, we no longer realize that we're trapped in a hole with fettered hands and feet and with gags in our mouths. What do you call a *lawful state?* A law that transforms the great masses of citizens into toiling cattle in order to satisfy the unnatural needs of an unimportant and decadent minority? Supported by raw military might and by the stupid conniving of its agents, this law is *eternal, brute force,* insulting justice and good sense, and I will fight *tooth and nail* against it wherever I can. If I do not take part in whatever has happened or might happen, I do so neither out of disapproval nor out of fear, but only because at the present time I regard any revolutionary movement as a futile undertaking, and I do not share the delusion of those who see in the Germans a people ready to fight for its rights. This foolish idea led to the events in Frankfurt, and the error was dearly paid for. Error is no sin, incidentally, and the indifference of the Germans really thwarts every plan. I deeply pity the unfortunate ones. Might any of my friends have been involved in the incident? [. . .]

To his parents

[Strassburg, spring 1833]

[. . .] You needn't worry about me, I won't go to Freiburg, and like last year I won't take part in any political meetings. [. . .]

To his parents

Strassburg, [after May 27], 1833

[. . .] We just heard the news that in Neustadt a gang of soldiers attacked a peaceful and unarmed assembly and indiscriminately cut down several people. Similar things are said to have happened in the rest of the province. The liberal party can't really complain about such things; it's an eye for an eye, violence for violence. It remains to be seen who is the stronger. — If on a clear day recently you had been able to see as far as the Strassburg Cathedral, you would have found me sitting with a longhaired, bearded young man. He had a red beret on his head, a cashmere shawl around his neck, a short German coat on his cadaverous frame, on his vest was embroidered the name "Rousseau," on his legs tight pants with straps, a fashionable cane in his hand. You can see that the caricature is assembled from various centuries and parts of the world: Asia around his neck, Germany on his body, France on his legs, 1400 on his head, and 1833 in his hand. He is a cosmopolitan—no, he is more: a Saint-Simonist! You may think I was talking to a fool, but you're wrong. He is a likable young man who has traveled much. Without his ghastly costume I would never have guessed him to be a Saint-Simonist, if he hadn't spoken of "la femme" in Germany. The Saint-Simonists believe man and woman to be equal, they have equal *political* rights. They have their "père," their founder Saint-Simon, but in fairness they also ought to have a "mère." She remains to be found, however, and they have set out like Saul after his father's asses, with the difference that—for the world has truly made great progress in the nineteenth century—this time the asses are searching for Saul. Rousseau with one of his companions (neither understand a word of German) wanted to search for "la femme" in Germany, but the border guards with intolerable stupidity turned them back. I told him that he hadn't missed much with German women, the women, however, had missed something with him. He would have been bored by some, he would have laughed at others. Now he'll remain in Strassburg; he puts his hands in his pocket and preaches work to the people, is well paid for his talents and "marche vers les femmes," as he calls it. He is truly to be envied, has the most comfortable life under the sun, and out of sheer laziness I would like to become a Saint-Simonist, for they'd have to pay me suitably for my talents. [. . .]

To his parents

Strassburg, June 1833

[. . .] I shall always act according to my principles, but I have recently learned that only the essential needs of the masses can bring about change, that all activity and shouting by *individuals* is vain folly. They write but are not read; they cry out but are not heard; they act but are not helped.—You can imagine that I won't become involved in clandestine politics and revolutionary children's pranks in Giessen.

To his parents (trip to the Vosges)

Strassburg, July 8, 1833

We wandered across the peaks and valleys of the charming countryside. On the second day we reached the so-called White and Black Lakes on a plain over three thousand feet high. There are two dark pools in a deep gorge under rock walls about five hundred feet high. The White Lake lies on the summit. At our feet lay the dark, still water. Beyond the closest peaks we saw toward the east the Rhine plain and the Black Forest, toward the west and northwest the mountains of Lorraine; in the south hung gloomy rainclouds, the air was still. Suddenly the storm drove the clouds up the Rhine plain, lightning flashed on our left, and under the ragged clouds over the dark Jura mountains, the alpine glaciers glowed in the evening sun. The third day granted us the same glorious sight, for we climbed the nearly five-thousand-foot-high Bölgen, the highest point in the Vosges range. One can survey the Rhine from Basel to Strassburg, the plain behind Lorraine to the mountains of the Champagne, the beginning of the former Franche-Comté, the Jura and the Swiss Alps from Rigi to the most distant Savoy Alps. The sun had almost set, the Alps like a pale afterglow over the darkened earth. We spent the night in a herdsmen's hut a small distance from the summit. The herdsmen have a hundred cows and nearly ninety heifers and bulls on the high slopes. At sunrise the sky was rather misty; the sun cast a red glow over the landscape. The clouds seemed to plunge over the Black Forest and the Jura like a foaming waterfall; only the Alps stood clear, like a glistening Milky Way.

Imagine over the dark chain of the Jura and over the clouds in the south, as far as the eye could see, a huge, shimmering wall of ice, pierced only at the top by the crags and peaks of individual mountains. We descended from the Bölgen down toward the right into the so-called Amarine valley, the final main valley of the Vosges. We went up the valley. It ends in a beautiful meadow in the wild mountain range. A good alpine road led us over the mountains toward Lorraine to the sources of the Mosel River. We followed its course for a while, then turned north and returned past several points of interest back to Strassburg.

For the last several days there has been some unrest here. A representative from the ministry, Herr Saglio, returned a few days ago from Paris. No one paid any attention to him. Bankrupt honesty is too common nowadays that a people's representative, who wears his frock coat on his back like a pillory, could attract anyone's interest. The police were however of a contrary opinion and placed a significant number of soldiers on the parade grounds and in front of Herr Saglio's house. This finally attracted the masses on the second or third day; last night and the night before there was some commotion in front of the house. The prefect and the mayor thought this to be a good opportunity to earn a medal, they ordered the troops to march out, clear the streets, to stab people with bayonets and club them with rifles, to arrest them, post proclamations, etc.

To Edouard Reuss

Darmstadt, August 31, 1833

Dear Edouard,

Shall I excuse my slothful hand? It's not necessary for my memory; I hardly ever worried about it, but now it's playing the ruminant and nourishes me with remembrances of happy days. I could continue in this style of lamentation in order to give you an idea of my current way of life, if you hadn't already had a taste of Darmstadt. I found my family in the narrower sense to be in the best of health, and my mother is recovering visibly from her serious illness. To see parents and siblings again was a great joy, but that doesn't compensate for the remaining awful, colossal, boring surroundings. There is something grand about this desert, this Sahara Desert in all heads and hearts. I know little about the other relatives. After my obligatory inaugural chatter I'll deliver toward the end of October my official farewell chatter, when I leave for Giessen. So much then for familial emotions. I expect little of Giessen; my friends are either in exile or in jail. Concerning me there's nothing to fear; I have been constitutionally, liberally enlightened since I know that the thousand-year Reich began with the constitutional era. Our legislature is proof of it, the question of its continuing existence has remained undecided for eight months. A human being needs at most an hour to be born (whereby civilization and enlightenment has not progressed as far as, for example, the Indians: ten minutes); a German legislature needs 5,760 days; a human lives sixty years, a legislature *41,272*. Oh, Lord! I can't tell you anything about its physiognomy yet, since it is not yet certain whether a child is born headfirst or assfirst.

But it will probably retain its family characteristics and thus resemble its French mama.

Considering our manner of correspondence, I hardly expect to receive a reply soon, but you could make an exception for me; such a complete separation from Strassburg pains me. I wrote to Boeckel, but no reply. Greet him for me and tell him he should answer soon and send me Goupil's thesis. I received the other one and thank him for it. Is Stöber in Strassburg? Best regards to him and to the other friends. And Wulfes? If he is still with you, then tell him I hope to see him here if his travels bring him into our area. You won't have forgotten me just because a month has passed without letters. I beg you and hope for a speedy reply.

Give my best regards to your mother, sister, and aunt, and tell them that the moments spent in their company belong to the happiest of my life. Farewell, your Georg.

Giessen and Darmstadt 1833–1835

To his parents

Giessen, November 1, 1833

[. . .] Yesterday two more students were arrested, the little Stamm and Gross. [. . .]

To his parents

Giessen, November 19, 1833

[. . .] Yesterday I was at the banquet in honor of the returning representatives. Nearly two hundred people, including Balser and Vogt. A few loyal toasts to get one's courage up, then the Polish hymn and the Marseillaise were sung, and a "vivat!" was shouted for those imprisoned in Friedberg. These people will go through fire—as long as it comes from a burning punch bowl! [. . .]

To August Stöber

Darmstadt, December 9, 1833

Dear August,

I write not knowing where this letter will reach you. I'm quite sure that Lambossy wrote me that you usually stay in Oberbrunn. Künzel said the same, having received from your father an answer to a letter addressed to you. You're the last to get a letter from me, because you're the last person I want to torment with my scowling face, and I'm always assured of your sympathy. I wrote often, perhaps you saw my letters; I lamented over myself and scoffed at others—both indicate to you how badly I felt. I didn't want to drive you into the hospital too, and so I remained silent. You may decide whether the memory of two happy years and the longing for all that made them happy or whether the repulsive circumstances in which I'm now living put me into this wretched mood. I think it's both. Everything is so narrow and small here. Nature and people, the pettiest surroundings, which don't interest me for a moment. At the end of October I went from here to Giessen. I spent five weeks there, half in the dirt and half in bed. I got an attack of meningitis; the illness was suppressed in its nascent state, yet I was forced to return to Darmstadt in order to recover fully there. I expect to stay here until the New Year and leave for Giessen again on January 5th or 6th.

A letter from you would make me very happy, and one doesn't refuse a convalescent anything, right? Since I last reached out my hands to you through the door of the coach on a Wednesday evening five months ago, I feel as if my hands had broken off, and I think we press each other's hands all the more firmly the less often we extend them to each other. I left three excellent friends in Giessen, and now I'm all alone.

Dr. H. K. is still here, to be sure, but I'm sick and tired of his aesthetic blathering; he has tried out all sorts of poetic obstetric chairs, all he can do now, I think, is to appeal for an emergency baptism from the critic in the evening paper.

I'm throwing myself with all my might into philosophy, the technical language is atrocious, for human affairs I think one should find human expressions; but that doesn't bother me, I laugh about my folly and tell myself that basically I'm doing nothing but cracking hollow nuts. But one has to choose an ass to ride under the sun, and so in God's name I'm saddling mine up; I'm not worried about fodder, there won't be a shortage of thistleheads, as long as the book printing business thrives. Farewell, good fellow. Greet our friends from me, then it will happen twice, for I've also asked Boeckel to do it.

The political situation could drive me insane. The poor people patiently draw the cart upon which the princes and the liberals play their comedy of apes. Every night I pray to the hangman's rope and to the lampposts.

What do Viktor and Scherb write?

And Adolph—is he back in Metz? I'll soon send you a few lines for him.

To his parents

Giessen, February 1834

[. . .] *I scorn no one,* least of all for his intellect or his education, for it lies in no one's power not to become an idiot or a criminal, because in similar circumstances we would all be equal and because the circumstances lie outside ourselves. *Intellect* is in fact only a very small part of our mental self, and education is only an incidental form of it. Whoever accuses me of such scorn maintains that I would kick a man because he wears a shabby coat. This kind of brutality, which one would never be considered capable of in the physical sense, is here transposed into the sphere of the mind, where it is all the more base. I can call someone an idiot without *scorning* him for that; idiocy belongs to the general characteristics of human nature. I can't change their character, but no one can keep me from calling everything that exists by its rightful name or from avoiding whatever I don't like. To offend someone is cruel, but to seek him out or avoid him is up to me. *That* explains my behavior toward old friends; I offended no one and spared myself much boredom. If they call me arrogant when I show a dislike for their entertainments or occupations, that's unjust; I would never think of reproaching anyone else for this reason. People call me a *scoffer.* That's true, I often laugh; but I do not laugh *about* a human being but *because* he is a human being, which he cannot help, and I thereby laugh about myself, for I share his fate. People call that ridicule; they do not tolerate it if one acts like a fool and talks to them familiarly. They are arrogant scorners and scoffers because they search for folly only *outside themselves.* I have in truth another kind of ridicule, but its origin is not contempt but hatred. Hatred is as acceptable as love, and I direct my hate in fullest measure against those *who scorn others.* There is a great number of them, endowed with an absurd superficiality called education or with that dead stuff, learning, who sacrifice the great masses of their fellow men to their scornful egotism. Aristocratic elitism is the most despicable contempt for the holy spirit in human nature. Against this contempt I turn its own weapons: arrogance against arrogance, ridicule against ridicule. — You had better consult my shoeshine-boy about me: my arrogance and contempt of those lacking intelligence or education would find their best subject there. I beg you, ask him sometime . . . I assume you don't consider me capable of the absurdity of condescension. I still hope that I have looked more often with pity at suffering, oppressed beings than I have said bitter words to cold, aristocratic hearts. [. . .]

To Wilhelmine Jaeglé

[Giessen, February 1834]

[. . .] I'm thirsting for a letter. I'm alone, like in a grave; when will your hand awaken me? My friends are abandoning me, we're screaming into each other's ears like deaf men; I wish we were mute, then we could only look at each other, and nowadays I can hardly stare at someone without tears coming to my eyes. Such continual watering of the eyes often results from staring. People call me crazy for saying that in six weeks I would arise from the dead but would first ascend to heaven, namely in the mail coach. Farewell, dear heart, and don't abandon me. Grief is your rival, I'm lying in its lap all day; poor soul, I believe you're in the same state. [. . .]

To Wilhelmine Jaeglé

[Giessen, around March 10, 1834]

[. . .] The first bright moment in a week. Incessant headaches and fever, barely a few hours of inadequate rest. I don't get to bed before two A.M., and then constant sudden awakenings, a sea of thoughts that consume my senses. My silence torments you as it does me, but I couldn't control myself. Dear, dear heart, do you forgive me? I've just come in from outside. A single, sustained tone from a thousand larks' throats resounds through the sultry summer air, heavy clouds wander over the earth, the deep roar of the forest sounds like their melodious footsteps. The spring air dissolved my paralysis. I was afraid of myself. The feeling of having died was always around me. Everyone had a Hippocratic face, with glazed eyes and waxen cheeks, and when the whole machine began to drone, the limbs twitched, the voice grated, and I heard the organ's song warbling endlessly and saw the little cylinders and gears jumping and turning in the organ-box—I cursed the concert, the instrument, the melody and—oh, we poor wailing musicians, is our groaning on the rack only meant to pierce through the clouds, resounding higher and higher, and finally to die away as a melodic breath in heavenly ears? Are we caged in the blazing belly of Perillus's bull as sacrificial victims, whose death-cries sound like the ecstatic shouts of the divine animal being consumed by the flames? I'm not blaspheming. But human beings blaspheme. Yet I'm being punished, I'm afraid of my own voice—and of my mirror. I could have sat for a portrait by Herr Callot-Hoffmann, right, my dear? For modelling I could have gotten travel money. I do believe I'm starting to become interesting.

The vacation begins two weeks from tomorrow; if I'm refused permission, I'll go secretly, I owe it to myself to put an end to an intolerable situation. My mental faculties are completely worn out. To work is impossible; I'm overcome by gloomy brooding, which hardly allows me a single bright thought. Everything eats away within me; if only I had an outlet for my inner self, but I have no scream for my pain, no shout for my joy, no harmony for my bliss. This inability to speak is my perdition. I've told you a thousand times: don't read my letters—cold, dull words! If only I could pour one full tone over you—I'm dragging you instead into my desolate aberrations. Now you're sitting in a dark room in tears, soon I'll join you. For two weeks your portrait has been constantly before me, I see you in every dream. Your shadow floats always before me, like a flash of light when one has looked into the sun. I'm thirsting for a blissful feeling—I'll have that soon, soon with you.

To Wilhelmine Jaeglé

[Giessen, after March 10, 1834]

There's no mountain here with an open view. Hill after hill and broad valleys, everywhere a hollow mediocrity; I can't get used to this landscape, and the city is abominable. Spring is here, I can always replace your sprig of violets, it's immortal like the Lama. Dear child, what's the good city of Strassburg doing? All sorts of things are happening there, and you don't say a word. Je baise le petites mains, en goûtant les souvenirs doux de Strasbourg.

"Prouve-moi que tu m'aimes encore beaucoup en me donnant bientôt des nouvelles." And I kept you waiting! Every moment for the last few days I pick up my pen, but I couldn't possibly write a single word. I studied the history of the Revolution. I felt as if I were crushed under the terrible fatalism of history. I find in human nature a horrifying sameness, in the human condition an inescapable force, granted to all and to no one. The individual merely foam on the waves, greatness sheer chance, the mastery of genius a puppet play, a ludicrous struggle against an iron law: to recognize it is our utmost achievement, to control it is impossible. I no longer intend to bow down before the parade horses and pillars of history. I accustomed myself to the sight of blood. But I am no guillotine blade. The word *must* is one of the curses with which man has been baptized. The dictum, "It must needs be that offenses come; but woe to that man by whom the offense cometh"—is terrifying. What is it within us that lies, murders, steals? I no longer care to pursue the thought. If only I could lay this cold and martyred heart on your breast! B. will have reassured you about my condition, I wrote him. I curse my health. I was ablaze, fever covered me with kisses and embraced me like a lover's arm. Darkness billowed over me, my heart swelled in infinite longing, stars pierced through the gloom, and hands and lips bent down. And now? And what else? I don't even have the ecstasy of pain and longing. Since I crossed the Rhine, I seem to be dead inside, not a single feeling comes to the surface. I'm an automaton; my soul has been removed. Easter is still my only solace; I have relatives near Landau, their invitation and permission to visit them. I've made the journey a thousand times already and won't get tired. — You ask me: do you long for me? Do you call it longing if a person can live only for one thing and is torn from it and then has nothing but the feeling of one's misery? Please send me an answer. Are my lips so cold? [. . .] This letter is a hodgepodge: I'll console you with another.

To his parents

Giessen, March 19, 1834

[. . .] More important is the inquiry concerning the fraternities; at least thirty students are threatened with expulsion. I wanted to testify that these conspirators were harmless. But the government must have something to do! They thank their lucky stars when a few children slide on the ice or swing on chains! — Those jailed in Friedberg are free, except for four. [. . .]

To Wilhelmine Jaeglé

[Giessen, March 1834]

[. . .] I'd be disconsolate, my poor child, if I didn't know what could cure you. Now I'm writing daily, just yesterday I began a letter to you. I almost feel like going directly to Strassburg, instead of to Darmstadt. If your indisposition takes a turn for the worse, I'll be there in a moment. But what kind of thoughts are these? They're inconceivable to me. — My face is like an Easter egg, which joy dots with red. But my writing is abysmal, it will harm your eyes, that will increase the fever. But no, I don't believe it, these are just the aftereffects of the old gnawing pain; the mild spring breeze kisses old and hectic people dead; your pain is old and emaciated, it will die, that's all, and you think you'll die along with it. Don't you see the new bright day? Don't you hear my footsteps coming back to you again? Look, I'm sending you kisses, snowdrops, primroses, violets—the earth's first shy glances into the flaming eye of the young sun-god. For half the day I sit in seclusion with your picture and speak to you. Yesterday morning I promised you flowers; here they are. What will you give me for that? How do you like my bedlam? When I want to do something serious, I feel like Punch in a comedy; when he tries to draw his sword, it's a rabbit's tail. [. . .]

I wish I had remained silent. An indescribable fear is coming over me. Write immediately, but for heaven's sake not if it strains you. You spoke to me about a cure; dear heart, it's been on the tip of my tongue for a long time. I did like our quiet secret—but tell your father everything—but with two conditions: *silence,* even around the closest relatives. I don't like to hear pots rattling behind every kiss, nor having to make a father-of-the-family face before various aunts. And: don't write to my parents before I do. I'll leave everything to you, do whatever comforts you. What can I say, except that I love you; what can I promise, except that which the word love already contains—fidelity? But can I be the so-called provider? A student for two more years; a stormy life is a certainty, perhaps soon on foreign soil!

In conclusion I come to you and sing you an old lullaby:

It's certain why she pined away:
She suffered from abandoned love.
In her small chamber high above
Her memories plagued her day by
  day;
Beside her cupboard near the door
He stood before her, evermore;
When sleep reclaimed her spirits, then
He came to her, again, again.

And then:

Forever does she feel the smart:
She sees an image on her wall
Of one who came one day to call,
And she, a child, lost her heart.
His face is almost faded now
But not the power of his vow;
The pains that hours of bliss have stilled,
The dreams so wondrously fulfilled—
Ah, pleasures that we wish would last,
But none of us can hold them fast.

To Wilhelmine Jaeglé

Giessen, March 1834

[. . .] I'll go directly from here to Strassburg without stopping at Darmstadt; I would have run into difficulties there, and my trip might have been postponed until the end of the vacation. I'm writing to you once more before that, though, otherwise I couldn't bear my impatience; this letter is in any case as boring as a calling card in an elegant house: Mr. Studiosus Büchner. That's all! How I'm shrivelling up here, my *awareness* almost makes me succumb; otherwise it wouldn't matter much. How can one possibly feel sorry for those who are insensitive or feebleminded? But what do you say to this invalid? I personally can't stand those people on half-pay. Nous ferons un peu de romantique, pour nous tenir à la hauteur du siècle; et puis me faudra-t-il du fer à cheval pour faire de l'impression à un coeur de femme? Aujourd'hui on a le système nerveux un peu robuste. Adieu.

To his parents

[Strassburg, April 1834]

[. . .] [In Giessen] I was outwardly calm, yet I was in a deep depression; I felt constricted by the political situation; I was ashamed to be a slave among slaves, at the mercy of a moldering race of princes and of a groveling civil-servant aristocracy. In Giessen I came into the vilest circumstances, worry and disgust have made me sick.

To his parents

Giessen, May 25, 1834

[. . .] The goings-on among the fraternity brothers concern me little; yesterday evening some of them were beaten up by the townspeople. Someone yelled "*Bursch* come out!" But no one appeared except some members of two fraternities, who however had to call the university magistrate to save themselves from the cobbler and tailor apprentices. The magistrate was drunk and cursed at the citizens; I was surprised that they didn't beat *him* up. The funniest thing is that the apprentices are liberal and therefore went after the loyalist fraternities. This is to be repeated this evening, there are rumors about a demonstration. I hope the brothers get beaten up again; *we're* supporting the citizens and are staying in town. [. . .]

To his parents

Giessen, July 2, 1834

[. . .] What is being said about Schulz's sentencing? I'm not surprised, it smells like a government plot. A propos, have you heard the funny story about Police Commissioner [. . .]? This fine Columbus was sent to discover a secret printing press in a cabinetmaker's house in X. . . . He surrounds the house, forces his way in. "My good man, it's all over, just show me the press." The man takes him to the winepress. "No! The press! The press!" The man doesn't understand him, and the commissioner ventures into the basement. It's dark. "Give me a light!" "If you want it, you'll have to buy it." But the commissioner spares the state unnecessary expenses. He runs like Baron von Münchhausen against a beam, fire flashes from the bridge of his nose, blood flows, he pays no attention and finds nothing. Our dear Grand Duke will make a nose-holder for him out of a Civil Order of Merit. [. . .]

To his parents

Frankfurt, August 3, 1834

[. . .] I'm using every excuse to free myself from my shackles. On Friday evening I left Giessen; I chose to go at night because of the great heat, and so I walked in the most pleasant coolness under a bright starry sky, lightning flashed constantly at the distant horizon. Partly on foot, partly traveling with mail carriers and other riffraff, I covered most of the distance during the night. I rested several times along the way. Toward noon I was in Offenbach. I made this small detour because it's easier to enter the city from this side without being stopped. There wasn't enough time to get the necessary papers. [. . .]

To his parents

Giessen, August 5, 1834

[. . .] I thought I had told you that Minnigerode was arrested a half hour before my departure; he was taken to Friedberg. I don't understand the reason for his arrest. It occurred to our clever university magistrate to suspect a connection between my trip and Minnigerode's arrest. When I arrived here I found my cabinet *sealed,* and I was told that my papers had been searched. Upon my demand the seal was immediately removed and my papers (nothing but letters from you and from my friends) were returned to me, only a few letters in French from W[ilhelmine], Muston, L[ambossy], and B[oeckel] were retained, probably because the officials had to hire a language teacher in order to read them. I am outraged by such behavior, it makes me sick to think of my most sacred secrets in the hands of these foul people. And all this—do you know what for? Because I left on the same day that Minnigerode was arrested. For the sake of a vague suspicion, my most sacred rights were violated, and all they wanted from me was to account for my journey!!! Of course I could do that with the greatest of ease; I have letters from B. that confirm every word I spoke, and there's not a line in my papers that could compromise me. You needn't worry about a thing. I'm a free man, and they couldn't possibly find a reason to arrest me. It's just that I'm deeply outraged about these legal procedures; on suspicion of a possible suspicion they break into the most sacred family secrets. The university court simply *asked* me about my whereabouts during the last three days, and to gain information on that they *break* into my desk on the second day of my absence and seize my papers! I'll talk to some legal experts and find out whether the law will allow me redress for such a violation! [. . .]

To his parents

Giessen, August 8, 1834

[. . .] I'm going about my business as usual, I wasn't interrogated further. They found nothing suspicious; however, the French letters don't appear to have been deciphered yet; Mr. University Magistrate surely has to take some French lessons first. They haven't been returned to me yet. [. . .] I already went to the court of appeals and asked for protection against the university magistrate's arbitrary actions. I'm eagerly awaiting their answer. I can't bring myself to renounce the compensation that is duly mine. Violating my most sacred rights, breaking into all of my secrets, laying hands on papers that I consider holy relics—this enrages me too greatly to prevent me from using any means to take revenge on the one responsible for this act of violence. I nearly killed the university magistrate with the politest sarcasm. When I returned to find myself barred from my room and my desk sealed, I went to him and in the presence of several people, I said coolly with the greatest politeness: I had heard that in my absence he had *honored* my room with a visit, I have come to ask him for the reason for his gracious visit, etc. It's too bad that I didn't come after lunch; even so, he almost blew up and had to respond to this biting irony with the greatest politeness. The law states that only in case of a *very strong* suspicion, in fact a suspicion that is already half proven, could a house be searched. You can see how the law is being interpreted here. A suspicion, least of all a strong one, cannot be under consideration, or else I would be arrested; while I'm here I could prevent any investigation with statements that confirm my own, and so on. The upshot is that I have not been compromised in any way and that my room was searched only because I don't look unkempt nor slavish enough not to be considered a demagogue. To endure in silence such an act of violence would make the government an accessory; it would declare that legal guarantees no longer exist, that there is no recompense for violated rights. I don't wish to subject our government to such a gross insult.

We know nothing about Minnigerode; the rumor about Offenbach is in any case a pure fabrication; that I was there too can compromise me no more than any other traveller [. . .]. If I'm to be arrested, as my papers were searched, without the required legal justification, then in God's name! I can do as little about it and am as guiltless as if I were detained, robbed, or murdered by a horde of bandits. This is brute force, to which one must succumb if one isn't strong enough to resist; no one can be blamed for weakness. [. . .]

To his parents

Giessen, end of August 1834

Almost three weeks have passed since the house search, and I still haven't received any notification whatsoever about it. The interrogation before the university magistrate on the first day has nothing to do with it; there is no *legal* connection; Mr. Georgi as *university magistrate* only demanded from me as a *student* that I account for my journey, while he ordered the house search as *state commissioner*. You can see how far *legal anarchy* has spread. If I'm not mistaken, I forgot to mention the important circumstance that the house search was carried out even without the three legally prescribed witnesses, and it therefore resembles a burglary all the more. The violation of our family secrets is in any case a more significant theft than stealing a few coins. Breaking in *in my absence* is likewise illegal; they were entitled only to seal my door, and only *then* to undertake a house search *in my absence* if I did not respond to a *subsequent subpoena*. Thus *three violations of the law* took place: a house search *without strong suspicion* (as I said, I haven't been interrogated yet, and three weeks have passed), a house search *without witnesses*, and finally a house search on the third day of my absence *without prior subpoena*.

My application to the court of appeals was basically superfluous, because the university magistrate as *state commissioner* is not subject to it. I took this step only to avoid being overhasty; I placed myself under its protection, I placed my grievance in its hands. Because of its position it *had* to take on my case, but the people are somewhat timid; I'm convinced that they'll refer me to another department. I'm awaiting their decision. . . . The circumstances are so simple and clear that I'll either receive full compensation or they'll have to state publicly that the laws have been suspended and that in their place rules brute force, against which there is no appeal other than alarm bells and cobblestones. [. . .]

To Sauerländer

Darmstadt, February 21, 1835

Most honored Sir:

I am honored to send you a manuscript along with this letter. It is an attempted dramatization of recent history. If you should be inclined to undertake its publication, then I beg you to inform me as soon as possible, or else to return the manuscript to the Heyer Bookshop in this city.

I would be much obliged if you would send the enclosed letter and the drama to Mr. Karl Gutzkow for his perusal.

Please be so good as to address any reply to me to: Frau State Councillor Reuss in Darmstadt. Various circumstances cause me to wish urgently that an answer would be forthcoming as quickly as possible.

I remain your obedient and faithful servant

G. Büchner

To Gutzkow

[Darmstadt, February 21, 1835]

Dear Sir:

You may have possibly observed, or in more unfortunate circumstances experienced, that a degree of misery exists that silences all deference and feeling. There are people who say that in this case one ought rather starve oneself to death, but I could find a refutation of this on the street: a captain, recently gone blind, explains that he would shoot himself if only he were not compelled to remain alive so that his salary could support his family. That is horrifying. You will realize that similar circumstances may exist which restrain one from throwing one's body from the wreck of this world into the water like an anchor, and you will therefore not be surprised that I open your door, step into your room, place a manuscript on your chest, and ask for alms. I beg you to read the manuscript as quickly as possible, to recommend it to Mr. Sauerländer if your conscience as a critic should allow you to do so, and to answer immediately.

Concerning the work itself, I can only say that unfortunate circumstances compelled me to write it in about five weeks. I say this to influence your judgment about the author, not about the drama itself. I don't know myself what I should do with it; I only know that I have every reason to blush before history, but I console myself with the thought that all poets, excepting Shakespeare, stand before history and nature like schoolboys.

I repeat my plea for a speedy response. In the event of a favorable reaction, a few lines from your hand—if they reach me before next Wednesday—would save an unfortunate man from a very sorry situation.

If the tone of this letter should disturb you, please consider that it is easier for me to beg in rags than to present a plea in a frock coat, and almost easier to say, with a pistol in my hand: la bourse ou la vie! than to whisper with trembling lips: may God reward me!

G. Büchner

Strassburg 1835–1836

To his parents

Weissenburg, March 9, 1835

I've just arrived here safe and sound. The journey was fast and comfortable. As for my personal safety, you needn't worry at all. According to reliable sources I have no reason to doubt that I'll receive permission to reside in Strassburg. [. . .] Only the most urgent reasons could compel me to leave my fatherland and my father's house in this manner. . . . I could surrender myself up to our political Inquisition; I would have nothing to fear from the result of an investigation, but everything to fear from the investigation itself. [. . .] I'm convinced that after two or three years have passed, nothing would stand in the way of my return. Had I remained, I would have spent this time in a dungeon at Friedberg; upon release I would have been a physical and mental wreck. I foresaw this so vividly, I was so certain of it that I chose the great misfortune of voluntary exile. Now my hands and head are free. [. . .] My future lies in my own hands. I'll study the sciences of medicine and philosophy with the greatest diligence; in *that* area there's still enough room to accomplish something of significance and have it properly acknowledged, for the times are right for this now. Since I crossed the border, I'm in high spirits; I'm now completely alone, but that increases my energy. It's a great blessing to be freed from the constant, secret fear of arrest and of other forms of persecution that tormented me in Darmstadt. [. . .]

To Gutzkow

Strassburg, [March 1835]

Honored Sir!

Perhaps you read in an arrest warrant published in the *Frankfurter Journal* about my departure from Darmstadt. I've been here for the last few days; I don't know whether I'll stay, that depends on various circumstances. I suppose my manuscript has been secretly making the rounds.

My future is so problematic that it's even beginning to interest *me,* and that's saying a lot. I can't easily bring myself to consider a subtle suicide by *working;* I hope to extend my laziness for another three months, and then I'll take a handout either from the Jesuits in the service of Maria or from the Saint-Simonists in the service of the "femme libre"—or I'll die with my sweetheart. We'll see. Maybe I'll be around when the Strassburg Cathedral puts on a Jacobin cap. What do you say to that? It's only a joke. But you'll find out what a German will do when he's hungry. I wish the entire nation were in my place. If we only had a bad year where only hangman's hemp would thrive! That would be fun—we would soon weave it into a boa constrictor. For the time being my Danton is a silk thread and my muse a disguised Samson.

To his parents

Strassburg, March 27, 1835

[. . .] I very much fear that the result of the investigation will adequately justify the step I took; there have been more arrests, and still more are expected. Minnigerode was caught red-handed; through him they hope to uncover all existing revolutionary conspiracies, they're trying to tear his secret out of him at all costs. How could his weak constitution withstand the slow torture they're subjecting him to? [. . .] Did German newspapers report about the execution of Lieutenant Kosseritz on the Hohenasperg in Württemberg? He was an *accessory* to the Frankfurt plot and was recently shot to death. The bookseller Frankh from Stuttgart and several others have been sentenced to death for the same reason, and it's believed that the sentence will be carried out. [. . .]

To his parents

Strassburg, April 20, 1835

[. . .] This morning I heard sad news: a refugee from outside of Giessen arrived here; he told me that several persons had been arrested near Marburg, and a printing press had been found in one of their houses. Furthermore, my friends A. Becker and Klemm have been incarcerated, and Rector Weidig of Butzbach is being prosecuted. Under these circumstances I don't understand why P[. . .] was released. Now I'm really happy to have left, I wouldn't have been spared in any case. [. . .] My mind is very much at ease about my future prospects. At any rate, I could earn a living from my writings. [. . .] I've also been asked to review the latest French literature for a literary journal—it pays well. I'd earn much more if I spent more time on it, but I'm determined *not to sacrifice my studies.* [. . .]

To his parents

Strassburg, May 5, 1835

I like Schulz and his wife very much; I met them some time ago and visit them regularly. Schulz is namely anything but the restless scourge of the bureaucrats that I imagined him to be; he is a rather quiet and very unpretentious man. He intends to go with his wife soon to Nancy and in about a year to Zurich, in order to teach there. [. . .] The situation of the political refugees in Switzerland is by no means as bad as one might imagine; only those have been severely punished whose unabated rage has seriously disturbed Switzerland's relations to foreign countries and has already nearly led to war. [. . .] Boeckel and Baum are still my closest friends; the latter is planning to publish his study of the Methodists, for which he received a prize of 3,000 francs and was publicly acclaimed. I recommended him to Gutzkow, with whom I've been continually corresponding. He's in Berlin right now but is supposed to return soon. He seems to think well of me; that pleases me, his literary journal is highly regarded. [. . .] In June he will come here, as he wrote me. From him I found out that several portions of my play had appeared in the *Phönix;* he also assured me that this had increased the paper's prestige. The whole drama is supposed to be published soon. In case you should come across it, I beg you to consider in your judgment of it that I had to remain true to history and present the men of the Revolution as they were: bloody, slovenly, energetic, and cynical. I view my drama as a historical portrait that must resemble its original. [. . .] Gutzkow asked me for reviews as a special favor; I couldn't refuse him, for I spend my leisure time reading, and if at times I then take pen in hand and write something about what I've read, that takes little effort and little time. [. . .] The King's birthday passed uneventfully; no one is eager to celebrate it, even the republicans remain quiet—they don't want any more uprisings, but their views are attracting more followers by the day, especially among the younger generation, and the government will therefore gradually collapse by itself, without violent upheaval. [. . .] Sartorius has been arrested, and so has Becker. Today I also found out about the arrest of Herr Weidig and Pastor Flick. [. . .]

To his parents

Strassburg, Wednesday after Pentecost, 1835

[. . .] What you've said about a rumor circulating in Darmstadt concerning a fraternity in Strassburg perturbs me greatly. At most there are eight or nine German refugees here; I hardly come into any contact with them, and there's no question of a political fraternity. They realize as well as I that under current conditions such an undertaking is wholly useless and highly dangerous for anyone involved. Their only goal is to improve the very poor reputation of German refugees through work, diligence, and high morals, and I find that most praiseworthy. Besides, our government considered Strassburg highly suspect and very dangerous, so I'm not at all surprised about the circulating rumors; I'm only concerned that our government plans to demand deportation of those found guilty. We have no legal protection here; we actually live here illegally, are only *tolerated* and are therefore wholly at the mercy of the prefect. If our government were to make such a demand, no one would ask: does such a fraternity exist or not?—whoever is around would simply be deported. I can count on enough protection to survive here, but that will only last until the Hessian government *specifically* demands my deportation, because in this case the law is *too* clear to permit the authorities to ignore it. But I hope all this is exaggerated. The following also concerns us: *Dr. Schulz was ordered several days ago* to leave Strassburg; he had lived in great seclusion here, had kept completely quiet—but *nevertheless!* I hope that our government considered me too insignificant to take similar measures against me as well, and so I'll remain undisturbed. Tell them I went to Switzerland. — Yesterday I spoke to Heumann. — Recently another five refugees from Darmstadt and Giessen arrived here and have already gone on to Switzerland. Rosenstiel, Wiener, and Stamm are among them. [. . .]

To Wilhelm Büchner

[Strassburg, 1835]

[. . .] I wouldn't tell you this if I could believe in the slightest possibility of a political upheaval at this time. For the last six months I've been utterly convinced that nothing is to be done and that anyone who sacrifices himself *right now* is foolishly risking his neck. I can't tell you anything more specific, but I know the situation; I know how weak, how insignificant, how fragmented the liberal party is; I know that purposeful, unified action is impossible and that any attempt won't have the slightest result. [. . .]

To an unknown recipient

[Strassburg, 1835]

[. . .] A close acquaintance with the activities of German revolutionaries outside Germany has convinced me that nothing is to be hoped from them either. They are in a state of tremendous confusion that will never be resolved. Let's hope for times to come! [. . .]

To Gutzkow

[Strassburg]

[. . .] The whole revolution has already divided itself into liberals and absolutists, and it will have to be devoured by the uneducated and poor classes; the relationship between poor and rich is the only revolutionary element in the world, hunger alone can become the goddess of freedom, and only a Moses, who brought the seven Egyptian plagues down on our heads, could become a messiah. Fatten the peasants and the revolution will have a stroke. A *chicken* in the pot of every peasant will kill the Gallic *rooster*. [. . .]

To his parents

Srassburg, July 1835

[. . .] By word of mouth I've heard a lot of troublesome news from Darmstadt. Koch, Walloth, Geilfuss, and one of my friends from Giessen named Becker recently arrived here; the young Stamm is here as well. Several others have also arrived, but they'll all go on to Switzerland or further into France. I consider myself lucky and sometimes feel really free and easy when I survey the wide-open space around me and then imagine myself in the Darmstadt detention center. Those unfortunate people! Minnigerode has been in jail for almost a year, he's said to be almost a physical wreck, but isn't his steadfastness heroic? I've heard they've beaten him several times already, I can't and don't want to believe it. A. Becker seems to be forsaken by God and man; his mother died while he was in jail in Giessen, they informed him *two weeks* later!!! Kl[emm] is a traitor, that's certain, but I still believe I'm dreaming when I think about it. Did you know that his sister and sister-in-law were also arrested and brought to Darmstadt, most likely because of his testimony? Besides, he's digging his own grave; he still won't achieve his goal, which was to marry Fräulein von [Grolmann] in Giessen, and the unavoidable public scorn will kill him. I very much fear, however, that the recent arrests are only a prelude; things will get hotter. The government can't control itself; it will abuse its current favorable status to the limit, and that's very unwise and of great advantage to us. The young von Biegeleben, Weidenbusch, and Floret are also involved in an investigation—it won't ever stop. Three pastors—Flick, Weidig, and Thudichum—are among those arrested. I very much fear, however, that our government won't leave us alone here, but I'm certain of the support of Professors

Lauth, Duvernoy, and Dr. Boeckel, who are all on good terms with the prefect. — I finished my translation a long time ago. I don't know what's happening with my drama; about five or six weeks ago Gutzkow wrote me that it was being printed—since then I haven't heard anything more. I believe it must have been published, and they'll only send me a copy together with reviews, once they've appeared. I can't imagine any other reason for the delay. I'm sometimes afraid for Gutzkow; he's a Prussian and has recently incurred the displeasure of his government because of a preface he wrote to an edition published in Berlin. The Prussians act quickly; maybe he's sitting in a Prussian dungeon now, but we'll hope for the best. [. . .]

To his parents

Strassburg, July 16, 1835

[. . .] I've been living here without any interference; some time ago a warrant came from Giessen, but the police appear to have ignored it. [. . .] My heart is heavy when I think of Darmstadt; I see our house and the garden and then involuntarily the horrible detention center. Those unfortunate people! How will that end? Probably like in Frankfurt, where one person after another dies and is secretly buried. A death sentence, a scaffold, what's that? One dies for one's cause. But to be worn down slowly like that in jail! That's terrible! Can't you tell me who's imprisoned in Darmstadt? I've heard much confused talk here, but I can't make sense of it. Kl[emm] appears to play a despicable role. I liked the boy very much, he was exceedingly passionate but open, lively, courageous, and bright. Has anyone heard anything about Minnigerode? Was he really beaten? That's unbelievable. His heroic steadfastness ought to command the respect of the most unregenerate aristocrat. [. . .]

To his parents

Strassburg, July 28, 1835

[. . .] I must say a few words about my drama: first I must point out that my permission to make several changes was used to excess.

Omissions and additions occur on almost every page, and almost always to the detriment of the whole. Sometimes the sense is completely distorted or missing entirely, replaced by almost sheer nonsense. Besides, the book is teeming with the most dreadful typographical errors. I received no *proofs*. The title is tasteless, and my name is under it, which I had explicitly forbidden; it was not on the title page of my manuscript. The editor has moreover credited me with several obscenities I never would have said in my life. I've read Gutzkow's splendid reviews and noticed, much to my pleasure, that I'm not inclined toward vanity. Regarding the so-called immorality of my book, I have the following to say: the dramatic poet is in my eyes nothing but a writer of history; he is *superior* to the latter, however, in that he creates history a second time for us, and instead of telling us a dry story, he places us into the life of an era, giving us characters instead of characteristics and figures instead of descriptions. His greatest task is to come as close as possible to history as it actually happened. His book must be neither *more nor less moral* than *history itself;* but God didn't create history to be suitable reading matter for young ladies, and for that reason I can't be blamed if my drama is equally unsuitable. I can't make a Danton and the bandits of the Revolution into virtuous heroes! To show their dissoluteness I had to let them be dissolute, to show their godlessness I had to let them speak like atheists. Should you discover any improprieties, then think of the notoriously obscene language of that time; whatever my characters say is only a weak approximation of it. One might reproach me for choosing such material. But such a reproach has long been refuted. If one were to let it stand, then the greatest masterpieces of literature would have to be thrown out. The poet is not a teacher of morality, he invents and creates figures, he brings past times to life, and people can learn from that, just as well as from the study of history and from observation of what is going on around them. If you wished it *otherwise,* you shouldn't be permitted to study history at all, for it tells of many immoral acts; you'd have to walk blindfolded down the street, for you might see indecencies, and you'd have to cry out against a God who created a world in which so much dissoluteness occurs. If someone were to tell me that the poet shouldn't depict the world as it is but as it should be, then I answer that I don't want to make it better than God, who certainly made the world as it should be. As far as the so-called idealistic poets are concerned, I find that they have produced hardly anything besides marionettes with sky-blue noses and affected pathos, but not human beings of flesh and blood, whose sorrow and joy I share and whose actions fill me with loathing or admiration. In a word, I think much of Goethe or Shakespeare, but very little of Schiller. Moreover, it's obvious that highly unfavorable reviews will appear, for the governments must have their paid writers prove that their opponents are either idiots or immoral people. I do not in any way judge my work to be perfect and will accept any truly aesthetic criticism with thanks.

Did you hear about the powerful lightning bolt that struck the Strassburg Cathedral a few days ago? I've never seen such a flash nor heard such a clap of thunder—I was deafened for several moments. The damage is the worst the watchman can remember. Bricks were shattered with incredible force and flung far off; roofs of neighboring houses a hundred paces away were pierced by falling bricks.

Three more refugees arrived here, Nievergelder is among them; recently two students were arrested in Giessen. I'm as cautious as possible. We don't know of anyone here who was arrested at the border. That story must be a fairy tale. [. . .]

To his parents

Strassburg, beginning of August 1835

[. . .] Above all I have to tell you that upon special application I've been promised a security-card if I can produce a *birth* (not country-of-origin) *certificate*. This is only a legally prescribed formality; I have to be able to produce a piece of paper, as trivial as that may be. [. . .] But I'm living here without any interference, I'm only taking a preventive measure with an eye to the future. Tell people anyway that I've gone to Zurich; since you haven't received any letters from me through the mail for some time now, the police can't possibly know for certain where I am, especially since I've written to my friends that I've gone to Zurich. Several more refugees have arrived here, a son of Professor Vogt is among them; they brought the news of recent arrests of three heads of families! One in Rödelheim, another in Frankfurt, a third in Offenbach. A sister of the unfortunate Neuhof, a pretty and amiable girl, so they say, has also been arrested. It's certain that a woman from Giessen has been brought to the Darmstadt detention center; they say it's [. . .]. The government must keep these things very quiet, because you seem to be very poorly informed. We hear everything from the refugees, who know more than anyone, because in most cases they were recently involved in investigations. I know for certain that Minnigerode's hands were chained in Friedberg; I know it from someone who was imprisoned with him. He's said to be mortally ill; would to heaven that his sufferings would cease! It's established that the prisoners are given prison rations and have neither light nor books. I thank heaven that I foresaw what would happen, I would have gone crazy in a hole like that. [. . .] The political situation is getting lively again here. The time bomb in Paris and the legislative bills concerning the press are causing a great stir. The government is proving itself to be highly immoral, for although it's been proven in court that the perpetrator is a shifty rascal who has served all political parties and probably did it for money, the government tries to saddle the Republicans and the Carlists with the crime and, by exploiting current sentiment, to impose the most intolerable restrictions on the press. The bill is expected to pass in the chamber, and it might even be made more severe. The government is very unwise; in six weeks the time bomb will be forgotten, and the government with its law will then find itself facing a people used to saying publicly for several years now anything that comes into its head. The cleverest politicians suspect connections between the time bomb and the military celebration in Kalisch. I can't say they're utterly wrong—Bonaparte's time bomb! The murder of the ambassadors in Rastatt!! [. . .]

When one sees how the absolutist powers try to reinstate the old chaos: Poland, Italy, Germany under their thumb again! Only France is missing, it's always hanging over their heads like a sword. One doesn't throw those millions spent in Kalisch out the window just for the fun of it. They would have taken advantage of the confusion following the death of the king, and they wouldn't have needed very many steps to reach the Rhine. I can't account for the assassination attempt in any other way. The Republicans have no money and are in such a miserable state that they couldn't have attempted anything even if the king had died. At most a few Legitimists might have been involved. I don't believe that the courts will get to the bottom of the matter. [. . .]

To his parents

Strassburg, August 17, 1835

I know nothing about intrigues. All of my friends and I are of the opinion that for now, everything has to await the passage of time; besides, the princes' misuse of their reacquired power only works to our advantage. You mustn't let yourself be confused by various rumors; they say you've even been visited by someone claiming to be a friend of mine. I don't recall ever having seen this person; others have told me that he's an inveterate rascal, who probably also circulated the rumor about the political fraternity here. The current presence of Prince Emil here could possibly have repercussions for us, in case he requests our deportation from the prefect, but we consider ourselves to be too unimportant for His Majesty to concern himself with us. Besides, almost all refugees have traveled on to Switzerland or further into France, and in a few days several more will leave, so that five or six at most will remain here. [. . .]

To Gutzkow

[Strassburg, September 1835]

[. . .] What you've told me about the report from Switzerland makes me laugh. I can tell where it comes from. A person who was very dear to me a long time ago, who later became an unbearable burden that I've been dragging around for years, and who clings to me—out of what compulsion I don't know—without affection, without love, without trust and tortures me and whom I've endured as a necessary evil! I felt lamed or crippled, and I had more or less gotten used to my affliction. But now I'm happy, it's as if I had been absolved from a mortal sin. I can finally throw him out in a decent manner. Until now I was unreasonably kind; it would have been easier for me to kill him than to say: scram! But now I'm rid of him! Thank God! Surely nothing in the world takes as much out of a person as being humane. [. . .]

To his parents

Strassburg, September 20, 1835

[. . .] A source of support has become available to me: a large literary journal called *Deutsche Revue,* which will appear at the beginning of next year in weekly installments. Gutzkow and Wienbarg will direct the enterprise; I've been asked to supply monthly contributions. Although perhaps this would have been an opportunity to secure me a steady income, for the sake of my studies I declined to commit myself to regular contributions. Something of mine may possibly yet appear before the end of the year. — Kl[emm] is free, then? He's a victim of adversity rather than a criminal, I pity him more than I scorn him; they must have played quite cleverly on his raving emotions. Otherwise he would have had some self-respect; I don't think he'll be able to bear his disgrace. His *family disowns* him, except for his older brother, who seems to have played a leading role in the affair. It has brought misfortune upon many people. Minnigerode's situation is said to have improved. Has Gladbach still not been sentenced? I'd call that burying someone alive. I shudder to think what my fate might have been! [. . .]

To his parents

Strassburg, October 1835

[. . .] I've obtained many interesting notes about a friend of Goethe, an ill-starred poet named Lenz, who resided here with Goethe and who went half-insane. I'm thinking of publishing an essay on this in the *Deutsche Revue.* I'm also looking around for material for a treatise on a topic in philosophy or natural history. Some uninterrupted research for a while yet, and my path will be set. Some people here predict a bright future for me. I have nothing against that. [. . .]

To his parents

Strassburg, November 2, 1835

[. . .] I know for certain that people are saying the wildest things about me in Darmstadt; they've already had me arrested at the border three times over. I think that's natural; the exceptional number of arrests and warrants must cause quite a stir, and since the public has no idea what is happening, it constructs weird hypotheses. [. . .]

I've gotten the best possible news from Switzerland. *It may be* that before year's end I'll receive my doctorate from the University of Zurich, in which case I'd begin lecturing there next Easter. At age twenty-two that's everything one could ask for. [. . .]

Recently my name was exhibited in the *Allgemeine Zeitung* in connection with a major literary journal, *Deutsche Revue*, for which I've promised to provide articles. Someone has already attacked this periodical before its publication by saying that one need only mention the names of Messrs. Heine, Börne, Mundt, Schulz, Büchner, etc. to get an idea of this journal's potential success. — An article in *Temps* reported on how Minnigerode is being mistreated. It seems to have been written in Darmstadt; one really has to go far to be allowed to utter a complaint. My unfortunate friends! [. . .]

To Gutzkow

[Strassburg 1835]

[. . .] Enclosed is a small volume of poems from my friends the Stöbers. The legends are pretty but I'm not an admirer of the style à la Schwab and Uhland, nor of the faction that always looks back to the Middle Ages because it can't find a place in the present. But I'm fond of this little book; if you are unable to say anything favorable about it, I beg you rather to say nothing. I've gotten quite accustomed to my surroundings; I love the Vosges mountains like a mother, I know every summit and every valley, and the old legends are so strange and mysterious, and the two Stöbers are old friends with whom I first wandered through the mountains. Adolph was undeniably talented; you'll have heard his name in connection with the *Musenalmanach*. August is less gifted, but his style is elegant.

The subject is not without importance for Alsace; it's one of the rare attempts, which some Alsatians still make, to maintain their German nationality as opposed to France and to preserve the spiritual bond between them and the fatherland. It would be a pity if the Strassburg Cathedral were once to stand on entirely foreign soil. The purpose which in part produced this little book would be well served if the enterprise could win approval in Germany, and I especially recommend it to you from this perspective.

The study of philosophy is making me quite dumb; I'm gaining insights from a new angle into the wretchedness of the human spirit. So be it! If we could only imagine that the holes in our pants were palace windows, we could live like kings, but as things are, we're miserably cold. [. . .]

To Ludwig Büchner

[Strassburg, end of December 1835]

Happy New Year, Mutton-mouse!

I hear that you've been a good boy, your parents are pleased with you. Be sure it's always like that! To hear this about you was a nice Christmas present for me. You draw nicely, keep it up. Louis Jaeglé was very happy to get your drawing and your [. . .], and he asked me to send you a book with drawings. You can practice from that. Is Lottchen Cellarius pleased with you, and did the piece go well on Christmas Eve? When you go to your piano lesson, give my best regards to Miss Lottchen, but for heaven's sake don't tell anyone else a word about it.

Next spring I'm going to Switzerland. If you're a good boy and if you've grown a little, you'll have to get a walking stick and a knapsack and come visit me. First you'll go up the Strassburg Cathedral and then we'll go to the Rhine Falls in Schaffhausen and to Tell's Ledge on the Lake of Lucerne and to Tell's Chapel. Adieu, little mouse—I bet you're a big mouse now and if you keep it up, you'll go far. I hope you're too big for the gray beaver coat now.

Farewell,

your brother Georg

To his parents

Strassburg, January 1, 1836

[. . .] The banning of the *Deutschen Revue* does me no harm. Several articles I prepared for it can be sent to the *Phönix*. It makes me laugh how pious and moral our governments are suddenly becoming; the King of Bavaria bans immoral books! Then he mustn't allow his biography to be published, because that would be the dirtiest thing ever written! The Grand Duke of Baden, First Knight of the Double Order of Blockheads, makes himself a Knight of the Holy Ghost and has Gutzkow arrested, and every good German believes it's being done for the sake of religion and Christianity and claps his hands. I'm not familiar with the books everyone is talking about; they're not in the lending libraries and they're too expensive for me to spend money on them. If it's all like they say, I can see in it only the misconceptions of a mind led astray by philosophic sophistries. The most common trick to get the masses on one's side is to scream "Immoral!" with a mouth full of food. Besides, it really takes courage to attack a writer who must answer from a German jail. Gutzkow has revealed a distinguished, stalwart nature, he has given proof of great talent; why then suddenly this outcry? It seems to me as if one were fighting for the worldly realm while one pretends to be saving the life of the Trinity. Gutzkow has courageously fought for freedom in his sphere; the few who still stand upright and dare to speak have to be silenced! *I* by no means belong to the so-called "Young Germany," the literary party of Gutzkow and Heine. Only a complete misunderstanding of our social conditions could lead these people to believe that a complete transformation of our religious and social ideas would be possible through our current literature. I also do not share *in any way their opinions about marriage and Christianity,* but it still annoys me when people who have sinned a thousand times more in practice than these men have in *theory* make moral faces and cast stones at a youthful, vigorous talent. I'm going my own way and staying in the field of drama, which has nothing to do with all of these disputes; I draw my figures as I see fit in accordance with nature and history, and I laugh about people who want to make me responsible for the morality or immorality of these characters. I have my own ideas about that. [. . .].

I just came from the Christmas displays; everywhere crowds of ragged, freezing children who were standing wide-eyed and with sad faces before those wonders of water and flour, dirt and gold foil. The thought that for most people even the most paltry delights and joys are unattainable riches made me very bitter. [. . .]

To Gutzkow

[Strassburg, January 1836]

My dear Sir!

I don't know whether these lines will reach you at this questionable address.

Did you receive Boulet's letter? I sent it to Mannheim. At the time I didn't dare to enclose a few lines to you. I thought the matter was more serious. According to the papers, you'll be free soon. Four weeks. That's over soon. I've also gotten direct news about you from Mannheim. Your confinement is easy. You may receive visitors, you may even go out on leave. Is this true?

Have you nothing *further to fear?* Let me know *as soon as possible!* This isn't an idle question. Do you believe they'll let you go free after the *announced time?* You're confined in the police station, right?

As soon as you are free, leave Germany immediately. It's lucky for you that things *seem* to be turning out this way. I'd be surprised.

In case you pass through Strassburg, ask for me at: Herr Schroot, innkeeper of the Grapevine Inn. I'm awaiting you with impatience.

Your G.

To his parents

Strassburg, March 15, 1836

[. . .] I don't understand how they can have evidence against Küchler; I thought he wasn't involved in anything besides expanding his medical practice and knowledge. Even if he remains in jail only a short time, his whole future is most likely ruined: they'll set him free on probation, release him from further charges, make him promise not to leave the country, and forbid him to practice medicine, which is permissible under the newest ordinances. — I'm as certain as can be that in Bavaria two young people, after being kept in close confinement for almost *four years,* were recently released and proclaimed *innocent!* Besides Küchler and Gross, three other citizens of Giessen have been arrested. Two of them run their own business, and one is moreover the head of a family. We also heard that Max von Biegeleben was arrested but soon thereafter released on bail. Gladbach is said to have been sentenced some time ago to prison for eight years, but the sentence was overturned, and the inquiry was beginning anew. You would do me a favor if you would give me information about both.

In return I'll tell you a bizarre story that Herr J. read in the English papers and that, it was noted, couldn't be reported in the German papers. The director of the theater in Braunschweig is the noted composer Methfessel. He has a pretty wife, whom the Duke likes; a pair of eyes, which he is pleased to shut; and a pair of hands, which he likes to open. The Duke has a peculiar mania to admire Madame Methfessel in costume. He therefore usually stands alone with her onstage before the play begins. Now Methfessel intrigues against a noted actor, whose name escapes me. The actor wants revenge, he bribes a stagehand, one pleasant evening the stagehand raises the curtain a quarter of an hour early, and the Duke is performing the first scene with Madame Methfessel. He loses his head, pulls his sword and stabs the stagehand to death; the actor has fled.

I can assure you that the refugees here are not engaging in any political activity whatsoever; the many examinations they take and their good grades are sufficient proof to the contrary. Moreover, we refugees and prisoners are not exactly the most ignorant, simpleminded, or disreputable people! I'm not exaggerating when I say that up to now the best secondary-school pupils and the most diligent and best informed students have met this fate, including those who have been banned from examinations and civil service. Those who walk around Darmstadt now are truly a pitiful young bunch, trying to worm their way into a mediocre civil position!

To Gutzkow

Strassburg, [1836]

Dear friend!

Was I silent long enough? What shall I tell you? I *also* sat in jail, in the most boring one under the sun—I wrote a dissertation lengthwise, breadthwise, and depthwise. Day and night over the ghastly affair, I don't know where I found the patience. I happen to be obsessed with the idea of teaching a course next semester in Zurich on the development of German philosophy since Descartes; for that I need my diploma, and people don't seem inclined toward putting a doctoral hood on my dear son Danton.

What's to be done?

You're in Frankfurt, without interference?

That you didn't knock at the Grapevine Inn makes me sad and then again happy. I know next to nothing about the state of modern literature in Germany; only a few scattered brochures that crossed the Rhine, I don't know how, have fallen into my hands.

The battle against you reveals a *fundamental* baseness, a downright *healthy* baseness—I can't fathom how we can still remain so unaffected! And Menzel's scorn about the political fools in German dungeons—and from people like that! My God, I could tell you some edifying stories.

That enraged me to the depths; my poor friends! Don't you agree that Menzel will soon get a professorship in Munich?

By the way, in all honesty it seems to me that you and your friends didn't exactly take the most sensible path. Reform society through *ideas,* through the *educated* classes? Impossible! Our times are purely *materialistic;* if you had ever worked along more directly political lines, you soon would have come to the point where reform would have stopped on its own. You will never bridge the chasm between the educated and uneducated classes.

I'm convinced that the educated and prosperous minority, as many concessions as it might desire for itself from the authorities, will never want to give up its antagonistic attitude toward the masses. And the masses themselves? For them there are only two levers: material poverty and *religious fanaticism.* Any party that knows how to operate these levers will conquer. Our times demand iron and bread—and then a *cross* or something like that. I believe that in social affairs one must proceed from an absolute *legal* principle, striving for a new mentality among the *people* and letting effete modern society go to the devil. Why should a thing like this walk around between heaven and earth? Its whole life consists only of attempts to dissipate its most dreadful boredom. Let it die out, that is the only new thing it can still experience. [. . .].

To his parents

Strassburg, May 1836

[. . .] I'm determined to remain here until this fall. The most recent incidents in Zurich are my main reason. You may know that several German refugees have been arrested under the pretext that they were planning to invade Germany. The same thing happened at other locations in Switzerland. Even here the foolish story had repercussions, and we were fairly uncertain whether we would be allowed to remain, because it was claimed that we (at most now seven or eight in number) would cross the Rhine armed to the teeth! But all was settled amicably, and we have no further difficulties to fear. At times our Hessian government seems to think of us with affection. [. . .]

I don't know what the whole affair is about; but since I know that the majority of refugees consider any overt revolutionary act to be senseless under current conditions, only a very insignificant minority, untutored by experience, could have thought of something like that. The leader of the conspirators is said to be a certain Herr von Eib. It's more than likely that this individual is an agent of parliament; the passports found in his possession by the Zurich police as well as the fact that he drew large sums from a Frankfurt trading house speak loudly for this supposition. The fellow is supposed to be a former shoemaker, yet he goes around with a disreputable woman from Mannheim, whom he passes off as a Hungarian countess. He really seems to have duped a number of donkeys among the refugees. The whole affair had no other purpose than to give parliament, in case the refugees could have been induced into overt action, a well-founded pretext to demand the expulsion of all refugees out of Switzerland. This von Eib had, moreover, already been under suspicion before, and people had already been warned about him several times. In any case, the plan failed, and the affair will remain without consequence for the majority of refugees. Nevertheless I wouldn't consider it advisable to go to Zurich at this moment; in such circumstances it's better to stay away. The

Zurich government is naturally somewhat uneasy and distrustful, and under current conditions my residency might be jeopardized. In two or three months, however, the whole affair will be forgotten. [. . .]

To Eugen Boeckel

Strassburg, June 1, [1836]

My dear Eugen,

I'm still sitting here, as you can tell by the date. "Very ill-advised!" you'll say, and I say: so what! Only yesterday was my dissertation finally completed. It grew to be much longer than I first thought, and I've lost a lot of good time on it; but I flatter myself to think that it has turned out well—and the Société d'histoire naturelle appears to be of the same opinion. In three different sessions I held three lectures on it, upon which the Society immediately decided to publish them in their protocol; moreover, it appointed me a Corresponding Member. You can see that fortune has gotten me out of a tight spot again, I owe fortune great thanks in any case, and my carefree nature, which is basically a boundless faith in God, has gotten a big boost again. I need it, though; when I've paid for my doctorate, I won't have a cent left, and I haven't been able to write anything during this time. For a while I'll have to live from dear old credit and see how in the next six to eight weeks I can cut a coat and pants for myself out of the large white sheets of paper that I have to scribble full. I think to myself: "Commend thy ways to God" and let nothing bother me.

Was I silent for a long time? But you know why and will forgive me. I was like a sick person who swallows loathsome medicine in one gulp; I couldn't do anything but get the damned thesis off my neck. I feel wonderful since I got the thing out of the house. — I'm thinking of staying here yet this summer. My mother is coming in the fall. To go to Zurich now, come back in the fall, lose time and money, that wouldn't make sense. At any rate, in the next winter semester I'll begin my course, which I'm now preparing at the most leisurely pace.

You seem to have had a good time on your journey. That pleases me. Life is indeed really beautiful, and in any case it's not as boring as if it were twice as boring. Hurry up a bit next fall, come on time, then I'll still see you here. Have you learned a lot on the way? Haven't you yet gotten tired of observing diseased and dead bodies? I mean, a tour through half the hospitals in Europe must make one very melancholy, and a tour through the lecture halls of our professors must make one half crazy, and a tour through our German states must make one quite furious. Three things—which by the way one can very easily become without the three tours, for example when it's rainy and cold, like now; when one has a toothache, like mine a week ago; and when one hasn't gotten out of one's four walls for an entire winter, like me this year.

You can see that I have to put up with a great deal, and before I had my hollow tooth pulled recently, in utter seriousness I contemplated shooting myself instead, which is in any case less painful.

Baum sighs every day, gets a monstrous belly, and makes such a suicidal face that I fear he secretly wants to die of a stroke. He worries on a regular basis every day, ever since I assured him that worrying is good for his health. He's stopped fencing and is so terribly lazy that to the great annoyance of your brother he hasn't attended to any of the tasks you ordered. What can one do with someone like him? He's got to become a priest, he's showing the best inclinations for it.

The two Stöbers are still sitting in Oberbrunn. Unfortunately the rumor about the priest's wife is proving to be true. The poor girl here is quite forsaken and down there people are said to be philosophizing about the poetic significance of adultery. I don't believe the latter—but the story is ambiguous.

What is our friend and cousin, Zipfel, up to? Have things been made hot for him again? Do you see my cousin from Holland once in a while? Greet both of them heartily from me.

Wilhelmine was indisposed for a long time, she suffered from chronic miliaria without ever being seriously ill.

A propos, she gave me your two letters unopened, but I would have thought it more fitting if you had for propriety's sake put your letter in an envelope; if it was not to be read by a woman, then it was improper to address it to one; with an envelope it's different. I hope you don't take amiss this little reprimand of mine.

At any rate, I'll be here for the next month, while my thesis is being printed. Will you cheer me with a letter before you leave

Vienna? A propos, your studies are truly aesthetic—Demoiselle Peche is an old acquaintance of mine. Farewell,

Your G. B.

To his parents

Strassburg, June 1836

[. . .] It's inconceivable that at this moment a nation would suspend the right of asylum, because such a suspension would politically invalidate the nation vis-a-vis those other nations that requested it. Through such a measure, Switzerland would renounce its ties to the liberal states, to which it is naturally related through its constitution, and affiliate itself with the absolutist states—a relationship unimaginable under prevailing political constellations. It's quite natural, however, that refugees are deported who threaten the security and the relationship to neighboring countries of the state that has admitted them—the right of asylum is thereby not voided. Moreover, the congress has already issued its decree. *Only* those refugees are deported who *had already been expelled earlier* as participants in the *Savoy campaign,* as well as those who *participated in the most recent incidents.* This is *authentic.* The majority of the refugees are therefore not in danger, and everyone is at liberty to travel to Switzerland. In several cantons, however, one is obligated to post bond, which has been the case for some time already. Hence my journey to Zurich is free of obstacles. — You know that our government is harassing us here, and that there was talk of deporting us because we were said to be in league with those fools in Switzerland. The prefect wanted exact information about our activities here. I gave the police commissioner my certificate of membership in the Société d'histoire naturelle as well as a testimonial from one of the professors. The prefect was *exceedingly* satisfied with this, and I was told that *I personally* needn't worry about a thing. [. . .]

To Wilhelm Büchner

Strassburg, September 2, 1836

[. . .] I'm quite cheerful, except when we have a steady downpour or a northwest wind, which turns me into one of those who, when they've taken off one sock before going to bed at night, are capable of hanging themselves on their chamber door because it's too much effort to take off the other one. [. . .] I'm now concentrating totally on the study of natural sciences and philosophy, and I'll soon go to Zurich to lecture to my fellow-beings in my capacity as a superfluous member of society on an equally superfluous topic, namely schools of German philosophy since Descartes and Spinoza. — Right now I'm occupied with letting several people kill each other or get married on paper, and I beg the dear Lord for a simpleminded publisher and a large audience with as little good taste as possible. Many things under the sun require courage—even being a Lecturer in Philosophy. [. . .]

To his parents

Strassburg, September 1836

[. . .] I haven't yet released my two dramas; I'm still dissatisfied with several things, and I don't want it to go like the first time. These are works that cannot be completed at a specific time, like a tailor with a dress. [. . .]

To Mayor Hess

Strassburg, September 22, 1836

Honored Sir:

You will, I hope, pardon a stranger who takes the liberty of appealing to your benevolence in a highly important matter.

Political conditions in Germany compelled me to leave my homeland about a year and a half ago. I had chosen an academic career. I could not bring myself to abandon a goal toward which all my energies had been directed, and I therefore continued my studies in Strassburg, hoping to be able to realize my aspirations in Switzerland. Indeed, I had the honor to receive my doctorate from the College of Philosophy in Zurich by unanimous vote. After so favorable a judgment of my scholarly qualifications, I could well aspire to be accepted as a Lecturer at the University of Zurich and at best begin my lectures next semester. I therefore applied for a passport from the local authorities. I was told, however, that they were prohibited by the Ministry of the Interior, at Switzerland's request, from issuing a passport to a refugee who could not produce written authorization from a Swiss office permitting residency in its district. In this circumstance I now appeal to you, honored Sir, as the highest city official of Zurich, for the authorization required by the local authorities. The enclosed certification can prove that since my departure from my homeland I have distanced myself from all political intrigue, and I therefore do not belong to the category of refugees against whom Switzerland and France have recently taken legal measures. I therefore look forward to the fulfillment of my request, which if refused would result in the destruction of my life's goal.

If you, honored Sir, would feel inclined to favor my request with a response, I beg you to address it to: Dr. Büchner c/o Herr Siegfried, wine merchant at the Custom-house in Strassburg.

With all due respect your humble servant

Dr. Büchner

[Enclosure: affidavit from the Strassburg Police]*

I, Jonathan Pfister, Police Commissioner of the South District of the city of Strassburg, hereby certify that:

Monsieur Georg Büchner, Doctor of Philosophy, age 23, born in Darmstadt, is registered in the rue de la Douane No. 18 as a resident of this city for the last eighteen months without interruption, and that his political and moral conduct during this time has given no cause for complaint.

Attested by the undersigned:
Strassburg, September 21, 1836
Pfister

To the Presidium of the Zurich Educational Council

Dear Mr. President, honored Sirs:

After submitting a thesis on a subject in natural history, I had

*(originally in French)

the honor to receive my Doctor of Philosophy degree from the College of Philosophy in Zurich by a unanimous vote taken on September 3. Supported by this judgment of my scholarly qualifications, I wish to apply for a Lectureship at the college of Philosophy in Zurich. I am therefore honored to request permission from you to hold the public inaugural address required for this application by §157 of the Organizational Statutes for Public Instruction.

With all due respect your humble servant

Strassburg, September 26, 1836 G. Büchner Ph.D.

Zurich
1836–1837

To his parents

Zurich, October 26, 1836

[. . .] Heaven knows what will happen to Switzerland's dispute with France. But I recently heard someone say: "Switzerland will make a small curtsy, and France will say it was a large one." I think he's right. [. . .]

To his parents

Zurich, November 20, 1836

[. . .] Regarding political activities, you needn't worry at all. Just don't be troubled by the fairy tales in our newspapers. Switzerland is a republic, and since journalists usually don't know what else to say besides: "every republic is barbarous," they tell the good Germans daily about anarchy, murder, and manslaughter. You'll be surprised when you visit me; already on the way friendly villages everywhere, and then, the closer you come to Zurich and along the lake, widespread prosperity; back home we have no concept of the appearance of these villages and small towns. The streets aren't full of soldiers, job applicants, and lazy bureaucrats, you don't risk being run over by a nobleman's coach; in contrast, a healthy, sturdy people, and for little money a simple, good, purely *republican* government, which sustains itself through a *property tax,* a kind of tax that would be denounced back home as the height of anarchy. [. . .]

Minnigerode is dead, as I've heard in a letter; that is, for three years he was tortured to death. Three years! The men of blood of the French Revolution killed people in a couple of hours—the sentence and then the guillotine! But three years! We have indeed a humane government, it can't stand the sight of blood. And nearly forty people are similarly imprisoned, and that's no anarchy, that's law and order, and the masters feel outraged when they think of anarchistic Switzerland! By God, these people are raising great capital, which may once have to be repaid with heavy interest, very heavy interest. [. . .]

To Wilhelm Büchner

Zurich, end of November 1836

[. . .] I'm sitting with my scalpel by day and my books by night. [. . .]

To Wilhelmine Jaeglé

[Zurich,] January 13, 1837

My dear child! [. . .] I'm counting the weeks until Easter on my fingers. It's getting ever bleaker. In the beginning it was all right: new surroundings, people, situations, employment—but now that I'm used to everything, now that everything has become routine, I can't be oblivious to myself anymore. The best thing is that my imagination is active, and the mechanical business of lecture preparations gives it room. I'm always seeing you partially through fish tails, frog toes, etc. Isn't that more touching than the story of Abelard, when Heloise always came between his lips and prayer? Oh, I'm getting more poetic by the day, all my thoughts are swimming in formaldehyde. Thank God I'm dreaming a lot again at night, my sleep isn't so heavy anymore. [. . .]

To Wilhelmine Jaeglé

[Zurich,] January 20 [1837]

[. . .] I caught a cold and was lying in bed. But now it's better. When one is a bit out of sorts like that, one has a great yearning for idleness; but the mill wheel turns without a stop. [. . .] Today and yesterday I've been granting myself a bit of rest and am not reading; tomorrow it'll be back to the old grind, you can't believe how regular and orderly. I'm running almost as well as a Black Forest clock. But it's all right: some rest after all that turbulent mental life, and in addition the joy of creating my poetic products. Poor Shakespeare was a scribe during the day and had to write his own works at night, and I, who am unworthy of untying his shoelaces, am far better off. [. . .] Will you learn to sing the *folk songs* by Easter, if it doesn't fatigue you? One doesn't hear any voices here; the *folk* don't sing, and you know how much I love those women who in a soiree or in concert sing or wail a couple of notes to death. I'm coming ever closer to the folk and to the Middle Ages, every day I feel more clearheaded—and you'll sing the songs, right? I become half homesick, when I hum a melody to myself. [. . .] Every evening I sit in the casino for one or two hours; you know my liking for beautiful halls, lights, and people around me. [. . .]

To Wilhelmine Jaeglé

[Zurich,] January 27 [1837]

My dear child, you are full of tender concern, and you say you'll get ill from fear; I do believe you'll die—but *I* have no desire to die and am healthy as ever. I think I was cured by the fear of the medical care here; in Strassburg it would have been very pleasant, and I would have gone to bed for two weeks in the greatest comfort, rue St. Guillaume No. 66, up the stairs to the left, in a somewhat oddly shaped room, with green wallpaper! Would I have rung there in vain? Inwardly I feel rather well today, I'm still enjoying yesterday, the sun was high and warm in the clearest sky—and I extinguished my lantern and embraced a noble human being, a little landlord who looks like a drunk rabbit and who rented me a large elegant room in his splendid house near the city. A noble human being! The house isn't far from the lake, my windows face the water and on all sides the Alps, like clouds gleaming in the sun. — You're coming soon? My youthly spirit is gone, I'll get gray hair otherwise, I'll soon have to rejuvenate myself from your inner bliss and your divine innocence and your dear carefree nature and all of your wicked attributes, wicked girl. Addio piccola mia!

To Wilhelmine Jaeglé

[Zurich, 1837]

[. . . I'll] release *Leonce and Lena* along with two other dramas for publication in a week at most. [. . .]

Notes

Most of Büchner's letters survive only in abridged form. Nearly all original copies were lost or destroyed; the existing texts, with a few exceptions, derive from Ludwig Büchner's 1850 edition of his brother's works. The translation combines more recently discovered letters with Ludwig Büchner's published selection of primarily those passages "that illustrate the political activities of the time and Büchner's participation in them."

245 **Ramorino:** Polish general, active in the revolution of 1830.
Marseillaise: French national anthem. **Carmagnole:** Jacobin
song popular during the French Revolution. **"Vive . . . milieu!":**
"Long live freedom! Long live Ramorino! Down with the ministers! Down with the juste milieu!" [i.e., the centrist policies
246 of the July Monarchy of Louis Philippe]. **Herr Perier:** Casimir
Perier, French prime minister under Louis Philippe; he helped
aid victims of the cholera epidemic of 1832 and subsequently
died of the disease. **Edouard Reuss:** Büchner's uncle, professor
248 of theology in Strassburg. **August Stöber:** August and Adolph
Stöber were among Büchner's closest friends in Strassburg.
They collected Alsatian folksongs and tales and provided
Büchner with materials for *Lenz.* **the other paper:** an invitation
to contribute to a literary magazine, the *Deutschen Musenalmanach für 1833.* **epistolas ex ponto:** letters from exile.
Drescher: Stöbers' house. **"Eugenides":** members of the "Eugenia" fraternity, to which the Stöbers, Eugen Boeckel, and
Johann Wilhelm Baum belonged. **deathly miasma . . . :** i.e.,
Darmstadt. Stöber was in Metz at the time this letter was
249 written. **those thirty hours:** traveling time between Strassburg
or Metz and Darmstadt. **the unrest in Holland:** rebellion was
occurring against the unification of Holland and Belgium. **the
news from Frankfurt:** the storming of the main guardhouse in
Frankfurt on April 3, 1833. In less than an hour the military
suppressed the revolt, which had been planned by members
of the *Burschenschaften* and several of Büchner's future col-
laborators in Giessen, including Friedrich Ludwig Weidig,
250 coauthor of *The Hessian Messenger.* **Freiburg:** considered at

251 the time to be one of the centers of political unrest. **Neustadt:**
in May 1833 a celebration took place in Neustadt of the an-
niversary of the "Hambacher Fest," at which many thousand
participants had cheered the declaration of democratic rights.
Rousseau: A. Rousseau, who preached the doctrines of Saint-
Simonism in front of the Strassburg Cathedral. **Saint-Simonist:**
follower of the teachings of Henri de Saint-Simon and B. P.
Enfantin, who advocated the nationalization of private industry and equal rights for women. **marche vers les femmes:**
252 sets out after the women. **Vosges:** mountain range southwest
of Strassburg. **Franche-Comte:** former county in Burgundy.
253 **Saglio:** a representative with monarchist sympathies. **Goupil's**
254 **thesis:** Goupil, a Strassburg doctor, wrote a study on muscular
255 contraction. **Stamm and Gross:** Karl Theodor Friedrich Stamm,
a fellow student of Büchner in Darmstadt, and August Gross
were arrested on suspicion of complicity in the Frankfurt revolt. **banquet . . . representatives:** after the legislature had been
dissolved on November 2, 1833, the oppositional representatives were honored in Giessen with a banquet. **Balser and**
Vogt: Georg Friedrich Wilhelm Balser and Philipp Friedrich
Wilhelm Vogt, professors of medicine at the University of
Giessen. **Friedberg:** the political prisoners jailed in Friedberg
included several suspected of participating in the Frankfurt
revolt. **Lambossy:** a fellow student of Büchner in Strassburg.
256 **Dr. H. K.:** Heinrich Künzel, one of the editors of the *Musen-*
almanach. **Viktor:** probably Viktor Jaeglé, one of Wilhelmine's
brothers. **Scherb:** a member of the "Eugenia" fraternity. **Adolph:**
258 Adolph Stöber. **Wilhelmine Jaeglé:** Luise Wilhelmine (Minna)
Jaeglé became Büchner's fiancée. She died unmarried in Strassburg in 1880. **Hippocratic face:** fascies hippocratica, the facial
expression of a dying person, first described by the Greek
259 physician Hippocrates. **we poor wailing musicians . . . flames:**
cf. *Danton's Death*, IV,5. **Perillus's bull:** the tyrant Phalaris
commissioned Perillus to construct a bronze bull in which
victims were roasted to death. Their screams, audible through
holes made for this purpose, sounded like the shrieks of a
dying bull. The first victim was said to be Perillus himself.
Callot-Hoffmann: in 1814–16 the Romantic writer E. T. A.
Hoffmann published "Fantasy-pieces in Callot's Manner," tales

based on engravings by Jacques Callot. **Lama:** Dalai Lama,
spiritual head of Buddhism in Tibet. **Je baise . . . des nouvelles:**
I kiss your little hands and taste the sweet memories of Strassburg. "Prove to me that you still love me very much by sending
me news of yourself" (quote from a lost letter from her to
260 Büchner?). **I studied . . . Revolution:** the French Revolution,
readings that eventually resulted in the writing of *Danton's
Death*. **"It must . . . cometh":** Matthew 18:7; cf. *Danton's
Death,* II,5. **B.:** Eugen Boeckel. **inquiry . . . fraternities:** the
politically active *Burschenschaften* had been banned since 1819.
262 **lullaby:** verses from J. M. R. Lenz's "Love in the Country"
263 (1798). **Nous . . . Adieu:** We'll act a bit romantic, to keep up
with the fashion of the times; and would I then need horseshoes
to make an impression on a woman's heart? Today we have
rather robust nervous systems. Good-bye. ***Bursch* come out!:**
"Bursch heraus" was the beginning of a song popular among
the *Burschenschaften*. **university magistrate:** Konrad Georgi,
also a Court Justice and an alcoholic, later prosecuted those
who wrote and distributed *The Hessian Messenger*. **Schulz's
sentencing:** Wilhelm Schulz was arrested for writing subversive
pamphlets. He escaped to Strassburg and eventually went to
Zurich. Büchner lived in his house there from October 1836
264 until his death in 1837. **I left Giessen:** immediately after Minnigerode's arrest (see below) Büchner went to Butzbach and
Offenbach to warn those who had helped produce and distribute *The Hessian Messenger*. **Minnigerode:** Karl von Minnigerode, son of the Hessian Chief Justice, was Büchner's friend
and fellow student in Darmstadt and Giessen. He was arrested
on August 1, 1834 while transporting copies of the just-
published *Hessian Messenger*. Released in 1837, he emigrated
265 to America. **Muston:** Jean-Baptiste Alexis Muston, an acquaintance from Strassburg. **letters from B.:** Büchner used a
meeting with Boeckel as an alibi for his absence from Giessen.
266 **the rumor about Offenbach:** *The Hessian Messenger* had been
267 printed in Offenbach. **Sauerländer:** Johann David Sauerländer,
book publisher with ties to the liberal "Young Germans." **a
manuscript:** *Danton's Death*. **Heyer Bookshop:** important
publishing house for oppositional writings. **Karl Gutzkow:**
liberal writer *(Wally the Doubter)*, editor, and critic, a leading

figure among the reformist "Young Germans." He later became a playwright at the Dresden Theater. **Frau . . . Reuss:**
Luise Philippine Reuss, Büchner's maternal grandmother. **various circumstances . . . :** Büchner was preparing to flee from
268 the Hessian authorities and badly needed money. **la bourse ou
270 la vie!:** your money or your life! **Saint-Simonists . . . femme
libre:** (see p. 298). **Samson:** Henri Sanson, executioner during
the French Revolution. **Lieutenant Kosseritz:** Lieutenant Ko-
seritz, a leader of the Frankfurt uprising in 1833, was in fact
pardoned and exiled at the last minute. **Frankh:** Gottlob Franckh,
member of the Hessian opposition, served his sentence and
271 later founded several publishing houses. **A. Becker:** August
Becker, theology student, collaborator in the production of
The Hessian Messenger, one of Büchner's closest friends in
Giessen. After his release from prison in 1839, he emigrated
to Switzerland for several years, returned to Hesse, and eventually emigrated to America after the failure of the Revolution
of 1848. **Klemm:** Gustav Klemm, student of theology and
pharmacy in Giessen, member of the "Society for Human
Rights." After his arrest in 1834, he gave police detailed
testimony about subversive political activities in Giessen, im-
plicating his former associates. **Rector Weidig:** Friedrich Ludwig Weidig, coauthor with Büchner of *The Hessian Messenger*
(see pp. 54–56). **a literary journal:** Karl Gutzkow edited a
literary supplement to the newspaper *Phönix,* published by
272 Sauerländer; Büchner had been invited to contribute. **Sartorius . . . Flick:** both Theodor Sartorius and Heinrich Christian
273 Flick were sentenced to prison for political subversion. **Heumann . . . Stamm:** Adolf Heumann (medical doctor), Ludwig
Rosenstiel (law student), Hermann Wiener (student of philology and theology), and Karl Stamm (medical student) all
fled from Hesse to avoid arrest for political subversion. **Wilhelm Büchner:** one of Georg's younger brothers (see p. 39).
274 **Koch . . . Becker:** Jakob Koch, Johann Friedrich Walloth, Georg
Geilfuss, and Ludwig Christian Becker, likewise political refugees from Hesse. **Kl[emm] is a traitor:** (see above). **von Biegeleben . . . Floret:** Ludwig Maximilian Freiherr von Biegeleben,
Karl Weidenbusch, and Theodor Floret were practitioners of
law in Hesse. **Thudichum:** Georg Thudichum, a member of

275 the liberal opposition. **Professors Lauth, Duvernoy:** Ernst
Alexander Lauth, Professor of Physiology in Strassburg; George-
Louis Duvernoy, Professor of Natural History in Strassburg.
my translation: upon Gutzkow's request, Büchner translated
Victor Hugo's dramas *Lucrèce Borgia* and *Marie Tudor* for
an edition to be published by Sauerländer. **preface . . . edition:**
in protest against the suppression of Friedrich Schleiermacher's
letters on Friedrich Schlegel's *Lucinde,* Gutzkow published
them himself and added a preface. His edition was banned
and confiscated in Prussia and Bavaria, which led to the ban-
276 ning of the "Young Germans" in December 1835. **the title is
tasteless:** Sauerländer's editor had added to *Danton's Death*
the subtitle: "Dramatic Scenes of the French Reign of Terror."
Gutzkow's splendid reviews: Gutzkow had published portions
of and commentary on *Danton's Death* in the *Phönix,* fol-
277 lowed by an enthusiastic review. **Nievergelder:** Ludwig Nievergelder, a student of forestry and a member of the "Society
for Human Rights" in Giessen, eventually emigrated to America. **letters . . . through the mail:** presumably Büchner entrusted numerous letters to his parents to messengers. **son of
Professor Vogt:** Carl Vogt, like Büchner a student of medicine
278 in Giessen. **Neuhof:** Georg and Wilhelm Neuhof had fled to
avoid political persecution; their sister had given aid to the
political opposition in Hesse. **time bomb in Paris:** on July 28,
1835, Giuseppe Fieschi attempted to assassinate King Louis
Philippe; his bomb spared the king but killed eighteen other
people in his vicinity. **Republicans:** a party on the far left.
Carlists: supporters of Don Carlos of Spain. **military celebration in Kalisch:** in the summer of 1835, Prussian and Russian
troops celebrated victory over Poland in the Polish city of
Kalisch, where the two countries had signed an alliance against
Napoleon in 1813. **Bonaparte's time bomb:** in December 1800,
an attempt was made on the life of Napoleon I. **murder . . . Rastatt:** two French ambassadors were murdered by
Hungarian soldiers in April 1799 in the town of Rastatt in
279 southern Germany. **Legitimists:** supporters of King Charles X,
who was ousted by Louis Philippe. **Prince Emil:** Prince Emil
of Hesse, brother of Grand Duke Ludwig II. **report from Switzerland:** Büchner's friend and fellow student Hermann Trapp

disparaged Büchner in an anonymous letter to Gutzkow. As
fellow exiles in Switzerland, Büchner and Trapp reconciled
280 their differences. ***Deutsche Revue:*** this journal was to be the
organ of oppositional literature in Germany. The ban against
the "Young Germans" in December 1835 ended the project
before it could be realized. **Wienbarg:** Ludolf Wienbarg, a
leading critic and theoretician of the "Young Germans." **Gladbach:** Georg Gladbach, acquaintance of Büchner's in Darmstadt and Giessen; arrested for political subversion in 1833
281 but not sentenced until 1838. **Heine, Börne, Mundt:** Heinrich
Heine, Ludwig Börne, and Theodor Mundt were among the
most prominent figures of the "Young Germany" movement.
Schwab and Uhland: Gustav Schwab and Ludwig Uhland belonged to the "Swabian School" of German Romanticism.
282 ***Musenalmanach:*** (see p. 296). **Ludwig Büchner:** Georg's brother
was eleven years old when this letter was written (see also p.
39). **Tell's Ledge . . . Tell's Chapel:** locations prominent in
283 the legend of William Tell. **King of Bavaria . . . books:** King
Ludwig I had banned Gutzkow's *Wally the Doubter* and several other of his works. **Grand Duke of Baden:** Grand Duke
Leopold had Gutzkow imprisoned for one month for alleged
284 "defamation of Christianity" in *Wally the Doubter*. **Boulet:**
editor of the *Revue du nord,* published in Paris. **Küchler:** Heinrich Küchler, medical doctor in Darmstadt, sentenced to eight
285 years for political subversion. **Methfessel:** Albert Gottlieb
286 Methfessel, composer of songs. **dissertation:** "On the Nervous
System of the Barbel" (a fish related to the carp). **Menzel's
scorn:** author and critic Wolfgang Menzel, once Gutzkow's
mentor, distanced himself from the political liberalism of "Young
287 Germany" and urged its suppression. **Herr von Eib:** Zacharias
Aldinger, alias Baron von Eib, was eventually exposed as an
288 agent of Metternich's secret police. **Societe d'histoire naturelle:**
the Society of Natural History in Strassburg. **sheets of paper:**
289 presumably a reference to *Leonce and Lena*. **cousin from Holland:** son of Büchner's uncle Wilhelm Büchner. **miliaria:** an
290 inflammation of the skin. **Demoiselle Peche:** Therese Peche,
an actress in Darmstadt and Vienna. **Savoy Campaign:** the
Polish general Ramorino led Italian, Polish, and German refugees in an attack against Savoy in support of revolutionary

291 forces in Italy. **several people . . . paper:** probably a reference
to *Woyzeck* and *Leonce and Lena.* **Mayor Hess:** Johann Jakob
Hess, mayor of Zurich. **my doctorate:** Büchner's dissertation
had attracted the attention of the noted scientists Lorenz Oken
and Johannes Müller at the University of Zurich, which granted
293 him both a degree and an academic position. **inaugural ad-**
dress: Büchner delivered his address, "On Cranial Nerves,"
on November 5, 1836. **Switzerland's dispute with France:** the
two countries had broken diplomatic relations over the issue
294 of political refugees. **Minnigerode is dead:** Büchner was mis-
informed (see p. 299). **my scalpel:** Büchner was preparing
dissections for his course on the comparative anatomy of fish
296 and amphibians. **two other dramas:** presumably *Woyzeck* and
the lost drama *Pietro Aretino.*

Bibliography

Listed below are books, essays, and articles on Georg Büchner in English, arranged chronologically within each category. Dissertations, reviews of theatrical performances, and short introductions to editions and anthologies are not included.

I. General

Vickers, L. "Georg Büchner." *Nation,* 32 (1880), 224.

Dunlop, Geoffrey, trans. "Introduction." *The Plays of Georg Büchner.* London: Viking Press, 1927, pp. 7–65.

Hauch, Edward E. "The Reviviscence of Georg Büchner." *Publications of the Modern Language Association of America,* 44 (1929), 892–900.

Kresh, Joseph G. "Georg Büchner's Reputation as an Economic Radical." *Germanic Review,* 8 (1933), 44–51.

Kresh, Joseph G. "Georg Büchner." *Dialectics,* 1, No. 6 (1938), 1–11; No. 7 (1938), 19–31.

Kaufmann, Friedrich W. "Georg Büchner." *German Dramatists of the 19th Century.* Los Angeles: Lymanhouse, 1940, pp. 103–11.

Meyer, Erwin L. *The Changing Attitude Toward Georg Büchner.* Bloomington, Ind., 1945.

Rosenberg, Ralph P. "Georg Büchner's Early Reception in America." *Journal of English and Germanic Philology,* 44 (1945), 270–73.

Zeydel, Edwin H. "A Note on Georg Büchner and Gerhart Hauptmann." *Journal of English and Germanic Philology,* 44 (1945), 87–88.

Knight, Arthur H. J. *Georg Büchner.* Oxford: Basil Blackwell, 1951.

White, John S. "Georg Büchner or the Suffering Through the Father." *The American Imago,* 9 (1952), 365–427.

Majut, Rudolf. "Georg Büchner and Some English Thinkers." *Modern Language Review,* 48 (1953), 310–22.

Jacobs, Margaret, ed. "Introduction." *Georg Büchner: "Dantons Tod" and "Woyzeck."* Manchester: Manchester Univ. Press, 1954, pp. ix-xxxiv.

Majut, Rudolf. "Some Literary Affiliations of Georg Büchner with England." *Modern Language Review,* 50 (1955), 30–43.

Furness, N. A. "Georg Büchner's Translations of Victor Hugo." *Modern Language Review,* 51 (1956), 49–54.

Closs, August. "Nihilism and Modern German Drama: Grabbe and Büchner." *Medusa's Mirror: Studies in German Literature.* London: Cresset Press, 1957, pp. 147–63.

Hamburger, Michael. "Georg Büchner." *Evergreen Review,* 1 (1957), 68–98.

Hamburger, Michael. "Georg Büchner." *Reason and Energy: Studies in German Literature.* London/New York: Routledge & Kegan Paul, 1957, pp. 179–208.

Peacock, Ronald. "A Note on Georg Büchner's Plays." *German Life and Letters,* 10 (1956–57), 189–97. Also in *The Poet in the Theatre.* New York: Hill & Wang, 1960, pp. 181–93.

Steiner, George. *The Death of Tragedy.* New York: Knopf, 1961; Hill & Wang, 1963, pp. 270–81.

Benn, Maurice B., ed. "Introduction." *Georg Büchner: "Leonce und Lena" and "Lenz."* London: Harrap, 1963, pp. ix-xxxi.

Hartwig, Gilbert F. "Georg Büchner: Nineteenth Century Avant-garde." *The Southern Quarterly,* 1, No. 2 (1963), 98–128.

Lindenberger, Herbert S. *Georg Büchner.* Carbondale, Ill.: Southern Illinois Univ. Press, 1964.

Stern, J. P. "A World of Suffering: Georg Büchner." *Seven Studies in Nineteenth-Century German Literature.* London: Thames & Hudson, 1964, pp. 78–155.

Spalter, Max. "Georg Büchner." *Brecht's Tradition.* Baltimore: Johns Hopkins, 1967, pp. 75–111.

Böll, Heinrich. "On Georg Büchner." *Delos,* 2 (1968), 105–10.

Cowen, Roy C. "Identity and Conscience in Büchner's Works." *Germanic Review,* 43 (1968), 258–66.

MacEwen, Leslie. *The Narren-motifs in the Works of Georg Büchner.* Bern: Lang, 1968.

Benn, Maurice B. "Anti-Pygmalion: An Apologia for Georg Büchner's Aesthetics." *Modern Language Review,* 64 (1969), 597–604.

Schmidt, Henry J. *Satire, Caricature, and Perspectivism in the Works of Georg Büchner.* The Hague: Mouton, 1970.

Bell, Gerda E. "Georg Büchner's Translations of Victor Hugo's *Lucrèce Borgia* and *Maria Tudor.*" *Arcadia,* 6 (1971), 151–74.

Bell, Gerda E. "Traduttore-Traditore? Some Remarks on Georg Büchner's Victor Hugo Translations." *Monatshefte,* 63 (1971), 19–27.

Burwick, Frederick. "The Anatomy of Revolution: Beddoes and Büchner." *Pacific Coast Philology,* 6 (1971), 5–12.

Murdoch, Brian. "Communication as a Dramatic Problem: Büchner, Chekhov, Hofmannsthal, and Wesker." *Revue de Littérature Comparée,* 45 (1971), 40–56.

Stern, J.P. *Idylls and Realities. Studies in 19th-Century German Literature.* New York: Ungar, 1971, pp. 33–48.

Bell, Gerda E. "Windows: A Study of a Symbol in Georg Büchner's Work." *Germanic Review,* 47 (1972), 95–108.

Brustein, Robert. "Büchner: Artist and Visionary." *Yale/Theatre,* 3, No. 3 (1972), 4–7.

Fischer, Heinz. "Some Marginal Notes on Georg Büchner." *Revue de Littérature Comparée,* 46 (1972), 255–58.

Gilman, Richard. "Georg Büchner: History Redeemed." *Yale/Theatre,* 3, No. 3 (1972), 8–34.

Schechter, Joel. "*Pietro Aretino:* Georg Büchner's Lost Play." *Yale/Theatre,* 3, No. 3 (1972), 94–98.

Benn, Maurice B. "Büchner and Gautier." *Seminar,* 9 (1973), 202–07.

Bell, Gerda E. "Georg Büchner's Last Words." *German Life and Letters,* 27 (1973–74), 17–22.

Hauser, Ronald. *Georg Büchner.* New York: Twayne, 1974.

Wells, George A. "Büchner as Tragedian." *Erfahrung und Überlieferung: Festschrift for C. P. Magill.* Cardiff: Univ. of Wales, 1974, pp. 100–12.

Benn, Maurice B. *The Drama of Revolt: A Critical Study of Georg Büchner*. Cambridge: Cambridge Univ. Press, 1976.

Richards, David G. *Georg Büchner and the Birth of the Modern Drama*. Albany: SUNY Press, 1977.

Benn, Maurice. "Büchner and Heine." *Seminar,* 13 (1977), 215–26.

Schmidt, Henry J. "The Hessian Messenger." *Georg Büchner: The Complete Collected Works*. New York: Avon, 1977, pp. 241–57.

Grimm, Reinhold. "Georg Büchner and the Modern Concept of Revolt." *Studi Tedesci,* 21, No. 2 (1978), 7–66.

Schwarz, Alfred. *From Büchner to Beckett: Dramatic Theory and Modes of Tragic Drama*. Athens: Ohio Univ. Press, 1978.

Hoelzel, Alfred. "Betrayed Rebels in German Literature: Büchner, Toller, and Koestler." *Orbis Litterarum,* 34 (1979), 238–58.

Reeve, William C. *Georg Büchner*. New York: Ungar, 1979.

Hilton, Julian. *Georg Büchner*. London/Basingstoke: Macmillan, 1982.

Grimm, Reinhold. "Fragments of a Dirge. On Georg Büchner, Gottfried Benn and others." *Erkennen und Deuten. Essays zur Literatur und Literaturtheorie*. Ed. Martha Woodmansee & Walter F.W. Lohnes. Berlin: E. Schmidt, 1983, pp. 143–71.

Grimm, Reinhold. *Love, Lust and Rebellion: New Approaches to Georg Büchner*. Madison/London: Univ. of Wisconsin Press, 1985.

II. *Danton's Death*

Rosenberg, Ralph P. "Problems in Translation with Reference to *Dantons Tod*." *German Quarterly,* 15 (1942), 19–27.

Knight, Arthur H. J. "Some Considerations Relating to Georg Büchner's Opinions on History and the Drama and to His Play *Dantons Tod*." *Modern Language Review,* 42 (1947), 70–81.

MacLean, H. "The Moral Conflict in Georg Büchner's *Dantons Tod*." *Journal of the Australasian Universities Modern Language Association,* 6 (1957), 25–33.

Baxandall, Lee. "Georg Büchner's *Danton's Death*." *Tulane Drama Review,* 6, No. 3 (1961–62), 136–49.

Fleissner, E. M. "Revolution as Theatre: *Danton's Death* and *Marat/Sade*." *Massachusetts Review,* 7 (1966), 543–56.

Cowen, Roy C. "Grabbe's *Don Juan and Faust* and Büchner's *Dantons Tod:* Epicureanism and *Weltschmerz.*" *Publications of the Modern Language Association of America,* 82 (1967), 342–51.

Cowen, Roy C. "Grabbe's *Napoleon,* Büchner's *Danton* and the Masses." *Symposium,* 21 (1967), 316–23.

Milburn, Douglas, Jr. "Social Conscience and Social Reform: The Political Paradox of *Dantons Tod.*" *Rice University Studies,* 53, No. 4 (1967), 23–31.

Lindenberger, Herbert S. "*Danton's Death* and the Conventions of Historical Drama." *Comparative Drama,* 3 (1969), 99–109.

Beacham, Richard. "Büchner's Use of Sources in *Danton's Death.*" *Yale/Theatre,* 3, No. 3 (1972), 45–55.

Houseman, John. "Orson Welles and *Danton's Death.*" *Yale/Theatre,* 3, No. 3 (1972), 56–67.

Simon, John. "On *Danton's Death.*" *Yale/Theatre,* 3, No. 3 (1972), 35–44.

Wessell, Leonard P., Jr. "Eighteenth Century Theodicy and the Death of God in Büchner's *Dantons Tod.*" *Seminar,* 8 (1972), 198–218.

Bodi, Leslie. "'Sensualism' and 'Spiritualism' in Büchner's *Danton's Death.*" *Komos,* 3 (1973), 17–19.

Malkin, Michael R. "*Danton's Death:* Büchner's Unidealistic Danton." *Studies in the Humanities,* 3, No. 2 (1973), 46–48.

Roberts, David. "Büchner and the French Revolution: Two Arguments." *Komos,* 3 (1973), 24–27.

Rose, Margaret. "Messianism and the Terror: Desmoulins' and Büchner's Use of a New Messiah *Figura.*" *Komos,* 3 (1973), 27–30.

Teichmann, Max. "*Danton's Death:* An Early Psychodrama." *Komos,* 3 (1973), 21–23.

Worrall, G. S. "The Historical Background to *Danton's Death.*" *Komos,* 3 (1973), 19–21.

Holmes, T. M. "The Ideology of the Moderates in Büchner's *Dantons Tod.*" *German Life and Letters,* 27 (1973–74), 93–100.

Waldeck, Peter B. "Büchner's *Dantons Tod:* Dramatic Structure and Individual Necessity." *Susquehanna University Studies,* 9, No. 4 (1974), 211–25.

Grimm, Reinhold. "The Play within a Play in Revolutionary Theatre." *Mosaic,* 9, No. 1 (1975), 41–52.

Swales, Martin. "Ontology, Politics, Sexuality: A Note on Büchner's Drama *Dantons Tod.*" *New German Studies,* 3 (1975), 109–25.

Wetzel, Heinz. "Revolution and the Intellectual: Büchner's Danton and Koestler's Rubashov." *Mosaic,* 10, No. 4 (1976/77), 23–33.

McColgan, M. "The True Dialectics of *Dantons Tod.*" *New German Studies,* 6 (1978), 151–74.

Milner-Gulland, Robin. "Heroes of Their Time? Form and Idea in Büchner's *Danton's Death* and Lermontov's *Hero of Our Time.*" *The Idea of Freedom: Essays in Honour of Isaiah Berlin.* Oxford: Oxford Univ. Press, 1979, pp. 115–37.

Reddick, John. "Mosaic and Flux: Georg Büchner and the Marion Episode in *Dantons Tod.*" *Oxford German Studies,* 11 (1979), 40–67.

Solomon, Janis L. "Büchner's *Dantons Tod:* History as Theatre." *Germanic Review,* 54 (1979), 9–19.

McInnes, Edward. "Scepticism, Ideology and History in Büchner's *Dantons Tod.*" *For Lionel Thomas. A Collection of Essays Presented in his Memory.* Ed. Derek Atwood. Hull: Univ. of Hull, 1980, pp. 53–69.

Pomar, Mark. "The Remaking of Historical Drama: Pushkin's *Boris Gudonov* and Büchner's *Dantons Tod.*" *Germano-Slavica,* 3, No. 6 (1981), 363–76.

Guthrie, John. "The True Dialectics of *Dantons Tod:* A Reply." *New German Studies,* 10, No. 3 (1982), 151–74.

James, Dorothy. *Georg Büchner's* Dantons Tod: *A Reappraisal.* London: The Modern Humanities Research Assn., 1982.

III. *Lenz*

Parker, John J. "Some Reflections on Georg Büchner's *Lenz* and Its Principal Source, the Oberlin Record." *German Life and Letters,* 21 (1968), 103–11.

Harris, Edward P. "J. M. R. Lenz in German Literature: From Büchner to Bobrowski." *Colloquia Germanica,* 3 (1973), 214–33.

King, Janet K. "Lenz Viewed Sane." *Germanic Review,* 49 (1974), 146–53.

Jansen, Peter K. "The Structural Function of the *Kunstgespräch* in Büchner's *Lenz*." *Monatshefte,* 67 (1975), 145–56.

Schmidt, Henry J. "Lenz." *Georg Büchner: The Complete Collected Works.* New York: Avon, 1977, pp. 317–28.

Pascal, Roy. "Büchner's *Lenz:* Style and Message." *Oxford German Studies,* 9 (1978), 68–83.

Sharp, Francis Michael. "Büchner's *Lenz.* A Futile Madness." *Psychoanalytische und psychopathologische Literaturinterpretationen.* Ed. Bernd Urban & Winfried Kudszus. Darmstadt: Wissenschaftliche Buchgesellschaft, 1981, pp. 256–79.

Furness, N.A. "A Note on Büchner's *Lenz:* '. . . nur war es ihm manchmal unangenehm, daß er nicht auf dem Kopf gehn konnte.' " *Forum for Modern Language Studies,* 8, No. 4 (1982), 313–16.

Mahoney, Dennis F. "The Suffering of Young Lenz: The Function of Parody in Büchner's *Lenz*." *Monatshefte,* 76, No. 4 (1984), 396–408.

Holub, Robert C. "The Paradoxes of Realism: An Examination of the *Kunstgespräch* in Büchner's *Lenz*." *Deutsche Vierteljahrsschrift für Literaturwissenschaft und Geistesgeschichte,* 59, No. 1 (1985), 102–24.

IV. *Leonce and Lena*

Shaw, Leroy R. "Symbolism of Time in Georg Büchner's *Leonce und Lena*." *Monatshefte,* 48 (1956), 221–30.

Hauser, Ronald. "Georg Büchner's *Leonce und Lena*." *Monatshefte,* 53 (1961), 338–46.

Macay, Barbara. "Leonce and Lena." *Yale/Theatre,* 3, No. 3 (1972), 68–82.

Lamb, Margaret. "That Strain Again: 'Shakespearean' Comedies by Musset and Büchner." *Educational Theatre Journal,* 27 (1975), 70–76.

Lukens, Nancy. *Büchner's Valerio and the Theatrical Fool Tradition.* Stuttgart: Heinz, 1977.

Schmidt, Henry J. "Leonce and Lena." *Georg Büchner: The Complete Collected Works.* New York: Avon, 1977, pp. 336–47.

McKenzie, John R.P. "Cotta's Comedy Competition (1836)." *Maske und Kothurn*, 26 (1980), 59–73.

V. *Woyzeck*

Blackall, Eric A. "Büchner and Alban Berg: Some Thoughts on *Wozzeck*." *German Quarterly*, 34 (1961), 431–38.

Kayser, Wolfgang J. "Woyzeck." *The Grotesque in Art and Literature*. Trans. Ulrich Weisstein. London/Bloomington, Ind.: Indiana Univ. Press, 1963; New York: McGraw–Hill, 1966, pp. 89–99.

Perle, George. "Woyzeck and Wozzeck." *Musical Quarterly*, 53 (1967), 206–19.

Stein, Jack M. "From *Woyzeck* to *Wozzeck:* Alban Berg's Adaptation of Büchner." *Germanic Review*, 46 (1972), 168–80.

Wiles, Timothy. "*Woyzeck*, immer zu." *Yale/Theatre*, 3, No. 3 (1972), 83–89.

Stodder, Joseph H. "Influences of *Othello* on Büchner's *Woyzeck*." *Modern Language Review*, 69 (1974), 115–20.

Baumgartner, Ingeborg. "Ambiguity in Büchner's *Woyzeck*." *Michigan Germanic Studies*, 1 (1975), 199–214.

McCarthy, John A. "Some Aspects of Imagery in Büchner's *Woyzeck*." *Modern Language Notes*, 91 (1976), 543–51.

Schmidt, Henry J. "The *Woyzeck* Manuscripts. *Woyzeck*." *Georg Büchner: The Complete Collected Works*. New York: Avon, 1977, pp. 348–61; 362–83.

Grandin, John M. "*Woyzeck* and the Last Judgement." *German Life and Letters*, 31 (1978), 175–79.

Heald, David. "A Note on Verbal Echoes in Büchner's *Woyzeck*." *German Life and Letters*, 31 (1978), 179–82.

Otten, Terry. "*Woyzeck* and *Othello:* The Dimensions of Melodrama." *Comparative Drama*, 12 (1978), 123–36.

Patterson, Michael. "Contradictions Concerning Time in Büchner's *Woyzeck*." *German Life and Letters*, 32 (1979), 115–21.

Rugen, Barbara. "*Woyzeck:* A New Approach." *Theatre Journal*, 32 (1979), 71–84.

Bloom, Michael. "Woyzeck and Kaspar: The Congruities in Drama and Film." *Literature/Film Quarterly*, 8 (1980), 225–31.

For books and articles in German consult:

Schlick, Werner. *Das Georg Büchner-Schrifttum bis 1965*. Hildesheim: Olms, 1968.
Hinderer, Walter. *Büchner Kommentar zum dichterischen Werk*. München: Winkler, 1977.
Knapp, Gerhard P. *Georg Büchner*. Stuttgart: Metzler, [2]1984.

ACKNOWLEDGMENTS

Every reasonable effort has been made to locate the parties who hold rights to previously published translations reprinted here. We gratefully acknowledge permission to reprint the following:

Translations of *The Hessian Messenger, Danton's Death, Lenz, Leonce and Lena,* and *Woyzeck* as well as the Glossary to *Danton's Death* and the Synopsis of *Woyzeck* have been adapted from *Georg Büchner: The Complete Collected Works,* translations and commentary by Henry J. Schmidt (New York: Avon Books, 1977). © Henry J. Schmidt and reprinted by permission.

The letters from Georg Büchner to Edouard Reuss of August 20, 1832, and August 31, 1833, have been translated by permission of Athenäum Verlag from Jan-Christoph Hauschild's *Georg Büchner. Studien und neue Quellen zu Leben, Werk und Wirkung.*

Lightning Source UK Ltd.
Milton Keynes UK
UKHW010249070622
404050UK00001B/4